D1446920

PLANTING A CAPITALIST SOUTH

PLANTING A CAPITALIST SOUTH

MASTERS, MERCHANTS, *and* MANUFACTURERS

in the SOUTHERN INTERIOR, 1790–1860

TOM DOWNEY

LOUISIANA STATE UNIVERSITY PRESS

BATON ROUGE

Copyright © 2006 by Louisiana State University Press
All rights reserved
Manufactured in the United States of America
FIRST PRINTING

DESIGNER: *Andrew Shurtz*
TYPEFACE: *Adobe Caslon*
TYPESETTER: *The Composing Room of Michigan, Inc.*
PRINTER AND BINDER: *Edwards Brothers, Inc.*

LIBRARY OF CONGRESS CATALOGING-IN-PUBLICATION DATA

Downey, Tom, 1965–

Planting a capitalist South : masters, merchants, and manufacturers in the southern interior, 1790–1860 / Tom Downey.

  p. cm.

Originally presented as the author's thesis (doctoral)—University of South Carolina.

Includes bibliographical references and index.

ISBN 0-8071-3107-5 (cloth : alk. paper)

1. Southern States—Economic conditions—19th century. 2. Southern States—Commerce—History—19th century. 3. Capitalism—Southern States—History—19th century. I. Title.

HC107.A13D69 2005

330.975'03—dc22

2005005427

Chapters 2, 5, and 8 appeared previously in slightly different form as "Riparian Rights and Manufacturing in Antebellum South Carolina: William Gregg and the Origins of the 'Industrial Mind,'" *Journal of Southern History* 65 (February 1999): 77–108.

The paper in this book meets the guidelines for permanence and durability of the Committee on Production Guidelines for Book Longevity of the Council on Library Resources. ∞

For Mom & Dad
Gram & Gramps
Jack & Lizzie
and Mary

Contents

Tables

Acknowledgments

At the completion of this project, I find myself in a situation not unfamiliar to many an antebellum planter; that is, buried under a mountain of debts and obligations that I can never hope to repay. Topping my list of creditors at the University of South Carolina is Lacy Ford. This book originated as a paper in one of Lacy's seminars, expanded into a dissertation under his direction, and culminated in the book now before you. Lacy guided this project at every stage, offering a myriad of timely and insightful comments with grace and good humor. In short, he has overseen my transformation from history buff to historian. Mark Smith, Larry Glickman, and Chuck Kovacik served on my dissertation committee, in which capacity I became the beneficiary of their vast knowledge and warm friendship. At sundry points during its evolution, portions of my manuscript also gained from comments provided by Tom Brown, Tom Terrill, Michael Gagnon, Joseph Reidy, Dan Vivian, and from the anonymous reviews at LSU Press. My thanks go out to them all.

The South Caroliniana Library is undoubtedly one of the finest research facilities in the Southeast, due in large measure to the skill and dedication of its wonderful staff. My particular thanks go out to manuscript librarians Brian Cuthrell and Henry Fulmer, Robin Copp and Thelma Hayes of the Books Division, and photo archivist Beth Bilderback. Similar thanks are due to Paul Begley and Patrick McCawley at the South Carolina Department of Archives and History. Frankie Cubbage at USC–Aiken generously granted access to the Gregg/Graniteville collection. A fellowship from the Harvard University Graduate School of Business Administration made possible a highly rewarding trip to Cambridge, Massachusetts, where Brent Sverdloff at the Baker Library provided invaluable assistance in navigating the R. G. Dun & Company Collection.

My parents made all this possible by making me possible. Even though they weren't always quite sure of what I was doing for all those years in South Carolina, they never flagged in their support for me and my meandering chosen path. The late Edmund and Marjorie Mooney deserve the credit for initiating my interest in history by providing a house full of antique toys, gizmos, and gadgets to dazzle the curiosity of their grandson.

Jack made his debut halfway through my first draft of chapter six. Progress on my dissertation all but ceased as he filled diapers, fought off naps, and rummaged through every nook and cranny of my study. Lizzie arrived three years later, and quickly proved equally adept at hampering her father's productivity. And I wouldn't trade them for the world.

Finally, there is Mary. It's difficult to sum up her contributions to this work. She didn't type, proofread, or assist my research, and encouragement generally came in the form of such pointed questions as "Did you write anything today?" Yet, she is present in every page that follows. She was with me before this project began and will hopefully be with me long after it is finished. After ten years of marriage, Mary remains the cream in my coffee and the measure of my dreams.

Abbreviations

SCDAH: South Carolina Department of Archives and History, Columbia
SCHM: South Carolina Historical Magazine
SCL: South Caroliniana Library, University of South Carolina, Columbia
SHC: Southern Historical Collection, University of North Carolina, Chapel Hill

PLANTING A CAPITALIST SOUTH

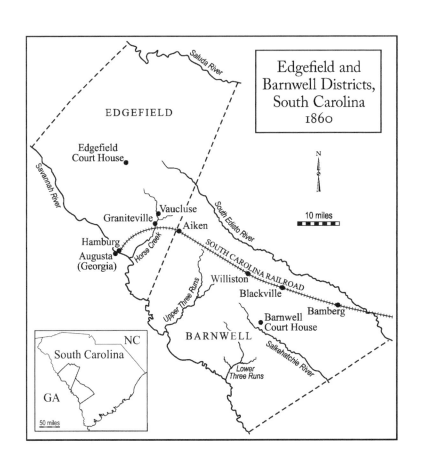

Edgefield and
Barnwell Districts,
South Carolina
1860

EDGEFIELD

Saluda River

Savannah River

Edgefield
Court House

N

10 miles

South Edisto River

Vaucluse
Graniteville
Aiken
Hamburg
Augusta
(Georgia)

Horse Creek

SOUTH CAROLINA RAILROAD

Williston
Blackville
Bamberg

Upper Three Runs

Barnwell
Court House

BARNWELL

Salkehatchie River

NC
South Carolina

GA

Lower
Three Runs

50 miles

INTRODUCTION

Come, let my carper to his life now look,
And find there darker lines than in my book
He findeth any; yea, and let him know,
That in his best things there are worse lines too.

JOHN BUNYAN, *The Pilgrim's Progress*

IT IS ONE OF THE GREAT perennials of southern historiography: What
was the basic economic nature of the Old South? Was it capitalist? Precapitalist? Noncapitalist? Seigneurial? Or something else entirely? Most historians of
the South can recite the historiographic debate by rote, with literature generally falling into two schools of thought that took shape in the 1960s. The first,
presented most forcefully in the writings of Marxist historians such as Eugene
Genovese and Raimondo Luraghi, maintained that the institution of slavery
created a noncapitalist society in the Old South, which was in fundamental opposition to the emerging bourgeois-capitalist ethos of its free-labor, industrial
counterpart in the North. Why else, such arguments posited, would the Old
South cling to such a backward and inefficient socioeconomic system? Planters
were more akin to feudal lords than modern entrepreneurs, and primarily
sought status, not profits, from slavery. In opposition, an alternate collection of
social and economic historians confronted precapitalist arguments with an
avalanche of manuscript and statistical data, which countered that cotton and
slavery were highly lucrative enterprises and their single-minded pursuit by

Epigraph from John Bunyan, *The Pilgrim's Progress* (New York, 1957), 5.

I

planters and yeomen made the South very much a capitalist society, fully imbued with the acquisitive, profit-seeking dictates of modern liberal capitalism.[1]

While this scholarly contest produced an abundance of pathbreaking literature, its usefulness in examining the political economy of the Old South has
waned as the debate has shifted from absolutes to degrees. Recent works admit the presence of both capitalist and noncapitalist traits in the antebellum
South, but disagree as to which predominates, if either. In their study of industrialization in the Old South, economic historians Fred Bateman and
Thomas Weiss presented copious data demonstrating that returns on manufacturing were generally higher than those in agriculture and that there was little in the way of economic barriers to prevent an increase in industrial development. Perplexed at the unwillingness of planters to invest in manufacturing,
the authors fell back on a very Genovesian explanation, suggesting planters
held an extreme aversion to financial risk and the possibility of "unagreeably
high social costs to industrial diversification." But even Genovese's early writings allowed that "a strong dose of capitalism" existed in the Old South, while
his later works tacitly admit that portions of the South-as-capitalist argument
are strong by abandoning explicit avowals of noncapitalist behavior and instead
presenting slaveholders as seeking "an alternate route to modernity."[2]

Ironically, the inspiration for revitalizing this debate may lay with an ex-

1. The feature works on the Old South as a noncapitalist/capitalist society are well known to
southern scholars and need not be repeated here in detail. The most sophisticated works arguing
the existence of a precapitalist society in the Old South remain Eugene D. Genovese, *The Political Economy of Slavery: Studies in the Economy and Society of the Slave South* (New York, 1965; Westport, Conn., 1989); idem, *The World the Slaveholders Made: Two Essays in Interpretation* (New York,
1969); and Eugene D. Genovese and Elizabeth Fox-Genovese, *Fruits of Merchant Capital: Slavery
and Bourgeois Property in the Rise and Expansion of Capitalism* (New York, 1983). See also Raimondo
Luraghi, *The Rise and Fall of the Plantation South* (New York and London, 1978). For the Old South
as capitalist society, see Robert Fogel and Stanley Engerman, *Time on the Cross: The Economics of
American Negro Slavery*, 2 vols. (Boston, 1974), and James Oakes, *The Ruling Race: A History of
American Slaveholders* (New York, 1982). For a recent in-depth review of the debate, see Mark M.
Smith, *Debating Slavery: Economy and Society in the Antebellum American South* (Cambridge, 1998),
esp. 12–14.

2. Fred Bateman and Thomas Weiss, *A Deplorable Scarcity: The Failure of Industrialization in the
Slave Economy* (Chapel Hill, 1981), 161; Eugene D. Genovese, "Marxian Interpretations of the Slave
South," in *Towards a New Past: Dissenting Essays in American History*, ed. Barton J. Bernstein (New
York, 1969), 90–121, quotation 119; idem, *The Slaveholders' Dilemma: Freedom and Progress in South-
ern Conservative Thought, 1820–1860* (Columbia, S.C., 1992), quotation 17.

amination of the North, for southern historians have by no means held exclusive provenance to the controversy over the presence or absence of capitalism in antebellum society. Indeed, the scholarly debate over the rise of capitalism in the American North has been one of the most fruitful and hotly contested topics among historians over the past quarter century, but one whose focus is on the timing and process of capitalism's ascent rather than identifying its existence. This dialogue offered serious challenges to the contention of post–World War II revisionists that America had been capitalist from its inception and essentially lacked a precapitalist past to overcome. A number of intensive local studies of northern communities argued instead for the perseverance of a precapitalist mentalité that survived the Revolution and persisted well into the next century. Most crucial have been works focusing on the early years of the American republic, which emphasized a transition to capitalism rather than the spread of a preexisting capitalist economy.[3]

This transition accelerated in the first half of the nineteenth century, leading many historians to define the era as that of a "market revolution"—one that did not mark the beginning of capitalism in America, but rather expanded and intensified capitalism's impact on a growing number of Americans. The result of this transition was a myriad of economic, social, legal, and political alterations, particularly during the rapid expansion of a national market in the years following the War of 1812. Such transformations were by no means restricted to changes in regional economies or the proliferation of factories and wage labor. Transition and conflict infiltrated almost every level of antebellum society.

3. The debate began in earnest with the publication of three now classic challenges to the wholly capitalist paradigm: Michael Merrill, "Cash Is Good to Eat: Self-Sufficiency and Exchange in the Rural Economy of the United States," *Radical History Review* 3 (1977), 42–71; James Henretta, "Families and Farms: Mentalité in Pre-Industrial America," *William and Mary Quarterly*, 3rd series, 35 (January 1978): 3–32; Christopher Clark, "The Household Economy, Market Exchange, and the Rise of Capitalism in the Connecticut Valley, 1800–1860," *Journal of Social History* 13 (winter 1979): 169–89. A number of good historiographical essays identify the participants and issues in the debate over the transition to capitalism. See Steven Hahn and Jonathan Prude, "Introduction," in *The Countryside in the Age of Capitalist Transformation,* ed. Hahn and Prude (Chapel Hill, 1985), 3–21; Allan Kulikoff, "The Transition to Capitalism in Rural America," *William and Mary Quarterly*, 3rd series, 46 (January 1989): 120–44; Gordon Wood, "Inventing American Capitalism," *New York Review of Books* 41 (June 9, 1994): 44–49; Michael Merrill, "Putting 'Capitalism' in Its Place: A Review of Recent Literature," *William and Mary Quarterly*, 3rd series, 52 (April 1995): 315–26; Paul A. Gilje, "The Rise of Capitalism in the Early Republic," *Journal of the Early Republic* 16 (summer 1996): 159–78.

Customary labor patterns altered, transportation networks grew, the role of government in economic development expanded, household patriarchy was undermined, shopfloor relations transformed, and a flurry of new legal interpretations of property rights subverted common law notions of public right. This juxtaposition of capitalist and precapitalist institutions and values placed proponents and opponents of change in a cultural and political confrontation over the course and shape of America's economic destiny.[4]

However, outside of a handful of perceptive works, studies of this type have been largely confined to communities in the highly industrialized Northeast, which seems particularly suited to the concept of a market revolution. Even though the early debate over the capitalist-noncapitalist nature of the slave South marked a preliminary challenge to the notion of America's inherently capitalist origins, the gridlock between the two camps has kept the Old South largely outside of the debate over the transition to capitalism. For if plantation agriculture is accepted as a capitalist activity, then the South was capitalist from

4. The two most prominent works advancing the idea of a market revolution are Charles Sellers, *The Market Revolution: Jacksonian America, 1815–1846* (New York, 1991), and Harry L. Watson, *Liberty and Power: The Politics of Jacksonian America* (New York, 1990). Also see Paul E. Johnson, "The Market Revolution," in *Encyclopedia of American Social History,* ed. Mary K. Cayton, Elliott J. Gorn, and Peter W. Williams, 3 vols. (New York, 1993), 1:545–60; Melvyn Stokes and Stephen Conway, eds., *The Market Revolution in America: Social, Political, and Religious Expressions, 1800–1880* (Charlottesville, 1996); Sean Wilentz, "Society, Politics, and the Market Revolution, 1815–1848," in *The New American History,* ed. Eric Foner (Philadelphia, 1990), 51–71; "A Symposium of Charles Sellers, The Market Revolution," *Journal of the Early Republic* 12 (1992): 445–71. Among the more representative works exploring the changes brought about during the market revolution era are Sean Wilentz, *Chants Democratic: New York City & The Rise of the American Working Class, 1788–1850* (New York, 1984); Jonathan Prude, *The Coming of Industrial Order: Town and Factory Life in Rural Massachusetts* (Cambridge, 1983); Mary P. Ryan, *Cradle of the Middle Class: The Family in Oneida Country, New York, 1790–1865* (Cambridge, 1981); Paul E. Johnson, *A Shopkeeper's Millennium: Society and Revivals in Rochester, New York, 1815–1837* (New York, 1978); Christine Stansell, *City of Women: Sex and Class in New York, 1789–1860* (Urbana, 1987); Morton J. Horwitz, *The Transformation of American Law, 1780–1860* (Cambridge, Mass., 1977); Ronald E. Seavoy, *The Origins of the American Business Corporation, 1784–1855: Broadening the Concept of Public Service During Industrialization* (Westport, Conn., 1982); Theodore Steinberg, *Nature Incorporated: Industrialization and the Waters of New England* (Cambridge, 1991). For critiques of the market revolution paradigm, see John Majewski, "A Revolution Too Many?" *Journal of Economic History* 57 (June 1997): 476–80, and Daniel Feller, "The Market Revolution Ate My Homework," *Reviews in American History* 25 (September 1997): 408–15.

the start. Likewise, if wage labor is invoked as the sine qua non of capitalism, then slavery kept the region noncapitalist until emancipation. On either side of the issue, however, the fundamental structure of southern society is presented as generally uniform and fixed. As such, some have questioned whether the term *transition* can be properly applied to the Old South, maintaining that the South's expanding but static slave and staple economy produced "more growth than change" and insulated the region from the deeper transformations wrought in the North during the market revolution era.[5]

But the inherent focus of such observations remains based within the older capitalist-noncapitalist paradigm. What market revolution studies offer are ways to examine a society in transition, where established and intruding features overlap and interact, with neither side wielding an absolute hegemony over the other. Southern historians have but rarely employed such an approach in their work in the antebellum era. When the theme of transition has been used at all, it is generally applied to works focusing on the transition from a frontier to a settled agricultural society or the postbellum transition from slave labor to free labor. Likewise, southern historians have largely approached the market revolution in sectional terms, with southerners on the outside looking in and attempting to avoid being caught up in the social, political, and economic upheavals ushered in by the capitalist tide washing over northern society. Fewer still are the scholars who accept the idea of a southern transition to capitalism in the antebellum era, which implies a tacit belief that slavery somehow obviated such a process. In one telling work on the capitalist transformation of rural America, each essay examining the northern states identified the trend as taking place prior to the Civil War. However, the three southern studies implied that the transition was an exclusively postemancipation phenomenon.[6]

5. Harry L. Watson, *Jacksonian Politics and Community Conflict: The Emergence of the Second American Party System in Cumberland County, North Carolina* (Baton Rouge, 1981); idem, *Liberty and Power;* idem, "Slavery and Development in a Dual Economy: The South and the Market Revolution," in *The Market Revolution in America,* ed. Stokes and Conway, 43–73; Johnson, "Market Revolution," 546–47, 553–58, quotation 547; Douglas R. Egerton, "Markets Without a Market Revolution: Southern Planters and Capitalism," *Journal of the Early Republic* 16 (summer 1996): 207–21; Peter Kolchin, *American Slavery, 1619–1877* (New York, 1993), 170–73.

6. James M. McPherson, *Battle Cry of Freedom: The Civil War Era* (New York, 1988), 861; Hahn and Prude, eds., *The Countryside in the Age of Capitalist Transformation.* For representative works on the "transition" from frontier to settlement in the South, see Rachel N. Klein, *Unification of a*

What follows is an attempt to inject the transition to capitalism focus of market revolution studies into the older historiographical debate over the capitalist-noncapitalist nature of the Old South. More specifically, this work examines how a portion of the region, the western South Carolina districts of Edgefield and Barnwell, came to terms with the capitalist features within their own borders during the antebellum era. Much literature exists on the efforts of planters to find an accommodation with capitalism outside the South, an accommodation they ultimately could not, or would not, achieve. But what of the "doses" of capitalism within their own region? Even leading proponents of southern distinctiveness admit the presence of such capitalist features as banks, railroads, and even a modest manufacturing sector in the South prior to the Civil War. Yet they also dismiss such intrusions as largely irrelevant to the southern political economy. Manufacturers and merchants were subservient to the needs and ideals of southern slaveholders, they argue, and were therefore forced to submit to the planters' dominant political and economic attitudes.

Antebellum Edgefield and Barnwell districts are particularly suited to challenge the tenet that merchants and manufacturers did little to alter the political economy of the Old South. First, both were firmly entrenched in the region's plantation society. Each participated aggressively in the initial cotton boom of the 1790s, and slavery and staple agriculture continued to expand in

---

Slave State: The Rise of the Planter Class in the South Carolina Backcountry, 1760–1808 (Chapel Hill, 1990); Harry L. Watson, "'The Common Rights of Mankind': Subsistence, Shad, and Commerce in the Early Republican South," *Journal of American History* 83 (June 1996): 13–43; and Daniel S. Dupre, *Transforming the Cotton Frontier: Madison County, Alabama, 1800–1840* (Baton Rouge, 1997). On the transition from slave labor to free labor, see Willie Lee Rose, *Rehearsal for Reconstruction: The Port Royal Experiment* (New York and London, 1964); Michael Wayne, *The Reshaping of Plantation Society: The Natchez District, 1860–1880* (Baton Rouge, 1983); and Julie Saville, *The Work of Reconstruction: From Slave to Wage Laborer in South Carolina, 1860–1870* (Cambridge, 1994). J. Mills Thornton and Lacy Ford both noted that the rapid commercial expansion of the 1850s touched off severe economic anxiety among southerners, as market fluctuations created tangible threats to personal liberty and heightened the susceptibility of yeomen to the radical remedies put forth by southern politicians. Thornton, *Politics and Power in a Slave Society: Alabama, 1800–1860* (Baton Rouge, 1978), and Ford, *Origins of Southern Radicalism: The South Carolina Upcountry, 1800–1860* (New York and Oxford, 1988). A handful of very recent works on the Old South, however, have made "transition" a central theme of their studies. Christopher Morris, *Becoming Southern: The Evolution of a Way of Life, Warren County and Vicksburg, Mississippi, 1770–1860* (New York and Oxford, 1995); Mark M. Smith, *Mastered by the Clock: Time, Slavery, and Freedom in the American South* (Chapel Hill, 1997).

both districts throughout the antebellum era. Not only did this make them typical of the Old South political economy familiar to historians, but the pantheon of states' rights and proslavery ideologues supplied by the region (including James Henry Hammond, Francis W. Pickens, George McDuffie, and William Gilmore Simms) made Edgefield and Barnwell extreme in their devotion to the South, its institutions, and its way of life. However, by the early 1820s, the districts also possessed one of South Carolina's leading inland commercial towns, Hamburg, situated across the Savannah River from the entrepôt of Augusta, Georgia. In addition, the region was among the first in the entire nation to possess a railroad, while the Horse Creek Valley of Edgefield became home to a thriving wage-labor industrial community, including the famous Graniteville textile mill of William Gregg, the South's leading advocate of industrial development. Taken together, the two districts provide a unique opportunity to analyze a variety of contrasting economic forces competing not as sectional interests, but solely within the boundaries of the South—slave labor versus free labor; industrial versus agricultural; urban versus rural.

In any study dealing with capitalism, qualifications are in order. The term has been consciously avoided in the work that follows, since its application to the antebellum South is largely anachronistic. The term did not gain currency until well after the Civil War and would have had little relevance to contemporaries of the era. *Capitalist*, however, was a widely used term and *capitalists* existed in abundance. Much of the antebellum era in Edgefield and Barnwell would be marked by a series of contests between different classes of capitalists. One class wielded influence through the agrarian capital of land and slaves, the other through the control of liquid capital in commercial and corporate forms. *Capitalism* might be applied with propriety to any political economy run by and operating in the interest of either of these classes. But it is not the purpose of this study to compel the reader to accept capitalism as a proper definition of the political economy of the slave South. Rather, it is to examine the antebellum interaction of agrarian, commercial, and industrial capitalists in Edgefield and Barnwell districts, how it shaped the local political economy, and in whose favor.[7]

It was not a contest over slavery. No merchant or manufacturer with any

7. On defining "capitalism," I have been influenced by the work of Michael Merrill. See "The Anticapitalist Origins of the United States," *Review* 13 (fall 1990): 465–97, and "Putting Capitalism in its Place."

hope for a future in Edgefield or Barnwell could possibly speak in opposition to the institution. Nor was there any reason to expect them to have done so. Members of both classes in the two districts had been reared on a militant defense of states' rights and unquestionably supported the rights of property in African slaves. But a shared commitment to slavery did not negate the possibility of conflict in other areas. In the antebellum era, agriculturists in Edgefield and Barnwell clashed with town merchants, the South Carolina Railroad, and Horse Creek factories in a series of local contests over the public responsibilities of entrepreneurship in the districts as well as the proper role of government in economic development. At the heart of the disputes lay an overriding question: in whose interest would the local political economy operate: agrarian men of property or commercial and industrial men of capital? By 1860, merchants, corporations, and factories in Edgefield and Barnwell succeeded not only in advancing their private interests over those of the local population, but also in recruiting state government as an active ally of commercial and industrial capital in South Carolina. The growing privilege granted to nonagrarian capital interests in the region during the antebellum period placed South Carolina in transition from merely being a society with capitalist features toward becoming a capitalist society. The transition was incomplete to be sure, but, by the outbreak of the Civil War, it was well under way.

CHAPTER ONE

THE AGRARIAN LANDSCAPE

It is impossible to shut our eyes to the wonderful superiority in permanence of capital invested in agriculture, over capital invested in machinery.

THOMAS COOPER, 1823

ON OCTOBER 29, 1858, U.S. Senator James Henry Hammond arrived at Barnwell Court House, South Carolina, to deliver a much-anticipated address to his neighbors and constituents. It was a homecoming of sorts. Earlier in the year, Hammond vaulted to the forefront of southern spokesmen with his castigation of northern free labor society and defense of slavery, immortalizing the assertion that "Cotton is King." Both sections of the nation echoed with his bold declaration of southern rights and northern wrongs, which earned comparisons to the revered John C. Calhoun in parts of the South while northern newspapers castigated his antidemocratic and confrontational stance. Now Hammond was back among his countrymen, indeed, among some of the very neighbors with whom he shared the tumultuous events of the previous three decades since taking up residence in Barnwell District.

As he looked at the assembly, Hammond waxed nostalgic. He saw a handful of old timers, veterans of the stirring days of nullification, now almost thirty

Epigraph from Thomas Cooper, *Two Tracts: On the Proposed Alteration of the Tariff; and on Weights and Measures. Submitted to the Consideration of the Members from South Carolina, in the Ensuing Congress of 1823–24* (Charleston, 1823), 22.

years past. But most of the faces were new, young men and "gallant spirits . . . whose kindling eyes and heaving bosoms" embraced the fire of his recent senatorial oratory. It was, Hammond felt, a propitious mix of young and old to whom he spoke that day. And if a younger generation had replaced many of their forefathers, the message Hammond delivered remained virtually unaltered with the passage of time. "Our battle then was for the Constitution and our rights, in the Union, if possible—out of it, if need be," he declared. "And this is our battle now." The issue then was nullification and the despised Tariff of 1828. Now it was Kansas, and whether or not the territory would be admitted as a slave or free state.

But while many of his fellow countrymen felt that southern interests had suffered an unbroken string of defeats and concessions to the North since the nullification crisis, Hammond had reason to feel optimistic about his region's accomplishments. "The South has long been undervaluing and doing great injustice to herself," he opined. Retracing the events of the previous three decades, southern successes were quite prominent. The protective tariff was largely repealed, as were plans for a federally funded system of internal improvements. The national bank was dead and buried and free trade was "pretty generally conceded now throughout the Union." Hammond felt especially proud of the South's successful defense of slavery. In the past, southerners—even powerful men such as Washington, Jefferson, Clay, and Marshall—expressed misgivings over slavery, believing it "to be an evil—weakness—disgraceful—nay, a sin." But a bold generation of slavery defenders—including a younger Hammond—came forth to take up the question anew. And the result? "Why, it would be difficult now to find a southern man who feels the system to be the slightest burthen on his conscience," Hammond declared proudly. He doubted if a southerner of any class did not now view slavery "as one of the main pillars and controlling influences of modern civilization; and who is not now prepared to maintain it at every hazard."[1]

1. "Speech delivered at Barnwell C.H., S.C., October 29, 1858," in *Selections from the Letters and Speeches of the Hon. James H. Hammond of South Carolina,* ed. Clyde N. Wilson (New York, 1866; Spartanburg, S.C., 1978), *passim,* quotations 323, 341, and 344–45. While Hammond immortalized the phrase *Cotton is King,* he did not coin it. Ironically, that honor goes to a northerner, David Christy, and his widely circulated treatise, *Cotton is King, or the Culture of Cotton and its Relation to Agriculture, Manufactures, and Commerce,* 2nd ed. (New York and Cincinnati, 1856; reprint, Clifton, N.J., 1975).

It would be difficult to find a region of the South that contributed more to the defense of southern institutions than the Savannah River Valley districts of Edgefield and Barnwell, South Carolina. Hammond was but one among a pantheon of proslavery, prosouthern spokesmen that the districts contributed to the state and national scene. Shortly after taking up residence in the Beech Island section of Barnwell District in 1831, Hammond won a seat in Congress, where the freshman representative boldly moved to ban abolitionist petitions and offered one of the earliest explicit defenses of slavery heard on the House floor. As governor, he penned a widely reprinted proslavery classic in response to criticisms of the institution made by the Free Church of Glasgow. And now, as a U.S. senator, Hammond put forward in his "mudsill" speech perhaps the most potent rebuke of free labor society ever offered by the South.[2]

In the corner of Barnwell District opposite Hammond's Silver Bluff plantation resided the senator's warm friend and confidant, the writer and sometime politician William Gilmore Simms. The popularity of his literary output had made him South Carolina's foremost man of letters. As the antebellum era advanced, Simms's work became a reflection of his growing political radicalism and social conservatism. Through his prolific writings, Simms hoped to inspire the southern nationalism both he and Hammond believed necessary to prepare the way for eventual secession. Residing between Hammond and Simms, at Barnwell Court House, Angus Patterson practiced law for four decades, entered the state senate in 1822, and remained there until his retirement in 1850, spending the final twelve years of his tenure as senate president. Patterson was an influential early champion of nullification, a political advisor to Hammond, and a longtime member of such influential senate committees as privileges and elections, federal relations, and the judiciary. Considering the volatile nature of upcountry politics, Patterson's electoral longevity provides strong testimony to his stature in state and local affairs until his death in 1854.[3]

2. Drew Gilpin Faust, *James Henry Hammond and the Old South: A Design for Mastery* (Baton Rouge, 1982), is an excellent analysis of Hammond's life and influence on southern thought. Also see Eugene Genovese, *The Slaveholders' Dilemma: Freedom and Progress in Southern Conservative Thought, 1820–1860* (Columbia, S.C., 1992), 85–107.

3. Jon L. Wakelyn, *The Politics of a Literary Man: William Gilmore Simms* (Westport, Conn., 1973). For Angus Patterson, see N. Louise Bailey, Mary L. Morgan, and Carolyn R. Taylor, eds., *Biographical Directory of the South Carolina Senate, 1776–1985*, 3 vols. (Columbia, 1984), 2:1237–39; John Livingston, *Portraits of Eminent Americans Now Living; Including President Pierce and his Cab-*

The conservative and intellectual demeanor of Barnwell's leading proslavery spokesmen contrasted starkly with the bombastic reputation of neighboring Edgefield District. George McDuffie helped set the standard. A brilliant young law partner of Edgefield congressman Eldred Simkins, McDuffie succeeded his legal mentor in Congress by virtue of his oratorical skill. He began as an ardent Calhoun nationalist in the early 1820s, but the protective tariff and rising abolitionist tide in the North forced a complete reversal of McDuffie's politics. The vehemence and vitriol of his defense of South Carolina in the nullification crisis made McDuffie appear to many Americans to be the "living embodiment of the wrath of the nullifiers." Even after he had relocated to neighboring Abbeville District, McDuffie's political legend loomed large over Edgefield for years to come.[4]

The loquacious Francis W. Pickens picked up in Congress where McDuffie left off, serving as a Calhoun lieutenant in the House of Representatives during the 1830s. His ambition and growing radicalism, however, caused a break with Calhoun. By the 1850s, Pickens had followed the lead of fellow Edgefieldian Louis T. Wigfall and they staked positions as "fire-eaters down to the ground." It would be Francis Pickens who occupied the governor's chair once South Carolina finally declared the dissolution of the Union. Preston Brooks clinched Edgefield's hotspur reputation by beating Charles Sumner of Massachusetts senseless on the floor of the U.S. Senate in 1856, defending, Brooks believed, the honor of the South as well as his cousin and fellow Edgefield planter Senator Andrew Pickens Butler. The "Bleeding Sumner" affair left the North aghast while simultaneously reinvigorating the militant defense of southern interests, touching off the final phase of sectional conflict that culminated in secession, civil war, and southern Armageddon.[5]

inet: With Biographical and Historical Memoirs of their Lives and Actions (New York, 1854), 221–25; John Belton O'Neall, *Biographical Sketches of the Bench and Bar of South Carolina*, 2 vols. (Charleston, 1859), 2:441–58.

4. William W. Freehling, *Prelude to Civil War: The Nullification Controversy in South Carolina, 1816–1836* (New York, 1965), 144–47, quotation 147; Edwin L. Green, *George McDuffie* (Columbia, 1936).

5. John B. Edmunds, *Francis W. Pickens and the Politics of Destruction* (Chapel Hill, 1986); Clyde W. Lord, "Young Louis Wigfall: South Carolina Politician and Duelist," *SCHM* 59 (April 1958): 96–112; William E. Gienapp, "The Crime Against Sumner: The Caning of Charles Sumner and the Rise of the Republican Party," *Civil War History* 25 (September 1979): 218–45. For a reappraisal of Edgefield's hotspur reputation, see Lacy K. Ford, "Origins of the Edgefield Tradition: The Late

Whether measured and rational or firebrand and reactionary, the defense of slave society was universal in Edgefield and Barnwell. Proudly emphasizing the distinctions—and, thus, the superiority—between their world and northern industrial society and corrupt European monarchies, the planters and yeomen of Edgefield and Barnwell made their claim as the true inheritors of the republican vision of their Revolutionary ancestors. Two institutions provided the bulwark of this society: agriculture and slavery. As an agrarian people in a slaveholding society, planter and yeoman alike believed themselves uniquely positioned to ward off the corruption, fanaticism, and anarchy that the rising tide of industrial capitalism seemed determined to conceive. Hammond's speech at Barnwell in 1858 merely came near the pinnacle of a world— and worldview—that his fellow Carolinians had embraced for generations.

As political entities, the districts of Edgefield and Barnwell came into existence in 1800, following a reorganization of the judicial system by state legislators. Edgefield District was simply a redesignation of Edgefield County, a 1,702-square-mile region between the Savannah and Saluda rivers. Originally laid out in 1785, Edgefield County previously constituted the southern portion of Ninety Six, a vast backcountry district comprising most of upper South Carolina. Bordering Edgefield on the south, Barnwell District was named in honor of the Barnwell family, a prestigious lowcountry clan that had provided military and civil leaders to South Carolina for almost a century. A slightly altered version of the former county of Winton, Barnwell District was nearly as large as Edgefield, occupying the part of the old judicial district of Orangeburg that lay between the Savannah and South Edisto rivers.[6]

At first glance, it appeared Providence did little to encourage the creation of a great agricultural society in either district. Three distinct landforms covered the region, none of which were ideally suited for intensive agricultural production. The piedmont predominated in most of Edgefield, with its gently rolling hills covering most of South Carolina above the fall line. With numerous swift-running rivers and streams, the region possessed fairly productive

Antebellum Experience and the Roots of Political Insurgency," *SCHM* 98 (October 1997): 328–48, quotation 330.

6. *Statutes at Large,* VII: 283–89; Robert Mills, *Statistics of South Carolina, Including a View of its Natural, Civil, and Military History, General and Particular* (Charleston, 1826), 211; Michael E. Stauffer, *The Formation of Counties in South Carolina* (Columbia, 1994).

surface soils. But underneath this thin layer of topsoil lay dense bands of clay and sand, neither of which were conducive to favorable drainage conditions. Combined with a sloping topography, the piedmont soils of Edgefield were notoriously susceptible to rapid erosion once cleared for farming. Its modest long-term productivity added to the dilemma. Much of the drive for agricultural reform and diversification that echoed out of Edgefield in the latter part of the antebellum period would be sparked by the dwindling productivity of this terrain, especially when compared with the phenomenally rich cotton lands of the Southwest.[7]

Unlike Edgefield, most of Barnwell was situated in the inner coastal plain, a level, featureless belt of land lying between the fall line and the seaboard, sometimes referred to as the "Middlecountry" by early inhabitants. Lacking the undulation of Edgefield's terrain, Barnwell was flat and its soil generally sandy, supportive primarily of the dense band of pine trees that blanketed the district. Although the soils drained well and proved fairly productive once cleared, the ubiquitous pine forest gave Barnwell lands a poor reputation. Residents and travelers alike commented frequently on the desolate appearance of the district's "pine barrens." Even after the railroad gave the area an air of modernity, locals still winced at the thought of travelers being exposed to such "an unluckily poor and desolate" portion of Barnwell, which left railroad passengers to "find only cause for depreciation, if not ridicule," from their narrow exposure to the district.[8]

Straddling the border between the two districts was a bleak ridge of land

7. Mills, *Statistics,* 520–21; William Gilmore Simms, *The Geography of South Carolina* (Charleston, 1843), 72; Robert L. Meriwether, *The Expansion of South Carolina, 1729–1765* (Kingsport, Tenn., 1940), 3–4, 113–15; Orville Vernon Burton, *In My Father's House Are Many Mansions: Family & Community in Edgefield, South Carolina* (Chapel Hill, 1985), 15–18; J. William Harris, *Plain Folk and Gentry in a Slave Society: White Liberty and Black Slavery in Augusta's Hinterlands* (Baton Rouge, 1985), 12; Charles F. Kovacik and John J. Winberry, *South Carolina: The Making of a Landscape* (Columbia, 1989), 16–17, 41; Carolyn Hanna Murphy, *Carolina Rocks! The Geology of South Carolina* (Orangeburg, 1995), 7–8, 63–65.

8. Mills, *Statistics,* 359–62; Simms, *Geography of South Carolina,* 34–36; Meriwether, *Expansion of South Carolina,* 9–10; Harris, *Plain Folk and Gentry,* 12; Kovacik and Winberry, *South Carolina: The Making of a Landscape,* 18–23, 41; *Edgefield Advertiser,* July 13, 1853; D. Huger Bacot, "The South Carolina Middle Country at the End of the Eighteenth Century," *South Atlantic Quarterly* 23 (1924): 50–60. See also H. Larry Ingle, ed., "Joseph Wharton Goes South, 1853," *SCHM* 96 (October 1995): 323–24.

overlapping the fall line, generally known as the sandhills. The moniker aptly described the locale, which contemporary observer John Drayton generously opined was "triflingly productive" at best. Millions of years earlier, the area marked the shoreline of the Atlantic, where silt from piedmont rivers collected to form ridges of sand and clay. After the ocean receded, the sandhills marked the transition zone between the piedmont and coastal plain, where the former dropped off sharply into the latter, with relief as much as several hundred feet in places. The sandy soil left behind was almost devoid of nutrients and drained so quickly that growing conditions were almost desert-like, supporting only a scrub forest of long-leaf pines and turkey oaks. Only the most desperate Carolinian attempted to scratch out a living on this uninviting strip of land, and the term *sandhiller* became synonymous with poverty and ignorance. The meanness of the region was summed up succinctly in a drunken bit of prose coined in the 1830s by an Edgefield resident:

Barnwell District, Aiken town;
O Lord in mercy do look down!
The land is poor, the people too;
If they don't steal what will they do?[9]

But despite these shortcomings, Edgefield and Barnwell held advantages as well. Both districts were very well watered, with annual rainfall totals reaching around forty-five inches. A myriad of rivers and streams crisscrossed both districts, which not only supplied convenient sources of transportation, but also swamp and bottom lands that, once cleared and drained, rewarded agriculturists with highly productive fields. The growing season was also long, numbering more than two hundred days on average. And while oppressive heat and humidity marked the summers, winters were quite mild. If one could find a better region in which to establish an agricultural economy than western South Carolina, one could do much worse as well.[10]

9. John Drayton, *A View of South-Carolina, As Respects Her Natural and Civil Concerns* (Charleston, 1802; Spartanburg, 1972), 9; Burton, *In My Father's House*, 15–18; Kovacik and Winberry, *South Carolina: The Making of a Landscape*, 18, 41, 44; David L. Carlton, *Mill and Town in South Carolina, 1880–1920* (Baton Rouge, 1982), 147; John A. Chapman, *History of Edgefield County: From the Earliest Settlements to 1897* (Newberry, S.C., 1897), quotation 77. For a more detailed description of the sandhills region, see Murphy, *Carolina Rocks!* 8–10; John M. Barry, *Natural Vegetation of South Carolina* (Columbia, 1980), 95–119.

10. Kovacik and Winberry, *South Carolina: The Making of a Landscape*, 31–38.

It took the better part of a generation to unlock the agricultural potential of Edgefield and Barnwell. Prior to the Revolution, an assortment of traders, trappers, and cattle drovers made up the initial white occupants of the region. Their transient nature did little to civilize the area. Indeed, coastal residents generally viewed the backcountry as a wilderness populated by ignorant squatters and murderous banditti, little removed in culture and mores from the Indian. English potter Thomas Griffiths traveled the region in 1767 in search of clay deposits suitable for porcelain production. Crossing the Edisto River into the backcountry, Griffiths was unfortunately obliged to sleep near a spot where only days earlier a set of "Virginia Crackers and Rebells" robbed and murdered five unlucky inhabitants. The wary Englishman traveled the primitive pathways with pistols "ready cock'd," which proved justified after encountering another set of robbers, who were caught only days later and subsequently executed in Charleston. The remainder of the population made little better impression on Griffiths, who found one family "all sick and Lay about the Room like dogs, and only one Bed amongst 'em, and that too a very Middling one."[11]

But among this dispersed assortment of squatters and nomads, distinct nodes of settlement also arose. Proprietary officials constructed Fort Moore on the Savannah River in the aftermath of the Yamassee War of 1715, which temporarily crippled the Indian trade and came uncomfortably close to eradicating the entire Carolina colony. As planned, the fort would protect coastal residents and trade routes from future Indian depredations. The fort later provided the nucleus for New Windsor Township in the 1730s, situated opposite the rising inland trading center of Augusta, Georgia. By 1753, Swiss entrepreneur John Tobler claimed the township's fertile soil made the place "famous," as did the exchange posts operated by Tobler and Indian trader George Galphin. Early arrivals at New Windsor were primarily Swiss immigrants, while small settlements of French Huguenots and Germans soon after occupied the areas of northern and western Edgefield along Stevens and Cuffytown creeks. At the same time, coastal planters began migrating up the Salkehatchie and Savannah rivers, encouraged in their efforts by English bounties on indigo production.[12]

11. Meriwether, *Expansion of South Carolina*, 10–16; Burton, *In My Father's House*, 35; "Account of a Voyage to Ayoree in the United States . . . in South Carolina in 1767 & 1768," Josiah Wedgewood Papers, mfm in SCL of original in the Wedgewood Museum, Barlaston, England.

12. Meriwether, *Expansion of South Carolina*, 66–76, 129–30; William Bartram, *Travels and other Writings* (New York, 1996), 259–61; Burton, *In My Father's House*, 18–19; Walter L. Robbins, trans. and ed., "John Tobler's Description of South Carolina (1753)," *SCHM* 71 (July 1970): 150; Rachel N.

While not insignificant, the influence of these pioneer communities paled in comparison to the wave of Scots-Irish migrants that washed across the South Carolina backcountry in the third quarter of the eighteenth century. Attracted by Carolina's generous land distribution policies, transplants from the northern colonies arrived in a steady stream and dispersed into Edgefield through peripheral settlements at Ninety Six and Augusta. Many newcomers had been small landholders before arriving in South Carolina and brought a familiarity with market agriculture into the backcountry. Whites arriving from Pennsylvania and Virginia were already well schooled in the cultivation of tobacco and assorted grains. Additional settlers also continued to push inland from coastal parishes, introducing the strong commercial orientation of lowcountry plantations. Some of these coastal arrivals worked their way up the Edisto, Salkehatchie, and Savannah rivers into Barnwell, while others went as far as Edgefield to develop new plantations out of vast land tracts acquired as speculations. A number of these aspiring agriculturists also brought a few slaves into the region with them.[13]

This myriad of classes and cultures proved a volatile mix. In the late 1760s, ancestors of Edgefield and Barnwell's antebellum planter elite participated in the Regulator movement, a violent vigilante campaign waged by those committed to commercial agriculture against lawless elements and subsistence hunters and drovers who kept the region in a perpetual frontier state. The Revolutionary War brought even further violence to the backcountry. Whig and Tory partisans repeatedly crisscrossed the Edgefield and Barnwell region, forcing residents to choose sides in a vicious guerrilla war. Few inhabitants emerged from the fighting unscarred. Later generations revered the heroes of this inland civil war, with leaders of one independence movement espousing the patriot cause of liberty over outside tyranny as analogous to their own struggles against northern manufacturers and abolitionists.[14]

Klein, *Unification of a Slave State: The Rise of the Planter Class in the South Carolina Backcountry, 1760–1808* (Chapel Hill, 1990), 9–15.

13. Burton, *In My Father's House*, 18–19, 65–66; Marjorie Mendenhall, "A History of Agriculture in South Carolina, 1790–1860: An Economic Study" (Ph.D. diss., University of North Carolina, 1940), 35–36, 67–68; Robbins, "John Tobler's Description of S.C.," 152–54; Joyce E. Chaplin, *An Anxious Pursuit: Agricultural Innovation & Modernity in the Lower South, 1730–1815* (Chapel Hill, 1993), 277–80, 287–90.

14. Burton, *In My Father's House*, 20, 65; Klein, *Unification of a Slave State*, 47–108; Harris, *Plain Folk and Gentry*, 133; Chapman, *History of Edgefield County*, 34–155 passim; Mills, *Statistics*, 533–36;

After nearly two decades of periodic warfare, the region emerged bloodied and badly shaken, but with the groundwork for its plantation society intact. Challenges, however, remained. Into the vacuum left by the disruption of civil authority, a new round of lawlessness struck the region in the years immediately following the Revolutionary War. In addition, the withdrawal of royal bounties left Barnwell indigo planters without a familiar means to revive their war-ravaged holdings. Finally, the postwar debtor crisis hit Edgefield and Barnwell farmers hard, causing further economic and political upheavals. Debtors in Winton (Barnwell) County took matters into their own hands and forcibly prevented county judges from sitting. Employing a grassroots variant of debt relief, Winton vigilantes tore up sheriff announcements and torched the county's first courthouse.[15]

After a half century of immigration, economic disruptions, and partisan conflict, however, Edgefield and Barnwell emerged firmly rooted in a market economy centered on the production of agricultural staples. Tobacco laid the groundwork, as Virginia and Pennsylvania immigrants spread their knowledge of the noxious weed's cultivation. Grown almost exclusively for trade, tobacco marked a step forward in carrying the commercial aspirations of backcountry farmers beyond the occasional surplus of foodstuffs. In the last two decades of the eighteenth century, tobacco production in South Carolina grew almost exponentially. Driven by strong postwar demand in Europe, state tobacco exports soared from 643 hogsheads in 1783 to almost 10,000 by 1799. Edgefield joined other parts of the upper Savannah River Valley as one of the boom areas of the postwar tobacco bonanza. At the request of local growers, the state government stepped in to encourage and regulate the trade by establishing inspection and warehouse facilities in Edgefield near the Savannah River across from Augusta. For a brief time, tobacco seemed destined to enter the pantheon of great South Carolina staple crops. But the trade dropped off sharply at the start of the nineteenth century. Poor quality and low yields took a toll on prices and outside competition hastened the decline. By 1801, owners of Edgefield's tobacco ware-

Tarleton Brown, *Memoirs of Tarleton Brown, A Captain in the Revolutionary Army, Written By Himself* (Barnwell, S.C., 1894), 4–28. The best book-length study of the Regulator movement is Richard M. Brown, *The South Carolina Regulators* (Cambridge, Mass., 1963).

15. Mendenhall, "A History of Agriculture in South Carolina," 33–35; Brent Holcomb, ed., *Winton (Barnwell) County, South Carolina, Minutes of Country Court and Will Book 1, 1785–1791* (Easley, S.C., 1978), 102–3.

houses complained that their once lucrative enterprises had devolved into "the worst species of real property at this time."[16]

Into the void left by tobacco's demise came cotton. The staple entered the state in the 1790s via the Caribbean. Sea island planters around Beaufort were the first to attempt production, focusing on the long staple, or black seed, variety with its delicate fibers ideally suited for laces and the very finest cloth. Northern textile manufacturer Amos A. Lawrence compared the silky strands of sea island cotton to Saxony wool. Highly prized, sea island cotton sold for several times the amount offered for other varieties. But the peculiar climatic requirements of the long staple variety limited its production to the coast south of Charleston. When production of sea island cotton was attempted inland, damper conditions and a shorter growing season rotted the fragile bolls.[17]

Instead, the upland cotton boom would be predicated by a hybrid cotton introduced at the end of the eighteenth century: green seed, or short staple, cotton. While lacking the long, silky fibers of the sea island variety, this upland cotton was heartier and thrived in backcountry soil and climatic conditions. A fortuitous crossroads of divine and secular forces ensured the staple's success. "If ever a crop and a place seemed well suited to each other," the historian J. William Harris aptly observed, "they were short-staple cotton and the lower piedmont." The loamy soil, long growing season, and ideal rainfall patterns combined to create an environment in which cotton thrived like nothing else in the South Carolina interior. With cotton introduced as tobacco production approached its nadir, growers benefited from the transportation and marketing infrastructure erected by the older staple. The two plants even shared similar cultivation methods. Both grew as freestanding stalks, and the planting, thinning, and topping practiced on tobacco transferred to cotton production as well.[18]

16. Chaplin, *An Anxious Pursuit*, 285–98; Lacy K. Ford Jr., *Origins of Southern Radicalism: The South Carolina Upcountry, 1800–1860* (Oxford, 1988), 6–7; Klein, *Unification of a Slave State*, 244, 248; "Petition of the proprietors of Hammonds, Campbells, & Pickens Ware Houses," Petitions, No. 1801–79, General Assembly Papers, SCDAH. On the initial attempt to establish tobacco culture in South Carolina, see Eldred E. Prince Jr., *Long Green: The Rise and Fall of Tobacco in South Carolina* (Athens and London, 2000), chap. 1.

17. Kovacik and Winberry, *South Carolina: The Making of a Landscape*, 88–91; Amos A. Lawrence Diaries, January 17, 1837, Massachusetts Historical Society, Boston.

18. Kovacik and Winberry, *South Carolina: The Making of a Landscape*, 89–90; Harris, *Plain Folk and Gentry*, 13–14, quotation, 13; Chaplin, *An Anxious Pursuit*, 297–98. Agricultural reformer

While climate made cotton production feasible, technology and market demand ensured its profitability. Whether in its patented or pirated form, Eli Whitney's cotton gin spread rapidly through the cotton districts. Almost overnight, the amount of cleaned cotton a hand could produce increased from five pounds a week to fifty pounds a day. These augmented yields found ready markets in the textile centers of England, as Manchester cotton mills devoured the staple with an almost insatiable appetite. Shortly thereafter, industrial development in the northeastern United States added to the consumption, creating a worldwide cotton demand that, aside from a few temporary slumps, continued throughout the antebellum era.[19]

This first cotton boom centered on the fertile soils straddling the upper Savannah River Valley in South Carolina and Georgia. In 1811 more than 30 million pounds of short staple cotton were exported from the South Carolina upcountry alone, and this from a region where the crop was raised in negligible quantities only twenty years earlier. By 1830, the total South Carolina cotton crop doubled to more than 60 million pounds, with the lower piedmont districts of Abbeville, Edgefield, Fairfield, and Laurens accounting for nearly one-half this total. Nor would output decrease as the antebellum era progressed. In the final cotton boom of the 1850s, production among piedmont farmers grew another 21.8 percent (31.2 percent in the lower piedmont). Most of the revered family names of the upcountry, such as Hampton, Calhoun, Brooks, and Butler, attained wealth and prominence on the shoulders of King Cotton. Yet the monarch proved surprisingly democratic as well. Cotton production required no special technological requirements or capital outlays. Nor did it benefit from any particular economy of scale. Any farmer with a few acres to spare could plant the staple and realize a tidy profit from it. Planters from across the state lauded the civilizing effects of cotton on the lower classes, deeming it the perfect incentive to produce a virtuous yeomanry of the purest Jeffersonian persuasion—industrious, independent, and residing in perfect harmony with their

---

Whitemarsh Seabrook advised that topping was an effective means of controlling the spread of caterpillars among cotton plants. Seabrook, *Memoir of the Origin, Cultivation and Uses of Cotton* (Charleston, 1844), 44.

19. Kovacik and Winberry, *South Carolina: The Making of a Landscape,* 89–90; Klein, *Unification of a Slave State,* 247; Chaplin, *An Anxious Pursuit,* 307–19; Gavin Wright, *The Political Economy of the Cotton South: Households, Markets, and Wealth in the Nineteenth Century* (New York, 1978), 90–97.

social betters. Rare indeed was the farmer of any class who withstood cotton's siren call.[20]

Cotton's most important impact, however, came in the new opportunities it opened for the acquisition of slaves. Virginia and coastal immigrants carried a handful of slaves into the South Carolina backcountry prior to the cotton boom, but cotton profits enabled slaveownership to expand beyond the bounds of this favored few. Thousands of farm operators in this first cotton generation crossed over to the ranks of slaveholder in the first decades of the 1800s. From 1790 to 1810, the inland slave population almost tripled, from 29,094 to 85,654. In parts of the interior, slave populations grew by as much as 300 percent and began to display black majorities in percentages previously found only in coastal parishes. Slave numbers also expanded dramatically in the upcountry, especially in the lower piedmont, even as the white population stagnated or even declined. From 1800 to 1860, the percentage of whites in the total upcountry population declined from more than four-fifths to just over one-half. In 1800 only one-fourth of white families in the upcountry owned slaves. By 1820, the number increased to almost two-fifths, and by 1850 almost one-half of all white families were slaveowners. The percentage of slaveowning whites was even greater in lower piedmont districts, where the local economy had a more substantial involvement in cotton production. There, by the eve of the Civil War, more than one-half of all agriculturists worked one hundred or more improved acres, with 20 percent possessing the score of slaves requisite to earn the title *planter*. By 1850, the population of every lower piedmont district in South Carolina had a black majority.[21]

The immersion of Edgefield and Barnwell into this cotton and slave economy closely paralleled the path taken by the rest of South Carolina. Indeed, if the piedmont cotton belt had a buckle, it may well have been Edgefield District. Situated in the very heart of the first inland boom, Edgefield quickly became a leading cotton district in the state and remained so throughout the antebellum era. Barnwell rose to cotton prominence at a slower, but no less determined, pace. With most of the district covered with dense pine forest and

20. Ford, *Origins of Southern Radicalism*, 7–14, 244–48; Kovacik and Winberry, *South Carolina: The Making of a Landscape*, 89; Klein, *Unification of a Slave State*, 248–49.

21. Klein, *Unification of a Slave State*, 251–54; Ford, *Origins of Southern Radicalism*, 12–14, 44–49. Ford defines the lower piedmont as consisting of the following districts: Abbeville, Chester, Edgefield, Fairfield, Laurens, Newberry, and Union.

TABLE I. Cotton Production

YEAR	LOCATION	BALES (RANK AMONG S.C. DISTRICTS)
	Edgefield	19,033 (3rd)
1840	Barnwell	7,010 (6th)
	South Carolina	154,276
	Edgefield	25,880 (2nd)
1850	Barnwell	10,138 (12th)
	South Carolina	300,901
	Edgefield	27,197 (1st)
1860	Barnwell	23,490 (2nd)
	South Carolina	353,412

SOURCES: Compendiums to U.S. Census, 1840, 1850, 1860.

NOTE: Bales are calculated as 400 pounds of ginned cotton.

meandering river swamps, clearing farmland was a much slower and more difficult process than in its piedmont neighbor. But as arable land opened up in Barnwell, its agriculturists dedicated an ever-increasing acreage to cotton. A dramatic jump during the 1850s saw Barnwell vault from twelfth to second among South Carolina districts in cotton output. By 1860, Edgefield and Barnwell accounted for nearly one-seventh of the state's cotton crop (table 1).[22]

Cotton profits led to a parallel increase in the slave population of the two districts. Even as outmigration caused white population growth to stagnate— and at times to even decrease—a steady influx of slaves kept African population figures rising throughout the antebellum era. Edgefield became a black majority district by 1830. A decade later, the slave population in Barnwell matched its white counterpart. In 1800, slaves constituted just over one-fourth of the total population in Edgefield and Barnwell. By 1860, the percentage reached almost three-fifths (table 2).

22. Lewis Cecil Gray, *History of Agriculture in the Southern United States to 1860*, 2 vols. (Washington, D.C., 1933), 2:683–86.

TABLE 2. Population

YEAR	DISTRICT	WHITE	SLAVE	TOTAL
1800	Edgefield	13,063	5,006	18,130
	Barnwell	5,575	1,690	7,376
1810	Edgefield	14,433	8,576	23,160
	Barnwell	7,969	4,153	12,280
1820	Edgefield	12,864	12,198	25,119
	Barnwell	8,162	6,336	14,750
1830	Edgefield	14,957	15,349	30,509
	Barnwell	10,456	8,497	19,236
1840	Edgefield	15,020	17,538	32,852
	Barnwell	10,533	10,503	21,471
1850	Edgefield	16,252	22,725	39,262
	Barnwell	12,289	14,088	26,608
1860	Edgefield	15,653	24,060	39,887
	Barnwell	12,702	17,401	30,743

SOURCES: White and total population figures taken from Julian J. Petty, *The Growth and Distribution of Population in South Carolina* (Columbia, 1943), Appendix F, 226–27. Slave population figures taken from compendiums to U.S. Census, 1810, 1830–60. Slave figures for 1800 and 1820 taken from Mills, *Statistics,* 359, 527.

NOTE: Errors have been adjusted. Total population figures also include free blacks.

The wealth garnered from cotton and slavery laid the foundation for a number of prominent planters and families in the districts, including such revered names as Brooks, Butler, Pickens, and Simkins. Arthur Simkins migrated from Virginia and arrived in what became Edgefield District in the 1770s. Obtaining grants for vast amounts of upcountry land, Simkins settled himself on Cedar Fields plantation in Edgefield, gradually enhancing his social standing and his estate, which grew to include fifty-nine slaves. His son, Eldred, took full advantage of his father's newly acquired wealth, attending Moses Waddel's prestigious upcountry academy and later studying law at the Litchfield academy in Connecticut. Through a successful law practice and the inheritance of his father's property, Eldred added further to the Simkins family wealth in land and slaves, which numbered 117 at his death in 1831. One of Eldred's sons, Arthur, carried on the family's influence in Edgefield as editor of the staunch states' rights newspaper, the *Edgefield Advertiser*. All three generations also represented Edgefield District in the state senate. Perennial Barnwell state senator Angus Patterson began his career as an itinerant teacher before arriving in the district to study law under the tutelage of Johnson Hagood. Patterson gradually parlayed his legal earnings into $30,000 in real estate, including plantations on the Edisto River and Lower Three Runs, as well as town lots in Barnwell Court House and Aiken. At the time of his death in 1854, the former school teacher owned 171 slaves.[23]

To be sure, not every member of the planter elite in Edgefield and Barnwell possessed the multigenerational roots of the Simkins family or were self-made men such as Patterson. Francis W. Pickens was already a scion of one of South Carolina's wealthiest and most influential upcountry families when he arrived in Edgefield in the 1820s to study law and wed a daughter of Eldred Simkins. His grandfather, General Andrew Pickens, was a Revolutionary War hero, while his father, Andrew Jr., became the first South Carolina governor from above the fall line. Establishing himself on his "home" plantation of Edgewood, the aristocratic Francis steadily expanded his family holdings and became one of South Carolina's wealthiest and most influential men. He owned plantations in three states, with his South Carolina holdings alone valued at $45,400 in real property and $244,206 in personal property. Near Edgefield Court House, his Edgewood plantation was home to 165 slaves in 1842, and at one point, he may have owned as many as 563 slaves. Levi Durand Wigfall tapped the inland cotton boom with an Edgefield plantation purchased with profits garnered from his successful mercantile career in Charleston, as well as his propitious marriage to the daughter of a wealthy lowcountry family.[24]

23. Bailey, Morgan, and Taylor, *Biographical Directory of the S. C. Senate*, 2:1237–38, 1457–61.
24. Edmunds, *Francis W. Pickens*, 4–9, 21–22; Burton, *In My Father's House*, 65–66; Ford, *Ori-*

Marriage often proved to be the quickest and most reliable way for an ambitious and impatient young man to join the elite in Edgefield and Barnwell. James Henry Hammond may have been the South's best example of such a planter parvenu. An extremely talented and ambitious son of a South Carolina College steward, Hammond was a struggling Columbia lawyer when a highly favorable marriage to lowcountry heiress Catherine Fitzsimons vaulted him to the very top of South Carolina society. Always sensitive about his modest beginnings, Hammond worked especially hard to prove himself a worthy member of the planter aristocracy and succeeded admirably. In 1831 his newly acquired Barnwell plantation, Silver Bluff, had earned a paltry $775 in the previous four years. Within a year under Hammond's management, however, Silver Bluff made a clear profit of more than $8,500. Within a decade, the plantation was earning Hammond $12,500 annually. Other prominent Edgefield and Barnwell planters likewise established themselves through marriage. William Gilmore Simms acquired his Barnwell plantation, Woodlands, through his marriage to the daughter of a successful Edisto River planter. Likewise, the Reverend Iveson L. Brookes inherited his plantation near Hamburg, Woodville, by marrying the widow of its former owner, James Myers.[25]

While few enjoyed the prosperity wrought by cotton and slavery to the degree of the districts' leading planters, many nevertheless saw their status advance markedly, if not so spectacularly. In 1770 Virginia native Tarleton Brown, his parents, and eight siblings arrived in the Barnwell region, where they initially occupied "a bark tent, which served for our use until we could erect a rude dwelling of logs." After serving the patriot cause during the Revolution, Brown gradually established his position in Barnwell, acquiring three tracts of land near the Lower Three Runs and twenty slaves by his death in 1845. The Ouzts family of Edgefield contained a number of small slaveholders, thanks in large part to bequeathments made by the family patriarch Peter Ouzts to his prodigious progeny. One of Peter's sons, Martin Ouzts, expanded his inheritance to $5,000 in real property and thirteen slaves, while another son, George, owned ten slaves and $4,000 in property. Many other descendants of Peter Ouzts were likewise among the slaveholding yeomen of Edgefield, making the family solid

gins of Southern Radicalism, 58; Bailey, Morgan, and Taylor, Biographical Directory of the S.C. Senate, 2:1272; Alvy L. King, Louis T. Wigfall: Southern Fire-eater (Baton Rouge, 1970), 8–9.

25. Faust, James Henry Hammond, 105–34; Wakelyn, Politics of a Literary Man, 60; Iveson L. Brookes to Tristram Tupper, March 21, 1837, Iveson L. Brookes Papers, SCL.

citizens in the community and recipients of the middle-class respectability that their economic status entailed.[26]

Like the Ouzts family, most slaveholders in Barnwell and Edgefield were not planters. In 1800 Barnwell District was already home to at least 290 slaveholders, but only thirteen of these held the twenty or more slaves that defined a planter. Eighty-seven percent of these slaveholders owned ten slaves or less, and 70 percent owned no more than five. The historian Orville Vernon Burton calculated that 54 percent of household heads in Edgefield owned slaves by 1860, with more than half this figure holding less than ten slaves. Although the final decade before the Civil War would show a marked concentration in wealth controlled by the largest slaveholders, overall slaveownership remained relatively broad. And while the skyrocketing price of slaves made their acquisition more difficult as the antebellum period proceeded, placement into the slaveholding class was never entirely out of reach of those who desired entry. If slaveholding created an aristocracy in Edgefield and Barnwell, then it was an aristocracy with a very broad base.[27]

Thus, cotton and slaves became the respective means and ends by which wealth, status, and economic mobility were measured in the agrarian landscape of Edgefield and Barnwell. For a handful, they paved the way to great plantations and family dynasties. Others entered the ranks of small planters and acquired respectable wealth and standing. The majority used cotton profits to earn clear title to their land, expand existing holdings, and, perhaps, have enough remaining to become masters themselves, albeit on a scale far more modest than a Hammond or a Pickens. And even though the wealth created by cotton and slavery was never distributed evenly, few households in Edgefield and Barnwell lacked a stake in their continuation and expansion.

While preeminent, cotton growers never completely dominated the early population of Edgefield and Barnwell, although they came close. Merchants resided in the region since colonial times, albeit in very limited numbers. Fewer still were those who gained the respect of interior dwellers. Before the Revolution, Charleston merchant-prince Henry Laurens advised ambitious immi-

26. Brown, *Memoirs*, 4; Bailey, Morgan, and Taylor, *Biographical Directory of the S.C. Senate*, 1:208–9; Burton, *In My Father's House*, 61–62; Chapman, *History of Edgefield County*, 287–89.

27. Wilma Copeland Kirkland and Dorothy Havens Wheeler, eds., *Winton County Tax List, 1800* (Greenwood, S.C., 1977); Burton, *In My Father's House*, 40–46. On the paradoxically aristocratic and democratic nature of slaveownership in the Old South, see James Oakes, *The Ruling Race: A History of American Slaveholders* (New York, 1982, 1998), 37–68.

grants against entering the inland retail trade, believing it "would Lessen them in the esteem of people whose respect they must endeavour to attract." By the latter stages of the eighteenth century, only a handful of merchants and Indian traders succeeded in gaining wealth and status in the Edgefield-Barnwell region. Upon his death in 1773, merchant Daniel Nail of New Windsor township left an estate that included forty slaves and a large quantity of improved farmland. Upcountry patriarch Andrew Pickens operated a substantial trading business before the Revolutionary War, which he later expanded in partnership with a pair of Charleston lawyers who, like Pickens, shared an interest in the Long Canes region along the Edgefield-Abbeville boundary. The leading merchant-entrepreneur of the region in the eighteenth century was undoubtedly LeRoy Hammond. Beginning in the 1760s with a store and ferry on the Savannah River near Augusta, Hammond expanded his estate steadily during the next quarter century to eventually include fifty-four slaves, more than 1,200 acres of land, a ferry, and a tobacco warehouse and inspection facility.[28]

But while a few merchant-planters succeeded in wielding influence, the overall impact of the merchant remained scant well into the nineteenth century. By the start of the second decade, the total value of merchant inventories in Edgefield and Barnwell districts amounted to a paltry $20,000. Surviving store accounts likewise demonstrate the limited scale and scope of trade in the region. William Daniel's store in rural Edgefield District seldom conducted transactions exceeding a few dollars, with many involving amounts less than a single dollar. Alcohol was by far the most common item purchased, and scarcely a sale was made that didn't include a quantity of whiskey, rum, hard cider, or other libation. Other merchandise consisted of the standard household commodities that planters and farmers couldn't produce for themselves: coffee, sugar, tobacco, salt, lead, powder, ink and paper, needles, buttons, and the occasional fancy item such as a bonnet, handkerchief, or pair of suspenders. Cash payments were rarely made at the time of sale and accounts usually carried over for extended periods without settlement. On several occasions no cash exchanged hands at all and Daniel settled accounts by accepting goods or services in payment or for store credit. For example, Abba Pike discharged part

28. Philip M. Hamer and George C. Rogers Jr., et al., eds., *The Papers of Henry Laurens,* 16 vols. (Columbia, 1968–2003), 4:338; Klein, *Unification of a Slave State,* 30–34; N. Louise Bailey et al., eds., *Biographical Directory of the South Carolina House of Representatives,* 5 vols. (Columbia, 1974–92), 3:301–3.

of her account with five yards of homespun cloth. Mrs. May Coxon likewise wove cloth for Daniel, acquiring $7.50 in store credit in exchange for ten and one-half yards of homespun. Another surviving Edgefield store ledger revealed an even less impressive trade, dealing mainly in alcohol and petty luxuries, such as cigars, candy, plums, and oranges. Like Daniel's store, transactions were conducted largely on credit, with accounts often settled by exchange or in kind through the performance of sundry labor by the customer. At the end of one year, total sales at the store amounted to a mere $663.37.[29]

To be sure, part of the merchants' dilemma in the early antebellum decades stemmed from a general lack of demand for their products. Besides growing and harvesting agricultural commodities, home manufacturing also occupied the time of Edgefield and Barnwell agriculturists. As in much of South Carolina, district planters and yeomen relied on their own households to provide necessary goods and services for themselves and their neighborhoods. Homespun long played a prominent role in clothing rural inhabitants, both black and white, well into the nineteenth century. In 1810 census takers counted 5,741 spindles and 1,196 looms active in Edgefield District households, producing more than $200,000 worth of wool and cotton cloth for area residents. While much of this production undoubtedly went toward home consumption, homespun also found its way to the shelves of rural stores, where local "piney woods weavers" either sold it for cash or bartered it for sundry commodities.[30]

Even more prevalent among local manufactures was the wide assortment of processing activities tied to district farms and plantations. Sawmilling flourished as a profitable adjunct to planting operations throughout the antebellum era, particularly in heavily forested Barnwell District. Equally numerous were the sundry gristmills abutting district waterways, operating on their own or in conjunction with a sawmilling enterprise. Larger planters owned and operated gins to clean their cotton, often providing ginning services to yeoman farmers

29. William Daniel Account Book, 1819–20, SCL; Cambridge Account Book, 3 vols., 1837–60, SCL.

30. Mills, *Statistics,* 527; Edgefield, *Anti-Monarchist and South Carolina Advertiser,* September 28, 1811; William Daniel Account Book, 1819–20, SCL. On home manufactures in the antebellum South, see Steven Hahn, *The Roots of Southern Populism: Yeoman Farmers and the Transformation of the Georgia Upcountry, 1850–1890* (New York and Oxford, 1983), 30, 67, 299–304; Ford, *Origins of Southern Radicalism,* 81–83; Klein, *Unification of a Slave State,* 153; Stephanie McCurry, *Masters of Small Worlds: Yeoman Households, Gender Relations, and the Political Culture of the Antebellum South Carolina Low Country* (New York and Oxford, 1995), 101–2.

in their neighborhood as well. More widespread were the many farmers who distilled a portion of their produce, turning surplus corn, peaches, and apples into whiskey, brandy, and cider for household consumption, sale, or barter. In 1810 Edgefield agriculturists produced more than 14,000 gallons of peach brandy and 7,940 gallons of whiskey. Given the district's enduring reputation for alcohol consumption, it seems likely that census takers underestimated the production of district stills.[31]

While all these undertakings fell well within traditional notions of manufactures, they remained so closely tied to the agrarian landscape that little of it fell far from the purview of agricultural activity. Distilling not only produced a salable commodity, but was also a convenient means to store and consume surplus grain and fruit. Land had to be cleared before it was fit for planting, an action that generally created marketable timber as a byproduct. Corn and wheat had to be ground before it was fit for consumption. Cotton had to be cleaned of seeds before it could be baled and sold. And while this processing activity prepared surplus farm production for market, much of it also remained implanted in the sphere of local exchange. Wealthy planters like Hammond frequently ginned and pressed cotton for poorer neighbors as an act of paternalism and noblesse oblige, seeing such transactions as legitimizing their preeminence in the local community. On the other hand, plain folk were more likely to view such transactions through the lens of reciprocity. In addition, compensation for grinding at local grist and flour mills was set by custom and the law, not the market, with services rendered exchanged for a fixed portion of the ground grain, not cash.[32]

While the profits wrought from raising cotton made the single-minded pursuit of agriculture in Edgefield and Barnwell understandable, few practitioners placed the benefits of agrarian life in such crude, materialistic terms.

31. Ford, *Origins of Southern Radicalism,* 65–66; Chaplin, *An Anxious Pursuit,* 338–45; Edgefield, *Anti-Monarchist and South Carolina Advertiser,* September 28, 1811; Chapman, *History of Edgefield County,* 73.

32. Ford, *Origins of Southern Radicalism,* 65–66; Faust, *James Henry Hammond,* 131–34. In 1841 Benjamin Gallman's flour and grist mill on Horn's Creek took a one-tenth toll for grinding ten or more bushels of grain and one-eighth toll for grinding less than ten bushels, which had been the legal rate of toll in South Carolina since 1785. Grain ground for hominy, feeding stock, or distilling was liable to a toll of only one-sixteenth part. *Edgefield Advertiser,* July 8, 1841; *Statutes at Large,* IV: 652.

More than mere material rewards were to be gained by district farm operators. Arthur Simkins, editor of the *Edgefield Advertiser*, admitted to the State Agricultural Society that agriculture was indeed an excellent path to wealth and status. But he also considered it "among the most honorable . . . the most useful of human pursuits." "A Planter" stated his case with greater vigor, considering agriculture to be "the Great Arch, and very Key-stone upon which all other interests and pursuits depend." Few people in either district would have accused him of hyperbole.[33]

Edgefield and Barnwell inherited the great country-republican ideology of the Revolutionary generation: a belief that only an agrarian society could sustain the liberty and virtue of a free republic. As envisioned by Jefferson and other republican theorists, farmers were the bulwark of this model society. As landowners, they were not beholden to another for their sustenance and thereby possessed the economic foundation necessary for personal independence. Without economic independence, men became dependent on others and subject to selfish manipulation. "Dependence begets subservience," Jefferson declared, "and venality suffocates the germ of virtue, and prepares fit tools for the designs of ambition." Only in an agrarian society, with its widespread ownership of productive property, could a virtuous society remain free from the corrupting influences of self-interest and exploitation. Such a society would certainly prosper economically, but not to the degree that it threatened the common good. If a population advanced into a commercial and manufacturing society, selfish and corrupting influences would undermine the liberty of its citizens. The result would be a dangerously dependent class of citizens, whose livelihoods were tied to wages controlled by scheming capitalists, rendering them susceptible to political manipulation and economic exploitation. The concentrated wealth of commercial and manufacturing interests would eventually wield influence in government, enriching and empowering the few at the expense of the many. To republican theorists, this scenario was no mere phantom. One only had to look at England or the northeastern United States, and the pauper labor of their manufacturing centers, to see the decline of a once virtuous society that strayed from the agrarian ideal. Given these widely held assumptions, Whitfield Brooks understandably assured his fellow Edgefield farmers that "the Agricultural class

33. Arthur Simkins, *An Address by Arthur Simkins, Esq., Before the State Agricultural Society of South Carolina, at its First Anniversary Meeting, Held During the Month of November, 1855 at Columbia S.C.* (Edgefield, 1855), 1; *Edgefield Advertiser*, October 10, 1839.

of every civilized community constitute the only sure and permanent foundation of all government, and upon which civil society and government must, in truth, depend for their continued support and preservation."[34]

South Carolinians of all classes embraced these principles as their own. Throughout the antebellum era, a panoply of politicians and orators lauded the agrarian ideal embodied in the planter and yeoman. "No pursuit is so well calculated to produce stern integrity and devoted patriotism, as agriculture," Francis Pickens told an audience. "Those who are engaged in it, are, for the most part, removed from the daily temptations that so often lead us astray from the path of rectitude and independence." Arthur Simkins agreed wholeheartedly. "The farmers and planters of the country are truly the bone and sinew of our bodies politic . . . Without them, who will deny that our experiment of Republican rule would have proven a farce?"[35]

While most of South Carolina, including Edgefield and Barnwell, fit the ideal of republican ideology, discrepancies were evident as well. The simple agrarian life of republican theory met a glaring inconsistency in the aristocratic pretensions of many planters. And while land generally remained available to all, an irritatingly large portion of the white population remained propertyless throughout the period. More ominously, outsiders cast an increasingly critical eye southward and saw a two-tiered, semifeudal white society, with patrician planters lording over both slaves and poor whites alike, leaving them with little opportunity or incentive to advance beyond their degrading state of indigence. Most galling to outside critics, however, was the hypocrisy inherent in a population of chattel slaves existing in a society that cherished liberty and opportunity above all.[36]

In response to emerging antislavery attacks, South Carolina's political leaders advanced a defense of the "peculiar institution" far beyond the traditional

34. Faust, *James Henry Hammond*, 40–41; Ford, *Origins of Southern Radicalism*, 49–51; Harris, *Plain Folk and Gentry*, 20–22, Jefferson quoted 21; *Edgefield Advertiser*, May 7, 1841. On the influence of republican theory in the development of early American government and society, see Drew R. McCoy, *The Elusive Republic: Political Economy in Jeffersonian America* (Chapel Hill, 1980; New York, 1982).

35. Francis W. Pickens, *An Address, Delivered Before the State Agricultural Society of South Carolina, In the Hall of the House of Representatives, November 29, 1849* (Columbia, 1849), 4; Simkins, *Address Before the State Agricultural Society*, 6.

36. On northern critiques of southern society, see Eric Foner, *Free Soil, Free Labor, Free Men: The Ideology of the Republican Party Before the Civil War* (Oxford, 1970, 1995), 40–72.

"necessary evil" arguments offered by their forefathers. In its place they fashioned a republican defense of the system, making slavery, in the words of Edgefield lawyer George McDuffie, "the corner-stone of our republican edifice." If landowning ensured a virtuous citizenry, explained the historian J. William Harris, then "slavery ensured that the poorest and most dependent people were permanently kept out of any role in government." As southern politicians looked to the North's burgeoning industrial society, they winced at what they observed: a throng of urban laborers, lacking land or any material stake in society, yet granted all the political privileges of citizenship. Not only were such rabble unfit citizens, they threatened to devolve into anarchy or fall under the fanatical sway of northern abolitionists. No republican society could long endure with such a large percentage of its dependent population enfranchised, slavery defenders argued. Mobocracy and demagoguery would be the inevitable result. By removing their propertyless, dependent population from the body politic, southerners believed they had ensured the peaceful, orderly continuation of their republican society.[37]

But slavery enhanced republican liberties in other ways as well. It allowed economic advancement beyond the subsistence level without creating a propertyless, politically active proletariat. And although they were removed from the body politic, masters argued that their slaves benefited from the physical and moral stewardship of their masters. While labor and capital in the North grew increasingly antagonistic to each other, southern slaveholders were obliged to their laborers beyond mere wages. Capital was labor in the South, creating a unified and inseparable interest between the two, a point on which Francis Pickens often expounded:

> Political slavery, where the masses are owned by capitalists, through the power of government, is heartless, remorseless, and cruel in its exactions, and delusive and fraudulent in its protection. Domestic slavery, where all the individual feelings of man are enlisted, generates mildness and mutual attachment; while the other system is full of arrogance and duplicity.[38]

Most crucial, however, was slavery's positive impact on all white men in South Carolina, regardless of whether they actually owned slaves. Slavery cre-

37. Harris, *Plain Folk and Gentry*, 36–39. On the intellectual defense of slavery, see Genovese, *The Slaveholders' Dilemma*.
38. Pickens, *Address Delivered to the State Agricultural Society, 1849*, 20.

ated a pervasive sense of equality among all whites on the simple basis of race. More than simply enjoying the psychological "wages of whiteness," the use of black slaves as a permanent dependent labor force freed common whites from becoming what they most feared: a wage laboring proletariat dependent on another for its daily bread. Thus, it was this ultimate paradox of slave society that non-slaveowning whites found most compelling: black slavery enhanced white freedom.[39]

Nor were politicians the only leaders to offer a defense of slavery. As abolitionists increasingly contended the sinfulness of slaveholders in perpetuating their institution, Edgefield minister William Bullein Johnson countered with numerous biblical passages to prove that slavery was tolerated by God. When northern Baptists began to join the abolitionist ranks, Johnson led the effort to persuade his fellow southerners to part company, culminating in 1845 with the formation of the Southern Baptist Convention, with Johnson serving as first president. Another Edgefield minister, Iveson L. Brookes, gained a reputation as an even more outspoken biblical defender of slavery. Not only weren't masters sinners, Brookes maintained they were actually practicing "one of God's favorite institutions—slavery." Slavery, especially Negro slavery, "is an Institution of heaven and intended for the mutual benefit of master and slave," contended Brookes, "as proved by the Bible and exemplified in the condition of the Society, and the prosperity of the Southern States."[40]

But if economic, political, or religious arguments in defense of slavery fell on deaf ears, then simple fear could be invoked. What would South Carolina be like without slavery? Francis Pickens could imagine: "Three millions of black slaves, turned lose upon the community . . . would work for little or nothing—a bottle of rum and twist of tobacco; what would become of the free artisans, enterprising mechanics, and industrious laborers of our country?" James Henry Hammond presented a more apocalyptic vision, believing emancipa-

39. Ford, *Origins of Southern Radicalism*, 353–54; Genovese, *The Slaveholders' Dilemma*, 10–40. On the psychological wage offered by race to white labor in antebellum America, see David Roediger, *The Wages of Whiteness: Race and the Making of the American Working Class* (New York, 1991).

40. Hortense Woodson, *Giant In The Land: A Biography of William Bullein Johnson, First President of the Southern Baptist Convention* (Nashville, 1950); Iveson L. Brookes, *A Defence of the South Against the Reproaches and Incroachments of the North, In Which Slavery is Shown to be An Institution of God Intended to Form The Basis of the Best Social State And The Only Safeguard to the Permanence of a Republican Government* (Hamburg, S.C., 1850), "Introduction," 2; also see Brookes, *A Defence of Southern Slavery Against the Attacks of Henry Clay and Alex'r Campbell* (Hamburg, S.C., 1851).

tion could never occur "without the extermination of one race or the other, through crimes and horrors too shocking to be mentioned—leaving a devastated land covered with ashes, tears, and blood." With such scenarios apparently ready to play themselves out if the South were ever denied its slaves, Hammond hoped anyone could understand the often startling degree to which his state carried out its defense of the institution. Emancipation would mean more than the loss of a labor force. It would mean the destruction of an entire way of life.[41]

Such attitudes were hardly unique to Edgefield and Barnwell. Indeed, slavery and agriculture were revered throughout the South as the economic and moral foundation of southern civilization. But the agrarian mentality of the region and its inhabitants was not solely manifest in the adulation heaped upon agriculture or the pathological defense of their "peculiar institution." As the planters and yeomen of Edgefield and Barnwell crossed into the nineteenth century, they carried with them not only a devotion to slavery and staple agriculture, but a shared set of assumptions about political economy that guided the initial stages of economic development in their districts. While participating—often boldly—in a burgeoning market economy, district agriculturists were simultaneously constrained by long-held community norms regarding the practice and purpose of entrepreneurship. While seldom, if ever, voiced with the frequency and vigor that district ideologues spewed in defense of agriculture and slavery, these values were nevertheless a cherished part of the agrarian landscape, and ones that found frequent, if less conspicuous, champions among the agriculturists of Edgefield and Barnwell.

41. Burton, *In My Father's House*, 38; James Henry Hammond, "Message to the Senate and House of Representatives of the State of South Carolina, November 26, 1844," in Wilson, ed., *Selections from the Letters and Speeches of the Hon. James H. Hammond*, 102.

CHAPTER TWO

Publici Juris

ECONOMIC DEVELOPMENT AND ENTREPRENEURSHIP

IN THE POST-REVOLUTIONARY ERA

It is evident, that, by the very act of the civil or political association, each citizen subjects himself to the authority of the entire body, in every thing that relates to the common welfare. The authority of all over each member, therefore, essentially belongs to the body politic, or state. . . . If the body of the nation keeps in its own hands the empire, or the right to command, it is a popular government, a *democracy.*

EMER DE VATTEL, *The Law of Nations*

TOURING THE SOUTH CAROLINA backcountry in the fall of 1784, Aedanus Burke was appalled by what his eyes beheld. Returning to Charleston, the circuit court judge reported to Governor Benjamin Guerard that people in the backcountry were "worried & half-ruined" by the lawlessness that dominated the region in the aftermath of the Revolutionary War. Roaming gangs of banditti robbed and plundered inhabitants at will. No property of any value was safe. Worst of all, in Burke's eyes, was the impact of this disorder upon the local economy. "As to trade and commerce, it is at an end in that district," he lamented. Wagons traveling to market routinely had their horses stolen, while those returning from Charleston were set upon as soon as they crossed the Saluda River. Only by forming armed escorts to guard wagons could some degree of commercial contact be maintained. "Thus the wretched people are precluded from improving their Estates," Burke lamented, "and as to pay Taxes, I cannot see how they will be able until some Security be established thro' the Settlements."

Epigraph from Emer de Vattel, *The Law of Nations; or, Principles of the Law of Nature, Applied to the Conduct and Affairs of Nations and Sovereigns* (Philadelphia, 1817), Book I, 1.

The "Security" Burke had in mind was government. He saw little chance for backcountry residents to improve their lot "unless Government take some Measures for exterpating the Outlyers." Indeed, Burke noted that except when judges such as himself went on circuit, "the influence of Government is felt but feebly," existing in little more than name only and providing "no sort of Security for life or property" for the desperate residents of the backcountry. Burke begged Governor Guerard to present his report to the legislature so that a course of action might be taken to relieve the situation of the backcountry.[1]

Burke's account of the post-Revolution backcountry, and his proposed solution, strongly echoed the prewar Regulator movement. Both were responses to the lawlessness that threatened the backcountry's blossoming commercial society, and that prevented industrious yeomen and a nascent planter class from reaping what they had sown. The overriding concern of the Regulators, as the historian Rachel Klein contends, was a shared interest "in making the backcountry safe for planting." Burke had the same concern, and saw government as the best means for not only establishing order, but a *commercial* order as well.[2]

However, an active government serving as a catalyst for economic development clashed with republican fears over the consequences of such a combination. In the years following the Revolution, backcountry republicans held deep suspicions of centralized political power, especially when allied with commercial interests. These fears took tangible shape in the form of the Federalist Party, whose ranks were dominated by an aristocratic and wealthy lowcountry elite who dreaded excessive democracy far more than a coalition of government and commerce. Upcountry republicans soon coalesced in the late eighteenth century into a vocal opposition, which sought to defend their interests by increasing backcountry representation and expanding the electorate. By the end of the first decade of the nineteenth century, the superior numbers of the republicans held sway. The Compromise of 1808 gave inland districts a larger—if still not proportional—voice in the legislature, while universal white manhood suffrage became a reality in 1810 with the repeal of property requirements for voting. By then, any upcountry candidate who wished the support of this

1. Aedanus Burke to Governor Benjamin Guerard, December 14, 1784, Governors' Messages-306, General Assembly Papers, SCDAH.

2. Rachel N. Klein, *Unification of a Slave State: The Rise of the Planter Class in the South Carolina Backcountry, 1760–1808* (Chapel Hill, 1990), 47–77, quotation 51.

rough-hewn white man's democracy needed to eschew aristocratic pretensions and vocalize a proper vigilance against efforts by private interests to turn the mechanisms of popular government toward selfish ends.[3]

Thus, state and local government in antebellum South Carolina needed to meet a series of potentially contradictory requirements. The electorate expected a government role in enhancing economic development, but wished such actions to be as unobtrusive as possible, both physically and fiscally. They desired that government permit its citizens economic autonomy, yet demanded a high degree of popular control over private economic institutions. They lauded the rights of the individual, yet demanded restraint be placed on those who sought to elevate individual over civic virtue. In short, they wanted government to enhance their opportunities in a market society, while defending participants from its pitfalls. And, to do both on a parsimonious budget and with as few manifestations of its presence as possible.

Much of the routine operation of government in South Carolina reflected the dual desires of this political economy, particularly at the local level. In the decades after the Revolutionary War, state and local government became active participants in the overall effort of South Carolinians to enhance the economic potential of themselves and their state. Legislatures authorized the laying out of roads and clearing of waterways. Local projectors received permission to build wharves, inspection stations, warehouses, bridges, and ferries. Additional aspects of economic activity fell under the regulatory purview of legislators, judges, and local custom. Charges for services rendered were often set by state legislators or local commissioners, not by the laws of supply and demand. Legislation frequently went so far as to set standards for packing and shipping produce, as well as assessing quality and weight and, thus, its value.

Such activity, however, cast the state in the role of regulator, not participant. Despite a desire for government to play a part in their state's development, South Carolinians still blanched at vast expenditures of public money or the creation of a vast, permanent administrative bureaucracy. Little in the way

3. On the political culture of the antebellum South Carolina upcountry, see Lacy K. Ford Jr., *Origins of Southern Radicalism: The South Carolina Upcountry, 1800–1860* (New York, 1988), 99–113. Ford challenges the long held view of planter domination of the antebellum South Carolina politics and aristocratic political culture, stated most succinctly in James M. Banner, "The Problem of South Carolina," in *The Hofstadter Aegis: A Memorial,* ed. Stanley Elkins and Eric McKitrick (New York, 1974), 60–93. In support of Ford's argument, also see J. Mills Thornton, *Politics and Power in a Slave Society: Alabama, 1800–1860* (Baton Rouge, 1978), esp. 3–58.

of state money went to public or private projects in the years immediately following the war. Likewise, responsibility for the construction, operation, and upkeep of such undertakings generally remained with local residents, who, in turn, were the primary beneficiaries of the same. Nevertheless, such modes of government involvement underscored the high degree of popular influence over economic activity at the local level. Little in the way of legislative action occurred in the economic sphere except at the behest of the local populace. The regulatory function of government served to stimulate a commercial economy, but also restrained self-interest in the name of the commonweal. The economic affairs of a community generally remained under private control, but with enough government and community oversight to render them *publici juris,* that is, operating under popular consent and in the public interest.[4]

The interplay between public interests, private entrepreneurship, and government was a prevalent combination in the development of Edgefield and Barnwell during the early decades of the nineteenth century. District residents eagerly worked to stimulate economic development and participate in the commercial expansion ushered in by the upcountry cotton boom: clearing land, planting cotton, and purchasing slaves. Simultaneously, however, they sought to place bounds on economic activity by maintaining a degree of quasi-public control over private entrepreneurship through the combined means of the petition, the law, and established custom. Such oversight not only worked to prevent individual interests from running roughshod over prescriptive rights and civic values, but also kept government from enhancing one interest to the detriment of others. The planters and yeomen of Edgefield and Barnwell were united—sometimes willingly, sometimes grudgingly—in making the economic maturation of their community a social compact, which turned entrepreneurship into a civic, as well as an individual, undertaking that bound citizens to their community and the community to each of its members.[5]

By far the most numerous demands made by Barnwell and Edgefield residents of their legislature was for internal improvements, primarily roads, bridges, and ferries. As the local economy began to thrive with the introduction of tobacco, and later boom with cotton, access to markets in Charleston and beyond became increasingly important to backcountry residents. An early Edgefield his-

4. Henry Campbell Black, *Black's Law Dictionary,* 5th ed. (St. Paul, Minn., 1979), 106.

5. Ruth Bogin, "Petitioning and the New Moral Economy of Post-Revolutionary America," *William and Mary Quarterly,* 3rd series, 45 (July 1988): 391–425.

torian asserted that the rising demand for roads and ferries clearly demonstrated "the needs and wants of the people and their progress in improvements." Furthermore, the means of authorizing and establishing these improvements also reflected the dual demands residents placed on their government: fostering development while remaining as unobtrusive as possible.[6]

By the end of the eighteenth century, a web of common roads already crisscrossed much of Edgefield and Barnwell. Primitive by modern standards—and the bane of contemporary travelers and residents alike—these avenues were anything but elaborate affairs. Like country roads nationwide, they were frequently little more than glorified horse paths, replete with stumps, rocks, and assorted ruts and gullies. After the shaft of her carriage fell victim to a stump-ridden Edgefield road, Mrs. S. Johnson exchanged her stylish barouche for a much sturdier wagon "that would stand a little racking." A visitor to Barnwell District in 1824 found that a popular means of improving roads was "to fall a tree on the bad part & oblige the traveller to turn rund through the woods, over the stumps." Roads through the sandhills region of the two districts were particularly notorious. The loose soil provided a poor foundation for vehicles and a team of horses could wear themselves out trying to drag a loaded wagon through axle-deep sand.[7]

Construction of these arteries mandated little in the way of engineering expertise and seldom required more than brute labor, though plenty of it. Frederick Law Olmsted noted the rudimentary skills needed for road repair on his journey through South Carolina: "driving the carts, loading them with dirt, and dumping them upon the road; cutting down trees, and drawing wood by hand, to lay across the miry places; hoeing, and shovelling." To make road maintenance a bit less strenuous, a Barnwell District ordinary advised that road commissioners work after heavy rainfalls, which would make the labor of filling ruts and grubbing roots "much easier than at a dry time."[8]

6. John A. Chapman, *History of Edgefield County, From the Earliest Settlements to 1897* (Newberry, S.C., 1897), 54. For an insightful local study of internal improvements in eighteenth-century South Carolina, see George D. Terry, "'Champaign Country': A Social History of an Eighteenth Century Lowcountry Parish in South Carolina, St. John Berkeley County" (Ph.D. diss., University of South Carolina, 1981), 176–242.

7. George Rogers Taylor, *The Transportation Revolution, 1815–1860* (New York, 1951), 15–17; Mrs. S. Johnson to Lucy Hamilton, May 8, 1834, SCL; James A. Padgett, ed., "Journal of Daniel Walker Lord, Kept While on a Southern Trip," *Georgia Historical Quarterly* 26 (June 1942): 190.

8. Frederick Law Olmsted, *The Cotton Kingdom: A Traveller's Observations of Cotton and Slavery*

However, the primitive condition and simple construction of public roads should not downplay their importance to the local community. These crude affairs supplied a basic transportation medium for the citizens of Edgefield and Barnwell, providing access to markets, churches, mills, court, and each other. Indeed, more than one contemporary acknowledged the humble road as one of the fundamental needs of civilized society. "For without public roads and highways," a South Carolina jurist observed, "there could be no convenient communication from one part of the country to another, unless men roamed like savages through a wilderness." Judges John Grimké and Elihu Bay stated the role of the public road in greater detail:

> That it was by the means of these roads and highways, that the citizens of the country had a convenient communication from one extremity of it to another; and between the intermediate towns and public places in the interior of it. It was along them also, that the citizens assembled with convenience and despatch in times of danger and alarm for defence and protection; and along these, the productions of the country were conveyed to a market, and the produce of the soil rendered valuable.

Forty years later, Judge Josiah Evans reaffirmed this view: "The existence of roads are essential to the well being of society, and the right to make them, has been exercised by the government of every civilized country." Understandably then, the layout, alteration, and upkeep of public roads commanded considerable attention from local residents, and through them, the state legislature as well.[9]

The practice of laying out public roads originated in the long-established common law doctrine of eminent domain: the authority of the state to expropriate a portion of private lands for the public's benefit. Although the state's power of eminent domain was seldom given explicit justification, it was generally reasoned that each citizen enjoyed his property subject to the sufferance

in the American Slave States, ed. Arthur Schlesinger Sr. (New York, 1984), 161; Orsamus D. Allen to Cornelius K. Ayer et al., June 11, 1830, Orsamus D. Allen Letterbook, 1826–47, SCL.

9. *Lindsay et al. v. Commissioners,* 2 S.C.L. (2 Bay, 1796) 42, 56; *State v. Dawson,* 21 S.C.L. (3 Hill, 1836), 104. On upcountry demand for internal improvements during the early stages of commercial development, see Joyce E. Chaplin, *An Anxious Pursuit: Agricultural Innovation and Modernity in the Lower South, 1730–1815* (Chapel Hill, 1993), 293, 295–97; Klein, *Unification of a Slave State,* 244–46. On early road development in Edgefield, see Chapman, *History of Edgefield County,* 20–21, 53–54.

of the sovereign, initially the Lords Proprietors, later the British crown, and finally the popularly elected representatives of South Carolina in the General Assembly. As such, when required, a portion of any person's private property could be taken to fulfill a public necessity. Roads, by far, became the most frequent catalyst in the exercise of eminent domain powers. Indeed, discussion of the tenet seldom came forward except in its relation to the power of the state to expropriate lands for public highways. The creation of all public roads, argued Judge Job Johnston in the 1827 case of *Eaves v. Terry*, "proceed[s] on the ground that there is a tacit reservation in every grant of a freehold, of so much as may be necessary for the ordinary purpose of making roads and public highways." And, under its reserved power of eminent domain, "the Legislature has a right to set it apart for that use, when the public convenience requires it."[10]

The invocation of eminent domain was by no means limited to the General Assembly of South Carolina, but was likewise asserted by every state legislature in the Union as part of the legal heritage inherited from the ancient doctrines of English common law. However, South Carolina did set itself apart by resisting the concomitant concept of just compensation for property taken under a claim of eminent domain. While other states began to provide "just" or "fair" compensation to property holders for lands taken, South Carolina courts resisted this emerging postcolonial legal doctrine. The authority of the state to appropriate land for roads under eminent domain, stated Grimké and Bay, "was one of the original rights of sovereignty, retained by the power of every community at its formation, and like the power of laying on, and collecting taxes, paramount to all private rights." In other words, judges argued that "all private rights were held and enjoyed, subject to this condition." If state or local authorities granted compensation to a property holder, it was more akin to an act of kindness or a favor rather than an express acknowledgment that a citizen had a right to such compensation. Judge Evans asserted that no citizen had a constitutional right to financial restitution "as a condition precedent to the use of the property." Besides, the property holder would also, presumably, be among the beneficiaries of the new road. Reciprocally, he also retained the right to pass through a portion of his neighbor's land as part of the common property of the community, if the public welfare so required.[11]

10. *Eaves v. Terry*, 15 S.C.L. (4 McCord, 1827), 127.

11. The most detailed statements on the theory and practice of eminent domain in the Palmetto State are found in the South Carolina Law Reports. See esp. *Lindsay v. Commissioners*, Grimké and Bay quoted 56; *Stark v. McGowen*, 10 S.C.L. (1 Nott & McCord, 1818), 387; *State v. Dawson*,

Although practiced since the organization of civil government in South Carolina in the late seventeenth century, taking private property for public purpose never became an act undertaken lightly. In the agrarian landscape of the state's deeply republican political economy, property ownership was held akin to a natural right, upon which rested the right of citizenship and the health of the republic. Any action that threatened to injure a resident in the private enjoyment of his property was liable to extremely close scrutiny, by both the landholder and the members of his community. Therefore, convincing arguments needed to be made that the action was of direct benefit to the community.

More specifically, when pertaining to proposed public roads, residents had to convince the legislature that the route was of public utility and promoted the general welfare of the locality. Residents of Winton County claimed that shortening the route from Kellies Cowpen to Augusta would "be of publick Benefit and . . . Redound to the Benefit and welfare of this Republick." A petition from more than one hundred Edgefield residents prayed the reestablishment of a road from the Saluda River to Barnwell Court House, trusting that the legislature would "promote the common interest of your fellow citizens" by granting their "reasonable and Laudable demand." In 1821 John Fox sought to alter the route of the Five Notch Road through his Edgefield property, alleging the current route was difficult to maintain, liable to flooding, and "very injurious to travers." The new route, he claimed, would not only be less detrimental to the lands through which it passed (including his own), but would also be "much to the advantage of the community & public at large."[12]

While a well-placed and well-laid-out road was a boon to the community, too many public roads could become onerous. Inhabitants sought to discon-

---

Bay quoted 103. On the role of eminent domain and property expropriation in the economic development of the early republic, see Morton Horwitz, *The Transformation of American Law, 1780–1860* (Cambridge, Mass., 1977), 63–66; William E. Nelson, *Americanization of the Common Law: The Impact of Legal Change on Massachusetts Society, 1760–1830* (Cambridge, Mass., 1975), 51–52; Harry Scheiber, "The Road to Munn: Eminent Domain and the Concept of Public Purpose in the State Courts," *Perspectives in American History* 5 (1971): 329–402, esp. 360–76; idem, "Property Law, Expropriation, and Resource Allocation by Government: The United States, 1789–1910," *Journal of Economic History* 33 (March 1973): 232–51; Carol Sheriff, *The Artificial River: The Erie Canal and the Paradox of Progress, 1817–1862* (New York, 1996), 79–109.

12. "Winton County, Road Petition," Petition, 1792–211; "Petition of Sundry Inhabitants of Edgefield District," Petition, 1823–91; "Petition of John Day," Petition, 1821–89; all in General Assembly Papers, SCDAH.

tinue any road deemed unnecessary for the public welfare, which burdened residents with its upkeep but with little remuneration for their labors. In 1809 road commissioners and a number of Edgefield residents sought to have an old public road between Edgefield Court House and Augusta discontinued. A new road rendered the old route *"unnecessary* and *oppressive,"* by requiring residents to continue its maintenance "without any publick necessity or advantage for such Labour and expense." Similarly, another Edgefield petition asked to close a further section of public road that was "of little or no advantage to the public," yet still worked by local residents "without the Public having rec^d any benefit."[13]

A more serious charge against certain public roads was that they were a means of private emolument at the public's expense. Several Edgefield property owners protested the blocking of a public road by one local landowner, who sought to have it discontinued "just through anger and malice because said road did not go by his door." Another petition from Edgefield sought to discontinue a new road from Lee's ferry on the Saluda River to the Columbia Road. The memorialists claimed the old route served a populous section of the district well, while the new road passed through a thinly settled region "for no other purpose as we apprehend but to accommodate Mr. Williams in passing his store house and distillery." No public road, they believed, should be laid out "for the convenience and imolument of the few at the detrimental and [im]pediment of all others concerned." A petition from another group of Edgefieldians condemned a different road in similar language: "The truth is the present road, was opened at the benefit of individual interest, and wholly against the public good." At times, protests went beyond mere rhetoric. In 1822 public outcry against a new road in one Edgefield neighborhood was so great that commissioners were prevented from laying out the new route "by the universal opposition of those persons holding land through which the road was to run."[14]

13. "Petition of the Commrs. of Roads and some of the Citizens of Edgefield," Petition, 1809–78; "Petition of Sundry in habitants of Edgefld. District to discontinue a Road," Petition, ND-1271; both in General Assembly Papers, SCDAH.

14. "Petition of the Commissioners, Land Owners and Many Citizens of Edgefield District," Petition, ND-3079; "Petition of Sundry Inhabitants of Edgefield District," Petitions, 1823–108, ND-1393; "Petition of Sundry Inhabitants of Edgefield District Praying for the Re-establishment of the Old 5 Notched Road," Petitions, ND-1352, ND-1354; all in General Assembly Papers, SCDAH.

High social or economic standing in a neighborhood offered little in the way of special privilege in deciding the route of public roads, and even less in exempting wealthy residents from the public responsibilities of road building and maintenance. In 1803 Lewis Malone Ayer was a prominent Salkehatchie River planter in lower Barnwell District, soon to embark on a decade of service as a representative and senator in the state legislature. Yet his prominence offered little defense against an angry board of barely literate road commissioners responding to complaints made against Ayer for blocking a public road passing through his land. The commissioners bluntly ordered Ayer to clear the old road or build a replacement route at his own expense. If he failed to comply, the board informed him, "we shal be obliged to pull down your fence and keap the Rod as it was laid out."[15]

Disputes over whether roads served a public or merely private interest could become quite heated. In 1809 Samuel Maner asked to discontinue a public road to a Savannah River landing, which passed through his Barnwell lands, asserting it injured his corn and cotton fields and stopped up ditches needed to water his lands. Furthermore, Maner claimed the road only benefited James Overstreet and his mother, "as the said road can only be of service to them and others for driving their stock . . . and can never be of General or public utility." A counterpetition by more than one hundred Barnwell residents demanded the road be kept a public highway, arguing that the route had been "enjoyed at all times by all inhabitants of this place" for upwards of forty years. Maner, they contended, only recently purchased the land over which the road passed, giving him "no Interest in, or affection for the society of the place." By asserting his rights of private property, the petitioners claimed Maner had "in contempt of Justice and defiance of Law, assailed our rights and privileges of ancient existence and *peculiar* utility." No convenient alternative existed and their reliance on the existing artery as a market road made it a "public necessity."[16]

Being removed from the scene of the conflict, the state legislature often had a difficult time deciding such disputes in an equitable manner. In the above case, the legislature ordered Maner to lay out a new road, at his own expense, to run above his fields, and appointed several local residents to oversee its lay-

15. Joseph Harly Sr. et al. to Lewis Malone Ayer, January 8, 1803, Lewis Malone Ayer Papers, SCL.

16. "Petition of Samuel Maner," Petition, 1809–75; "Petition of Sundry Inhabitants of Barnwell District," Petition, 1809–76; both in General Assembly Papers, SCDAH.

out and construction. The new route ensured public access to the Savannah River landing, but not through Maner's cotton and corn fields. But such examples of state government micromanaging local internal improvements became increasingly rare, particularly as the demand for new improvements continued to grow in proportion to the rapidly expanding population of upcountry districts. More and more, legislators delegated decisions regarding the planning, layout, and upkeep of roads to local authorities.[17]

By 1825, the General Assembly combined the myriad of road statutes into a general law. The act created permanent highway commissioners for each district, which met at specific intervals throughout the year and whose recommendation would be required before any road would be declared, or discontinued, as a public highway. In addition, before opening a new road, commissioners had to give three months' notice in local newspapers so that potential opponents could have their say. In theory, final authority to establish new roads lay with the General Assembly. But in practice, state solons seldom questioned the decision of local commissioners and combined all recommendations to open, alter, or discontinue roads into an omnibus annual act, which usually became law with little scrutiny or debate by legislators.[18]

While one part of the act devolved practical responsibility for laying out roads to local commissioners, other parts of the act illustrated the concomitant duties of the local community in the construction and maintenance of public roads in their neighborhood. Little in the way of public funding went toward road building and upkeep. Rather, the system continued to be carried out largely via the long-established system of taxing local residents in kind. All male residents, both white and slave, residing within ten miles of a public road were required to contribute a certain amount of labor annually, usually no more than twelve days. In addition to the labor of local residents and their slaves, commissioners were also authorized to take timber, earth, stone, or other materials from adjacent lands as needed. Public funds, when used at all, came largely through fees collected from tavern licenses, or from fines levied on those negligent in fulfilling their public road duties. These seldom added up to much. Even as late as 1850, when a dense web of local roads covered almost every part

17. "Report on the Petitions of Saml. Maner & the Counter Petition of Sundry Inhabitants of Barnwell Dist.," Committee Reports, 1809–116, General Assembly Papers; *Statues at Large*, IX: 442.

18. Ibid., IX: 558–66.

of Edgefield (the second largest district in the state), the total amount of moneys collected by the commissioners of roads amounted to just $1,693.43, or the equivalent of ten cents for every white inhabitant of the district.[19]

Whereas the practice of eminent domain demonstrated public authority over private property holders, public levies showed the reciprocity inherent in internal improvement. A property holder might be required to turn over a strip of his land for a public highway, but his neighbors were similarly bound to give their time and labor to maintain the same. As Judge Pringle asserted, since all members of a community held their property subject to the right of the sovereign to create public roads, "so all ought to contribute, either in money or labour, to keep them in order, and fit for use." As eminent domain made individuals subject to the needs of the community, so public road levies bound the community to the welfare of the individual.[20]

The layout and upkeep of public roads in Edgefield and Barnwell demonstrated a reciprocity inherent in the economic development of their districts, as well as the state's role as mediator. While the republican ethos held by district agriculturists lauded the independence and security that property provided, claims of private property rights could not be invoked to pursue personal ends detrimental to community interests. All public roads entailed a certain degree of individual inconvenience, whether by bisecting a farmer's land, requiring the labor of one's slaves or oneself, or taking timber from adjacent lands. But such nuisances were offset by the benefits a road bestowed to the community and the responsibility of its members toward maintaining their basic transportation infrastructure. The designation of a road as "public" not only gave the community the benefit of it, but the responsibility for it as well.[21]

Like roads, the creation of bridges and ferries was also of prime concern to Edgefield and Barnwell residents, serving to improve transportation networks which, in turn, contributed to the economic development and commonweal of

19. Ibid., IX: 558–66; *Edgefield Advertiser*, October 24, 1850; for population figures, see table 2. Milton Sydney Heath and U. B. Phillips described similar systems of road construction and oversight elsewhere in the antebellum South. Heath, *Constructive Liberalism: The Role of the State in Economic Development in Georgia to 1860* (Cambridge, Mass., 1954), 233–34; Phillips, *A History of Transportation in the Eastern Cotton Belt to 1860* (New York, 1908; New York, 1968), 59–61.

20. *Lindsay v. Commissioners*, 46.

21. William E. Nelson found similar public constraints on private property and entrepreneurship in prerevolutionary Massachusetts. Nelson, *Americanization of the Common Law*, 46–63.

their districts. In 1791 Thomas Chappell erected a bridge over the Saluda River, asserting it to be "a very great Convenience as well to the settlements on both sides of the River as to travellers for Transporting Produce to the Different markets." A decade later, Robert Ware sought to establish a ferry on his Savannah River lands, noting none existed within six miles of his place and that it would provide "important advantages that would necessarily result to the public and particularly farmers carrying their produce to market." Sixty-two residents supported Ware's petition, maintaining his ferry would be placed in "a convenient, proper, and advantageous place" for public use.[22]

Unlike roads, however, the construction and operation of bridges and ferries generally devolved upon individuals, not public levies. Smaller bridges, especially those over minor creeks and streams, fell under the provenance of local road commissioners, who contracted with private citizens to build or repair these structures. Though small, bridges of even a minor span could cost up to several hundred dollars to construct. As such, funding even a few of these basic improvements could claim the lion's share of a district's paltry highway funds. By 1850, road commissioners in Edgefield District collected $1,693.43 in highway funds, but spent almost $2,000 for bridge construction and repair, which forced commissioners to dip into surplus funds from the previous year. Rare indeed was the year in which other expenses in the local transportation network competed with those required for bridge building and repair.[23]

However, being generally cash poor—as much by choice as by circumstance—state government encouraged private entrepreneurs to undertake public ventures, such as bridges and ferries, by offering vested franchise rights in return for building and operating their respective enterprises. Granting franchises was a long-established means of encouraging private capital to be risked on public projects. The obligations and rewards of such ventures fell on both the owner and the public. By establishing a public bridge or ferry, owners were required to maintain and operate the franchise at their own expense. In return, the state permitted the collection of tolls to compensate owners for costs in-

22. "Petition of Thomas Chappell," Petition, 1791–229; "Petition of Robert Ware," Petition, 1802–102; both in General Assembly Papers, SCDAH.

23. *Edgefield Advertiser*, October 24, 1850. For other annual reports of the Commissioners of Roads and Bridges for Edgefield District, see *Edgefield Advertiser*, November 10, 1847; October 25, 1848; October 17, 1849; October 23, 1851; October 27, 1852; October 26, 1853; November 9, 1854; November 7, 1855; November 5, 1856; October 21, 1857; November 10, 1858; November 2, 1859; December 12, 1860.

curred and services rendered. Moreover, franchises often received exclusive privilege to operate a venture in a particular locale, preventing competition and increasing the likelihood that remuneration would be attained by the franchise holder for risking his private funds. In effect, the state harnessed private monopolies to the public's interest, although the odious term *monopoly* was rarely invoked explicitly. In 1799, for example, the South Carolina legislature permitted William Weekley to erect a bridge across the Salkehatchie River, authorizing the collection of tolls and declaring it unlawful for any competitor to construct another toll bridge or ferry within three miles of Weekley's enterprise. Robert Ware's petition sought exclusive right to operate a ferry across the Savannah River for a period of fourteen years, further requesting that the legislature "prohibit an invasion by any person within the distance of three miles." In lieu of public compensation for erecting a bridge over the Edisto River, John Holman instead asked that it be vested in him with permission to collect a reasonable toll in order to indemnify him for the undertaking.[24]

Though quasi-public, these ventures could still prove quite profitable for the franchise holder. If operated to the satisfaction of local residents and the legislature, a franchise might be renewed almost ad infinitum, providing the original holder, as well as his heirs and assigns, an enviable income for several decades. Thomas Lamar secured his initial charter to operate a Savannah River ferry at Fort Moore Bluff in 1795, which passed to his heirs, who, in turn, received recharters from the legislature throughout the antebellum period. When his daughter, Elizabeth Whatley, offered to sell the ferry some time later, she enticed prospective buyers in her area with the claim that the ferry had earned between $2,000 and $2,500 per annum over the previous ten years. John Murphy's Barnwell District ferry earned a steady annual income from ferrying residents, horses, slaves, and livestock. The ferry proved most profitable late in the fall with the collection of larger tolls on loaded wagons traveling to market with the year's harvest. Henry McGowen's ferry over the Saluda River earned an average of $15 to $20 per week, rising as high as $60 during the lucrative winter months.[25]

24. *Statutes at Large,* IX: 395; "Petition of Robert Ware," Petition, 1802–102; "Petition of John Holman," Petition, 1801–67; both in General Assembly Papers, SCDAH. On legal aspects of franchises and competition in early America, see Horwitz, *Transformation of American Law,* 109–39; Nelson, *Americanization of the Common Law,* 46–54.

25. *Statutes at Large,* IX: 365, 449, 538–39, 591, 613; XI: 374; XII: 75, 698; *Edgefield Advertiser,* February 1, 1854; Account: July 25, 1830, to September 28, 1831, David Montague Laffitte Papers, SCL; *Stark v. McGowen,* 396.

While remunerative, a bridge or ferry franchise also carried a high degree of public accountability. Justice Bay deemed a ferry operator as a man of "high public trust and confidence; and the lives of the passengers, as well as the goods, are entrusted to his good conduct and management." In the 1818 case of *Stark v. McGowen,* Justice Charles J. Colcock asserted the bestowment of privileges and responsibilities on operators was "an incident of sovereignty" by state government, providing a means to ensure that individual interests operated within those of the community at large:

> When a ferry is established by the government, certain duties are imposed on the person to whom the grant is made. He is obliged to make a sufficient boat; to employ a *white man;* to keep-up the banks of the river; to transport the citizens at all times of the day and night. He is subjected to fines for the neglect of duty; and is answerable in damages for any injury or loss which results from his negligence; all of which is necessary for the public convenience; and as a remuneration for his services, and these liabilities, is allowed a fixed rate of ferriage.[26]

To prevent abuse by franchise holders, charters held a number of conditions regarding the operation of respective enterprises. Setting the rate of toll was foremost among the prerogatives claimed by the legislature. John Holman, for example, acquired a charter vesting a bridge over the South Edisto in him and his heirs for a term of seven years, but which stipulated very specific rates of ferriage: three cents per head of livestock, six cents for a foot passenger or horse, twelve cents for a horse and rider, twenty-five cents per horse and cart or rolling hogshead, and fifty cents for each wagon and team or carriage and horses. Furthermore, state law required that rates be made known to the public. A 1799 statute mandated that every operator of a toll bridge or ferry post the rates prescribed by law, forfeiting the right to collect toll from the user if he failed to do so. The purpose of the law, as Justice Colcock pointed out, was obvious: to afford citizens "a shield to protect them from the imposition of ferry owners." If a ferry operator tried to extort a toll greater than his charter permitted, he became liable to forfeit triple the rate he attempted to charge.[27]

Statutes also defined categories of persons exempt from tolls altogether.

---

26. *Cook v. Gourdin,* 11 S.C.L. (2 Nott & McCord, 1819), 21; *Stark v. McGowen,* 394; Horwitz, *Transformation of American Law,* 116–22.

27. *Statutes at Large,* IX: 364, 396, 403; *Addison v. Hard,* 17 S.C.L. (1 Bailey, 1830), 433.

The president of the United States and governor of South Carolina were not required to pay tolls, nor were legislators traveling to or from a session of the General Assembly. But exemptions were not the exclusive privilege of high public officials. Rather, they were bestowed upon any person, or persons, carrying out a public function: men on militia or patrol duty, jurors summoned to state and district courts, government couriers, or witnesses called to give evidence in a legal prosecution. Ministers of the gospel and all persons traveling to or from religious services were also exempt from paying tolls to use public ferries and bridges. Statutory exemptions such as these further underlined the public boundaries placed on private entrepreneurs, preventing franchise holders from profiting off those carrying out civic responsibilities.[28]

Reciprocity was not confined to ferries, nor were ferry owners the only entrepreneurs ready to accept the public responsibilities of private enterprise. A variety of private ventures in the public sphere sought, and received, legislative charter. In 1838 John Chappell undertook to build a bridge across the Saluda River, "to subserve the public convenience" by furnishing "a safe & expeditious transportation over the river." The legislature granted a charter for the undertaking, permitting the collection of tolls in order that Chappell could "be indemnified for the labour & expense which he has bestowed on the undertaking." Isaac Randolph petitioned for the exclusive right to run a line of stages through Barnwell District, assuring the legislature that the enterprise would be "an accommodation to the citizens of this State." Without exclusive privilege, competitors might duplicate the venture and "the profits of it might be taken from the original undertaker," and thereby undercut the recompense that Randolph "would be fairly entitled to for having encountered the hazard of loss in making the experiment." The General Assembly agreed. Deeming his stage line a "public benefit," the legislature granted Randolph exclusive right to carry passengers along his proposed route, fixing rates at ten cents per mile for passengers and "the customary allowance" for the conveyance of baggage. The only exemption to Randolph's privilege went to persons contracted to carry the U.S. mail.[29]

Chartered monopolies did not go unchallenged by members of the Edgefield and Barnwell community, particularly by those who sought to establish a

28. *Statues at Large,* IX: 357.

29. "Petition of Jon. Chappell," Petition, 1838–126; "Petition of Isaac Randolph," Petition, ND-1493; both in General Assembly Papers, SCDAH; *Statutes at Large,* VIII: 321.

competing enterprise or those who felt entitled to a share of the privileges granted by the legislature. In 1814 Azariah Abney protested against Francis Higgins, claiming that gentleman had "enjoyed all the proffits" of a ferry over the Saluda River established some two decades earlier by Higgins and Abney's father, Nathaniel. In 1800 Higgins succeeded in having the ferry vested solely in his name, even though it still landed on Abney's Edgefield property. Azariah Abney and his supporters now maintained that Higgins enjoyed too much privilege, benefiting from what should be a joint charter and reaping profits through the exploitation of another man's property. The privilege Higgins enjoyed was unjust, they argued, and further suggested that "it is Contrary to the principles and Spirit of a Republican Government to grant exclusive privileges of this kind, and to enrich one part of its Citizens and to impoverish the others."[30]

The committees considering Abney's allegations felt little sympathy with the petitioners. To them, there appeared little reason to justify the revocation of Higgins's franchise. The house committee on roads believed Higgins "had been at the trouble and expense of the original establishment, had expended considerable work on the Banks," and furthermore "had always well conducted the said Ferry for the public utility." Rather than revoke Higgins's franchise, the committee recommended that his record of responsible public service be rewarded by vesting the ferry in Higgins for another seven years. A senate committee likewise agreed, but the full General Assembly rejected the reports and instead ordered that the ferry be established jointly in Higgins and Abney.[31]

The legislature's decision, however, should not be taken as an admission of the strength of Abney's assertions. While Abney referred to the "Spirit of Republican Government," undoubtedly hoping to invoke the sense of antiprivilege inherent to republican ideology, he miscalculated. Abney received a share of the ferry franchise due to his being an heir to one of the original proprietors and the owner of its south side landing, not because the assembly believed Higgins held an unjust monopoly or that "Republican Government" had no right to grant "exclusive privileges." The actions of the General Assembly were

30. "Petition of Azariah Abney," Petition, 1814–49; "Petition of Sundry Inhabitants of Edgefield District," Petition, ND-780; both in General Assembly Papers, SCDAH.

31. "Report of the Committee on Roads, Bridges, &c.," Report, 1814–96; "Report of Committee on Roads, &c.," Report, 1814–109; "Report on the Petition of Azariah Abney," Report, 1814–98; all in General Assembly Papers, SCDAH.

guided by the common law tradition of Blackstone, not the economic liberalism of Adam Smith, and demonstrated a greater concern for stability and public rights than for competition and private enterprise. Ferry and bridge charters were viewed as extensions of government sovereignty, not private privilege, and underscored the blurred line between public and private enterprise in the early stages of South Carolina's post-Revolution economic development. By explicitly harnessing an individual's interest to those of his entire community, the operation of ferry and bridge franchises in Edgefield and Barnwell provided a further display of the public responsibilities of private entrepreneurship in the agrarian landscape.

Passing through South Carolina in 1791, President George Washington's route of travel from Augusta to Columbia took him through the sandhills of the Barnwell and Edgefield borderlands. After viewing the region firsthand, Washington declared it to be "a pine barren of the worst sort," and his agricultural instincts wrote the region off as worthless. A half century later, William Cullen Bryant rode the railroad through Barnwell District and decided that anyone taking the same route "might naturally take South Carolina for a vast pine-forest . . . and would wonder where the cotton which clothes so many millions of the human race, is produced." But many planters and yeomen saw benefits to be derived from the vast forests covering their districts. Indeed, after agriculture, district forests were among the most important contributors to the local economy and many an agriculturist sought to supplement his income through the judicious use of the ax and saw.[32]

They were by no means the first to charter this course of economic betterment. One of the earliest resources South Carolina colonists worked to exploit was the colony's lush forests. Throughout the proprietary and colonial eras, lumber played a supporting role in the economic development of South Carolina, albeit not so spectacular as rice and cotton. Extensive stands of cypress, pine, and assorted hardwoods quickly came to the attention of English officials. The South Carolina lowcountry became a valued source of masts and naval stores for the Royal Navy, as well as a source of lumber, shingles, and staves for the British West Indies. To advance the trade, in 1712 the colonial as-

32. Donald Jackson and Dorothy Twohig, eds., *The Diaries of George Washington*, 6 vols. (Charlottesville, 1976–79), 6:145; William Cullen Bryant, *Letters of a Traveller; or, Notes of Things Seen in Europe and America* (New York, 1869), 82.

sembly passed an act that offered eight-year monopolies to those who would build a sawmill and "bring the same to complete perfection." The act encouraged other manufacturing enterprises by tendering similar local monopolies or bounties. By offering these inducements to manufacturing, the colony's leaders hoped to develop the economic potential of its virgin lands, believing "the erecting of mills of all kinds and other mechanick engines will greatly improve the country itself, and its trade, and navigation."[33]

But while fostering commercial development, South Carolina's colonial land policies simultaneously diffused economic opportunity, in particular by protecting public access to waterways, which served as the primary source of inland transportation until well into the nineteenth century. As early as 1669, the Lords Proprietors restricted possession of river frontage to no more than one-fifth the depth of any single tract of land in order to deter monopolization of valuable riverfront land. By 1726, South Carolina legislators enacted a law to protect navigable inland waterways from deliberate obstruction caused "by the ill practice of cutting down and falling trees in several rivers and creeks in this Province." To enforce the law, the assembly empowered local magistrates to levy fines of five pounds for each felled tree that obstructed a waterway for more than forty-eight hours.[34]

A century later, the South Carolina General Assembly was likewise using legislative means to protect navigable rivers from obstruction, with a particular emphasis on mill dams. During South Carolina's internal improvement campaign of the 1820s, the assembly passed several new acts to ensure that appropriations made for improving inland navigation would not be undermined by inconsiderate dam owners. An 1823 statute declared it unlawful "to keep up or erect any dam across any river which the legislature has ordered to be made navigable, or for improving which the legislature has made any appropriation so as to obstruct the passage of boats therein." Nor were dam owners singled out as the only potential offenders. In 1829 the assembly passed an act making

33. Peter A. Coclanis, *The Shadow of a Dream: Economic Life and Death in the South Carolina Low Country* (New York, 1989), 13–26, 48–110; Converse D. Clowse, *Economic Beginnings in Colonial South Carolina, 1670–1730* (Columbia, S.C., 1971), 83, 179–80; John A. Eisterhold, "Charleston: Lumber and Trade in a Declining Southern Port," *SCHM* 74 (April 1973): 61–62; *Statutes at Large*, II: 388.

34. Robert K. Ackerman, *South Carolina Colonial Land Policies* (Columbia, S.C., 1977), 30–31; *Statutes at Large*, III: 269–70.

persons who obstructed navigation with fish traps subject to a fine of one hundred dollars for each offense.[35]

The most comprehensive legislation protecting navigable waterways as public highways came in 1825 and remained the primary legal precedent on such matters until 1853. The 1825 act forbade erecting mill dams or other obstructions across streams used for navigation "by boats, flats, or rafts of lumber or timber" without creating "sufficient locks, slopes or canals" around the obstruction to allow "the free navigation of such streams." In essence, the act forced a balance between public and private interests. Owners of property through which a navigable stream flowed were allowed to build dams and use the waterpower to carry on private enterprises, such as grist or saw mills. But by requiring a means of access through such obstructions, the act also maintained the common use of waterways as a public highways.[36]

The catalyst behind the 1825 act was an ongoing expansion into the South Carolina interior by those seeking to exploit vast expanses of virgin timber. Production of lumber, shingles, and other wood products grew steadily in South Carolina during the first half of the nineteenth century, driven by demand in Charleston and Savannah as well as in the West Indies. As more inhabitants pushed into the backcountry, hundreds of sawmills sprang up along the state's numerous inland rivers and their tributaries. South Carolina Judge John Belton O'Neall explained the purpose of the 1825 act in light of this growing timber trade: "The Act was intended to encourage this spirit, by preventing the enterprise from being defeated by some churlish or revengeful man, who, as soon as the creek was opened, might, on his own land, throw a dam across it and thus deprive the mill owner above of the value of his mill and the fruits of his active industry." Thus, like other riparian acts passed before it, the 1825 law regulated competing interests by preventing a single mill owner or landowner from dominating a waterway and ensured open competition by allowing all persons to take advantage of the economic potential offered by area timber resources.[37]

The maintenance of navigable waterways as public highways also withstood legal challenges in the state courts. In 1822 the Constitutional Court of

35. *Statutes at Large,* VI: 219, 393.

36. Ibid., VI: 268.

37. Eisterhold, "Charleston: Lumber and Trade," 61–64, 69–71; idem, "Savannah: Lumber Center of the South Atlantic," *Georgia Historical Quarterly* 57 (winter 1973): 531–32, 538–41; Judge O'Neall quoted in *State v. Cullum, Toney v. Cullum,* 29 S.C.L. (2 Spears, 1844) at 490.

South Carolina ruled that no individual could possess sole right to a waterway capable of navigation, even if the river in question was not available for public use. No person held a monopoly on a river, and "the legislature may . . . declare it to be a public highway, whenever the obstructions are removed, and it becomes fit for public use." Property owners could utilize waterways passing through their property, but only "as far as is consistent with the right of the public."[38]

Throughout the 1840s, courts upheld the use of navigable rivers as public highways, overruling mill owners who sought to control traffic on streams passing through their private property. An 1844 decision by the Court of Appeals upheld the public right of access by disallowing a defendant's claim that the slope through his dam was private property and, therefore, he could collect tolls for allowing passage. The court ruled that the defendant's actions were "not of that public character contemplated by the [1825] Act," and that building a passage, but keeping the same closed to traffic that refused to pay his toll, constituted as much of an obstruction as constructing no passage at all. Three years later, the same court broadened the definition of navigable rivers included in the 1825 act, declaring that rivers traditionally used as public highways, even though not officially declared such by the state legislature, fell within the 1825 act if they were under the charge of local public functionaries and worked by public labor. Such circumstances rendered the river, "as like circumstances would have rendered a road—a public highway, for the obstruction of which, an indictment lies at common law."[39]

By 1850, South Carolina had well-established legislative and judicial precedents governing the private and public use of navigable waterways. Actions of both the General Assembly and state courts served to foster economic development and to prevent individual interests from undermining established notions of commonweal and public rights. Landowners were encouraged to cut timber, erect sawmills, and use local streams for power and transportation. Yet, by adamantly upholding the public use of waterways, even through private land, no individual interest would be permitted to prosper at the expense of others, despite the inconvenience such regulations might entail on landowners.

The initial blush of the upcountry cotton boom appeared as if it might stall development of the backcountry timber trade, and perhaps even snuff it out al-

---

38. *Ex'rs of Cates v. Wadlington*, 12 S.C.L. (1 McCord, 1822) at 583.

39. *State v. Cullum, Toney v. Cullum*, at 492; *State v. Thompson*, 33 S.C.L. (2 Strobhart, 1847) at 12.

together. Contemporary observer David Ramsay estimated that every pine tree brought to coastal towns "in a marketable form" would sell for at least $10, but feared that the "temptations" created by the spectacular rise in cotton prices might stifle the exploitation of this commodity. But while the lumber trade would not seriously challenge the reign of King Cotton, a significant number of backcountry arrivals included sawmills as part of the agricultural main chance. Most of Barnwell, as well as the southern portion of Edgefield District, were fabulously rich in timber. Savannah River tributaries possessed impressive stands of pine and hardwood, as did the Salkehatchie and Edisto basins. Land along the Upper and Lower Three Runs was "well stocked with White Oak & Pine Timber" and "a great quantity of good merchantable timber fit for Staves & Shingles." Property on the Salkehatchie abounded "with the best Timber Trees, such as Cypress, Ash, &c. &c." In particular, the Edisto River gained notoriety for its "great quantity of Eligible mill-seats" and lands "profusely loaded with the best timber." Robert Mills observed that Edisto pine timber "brings a higher price than any other brought to market."[40]

Edgefield and Barnwell soon counted themselves among the state's leading producers of timber and lumber. By the middle of the nineteenth century, no fewer than 128 sawmills operated within the two districts, each taking advantage of the forests and waterways that covered the local landscape. More than one observer was struck by the omnipresence of sawmills in the area. "Every stream of any size in this region is dammed to turn a saw-mill," commented agricultural reformer Edmund Ruffin as he passed through Barnwell District in 1843. The editor of the Barnwell *Palmetto Sentinel* likewise noted the near universal pursuit of timber in his district. "These forests," he declared, "we have discovered to be a mine of wealth, and the axe of timber-men ringing within them, declares that every tree must find its way to market." To meet this market demand, sawmill owners along the numerous tributaries of the Edisto and Savannah rivers eagerly cleared waterways to permit navigation by timber rafts.[41]

40. David Ramsay, *History of South Carolina, From its First Settlement in 1670 to the Year 1808*, 2 vols. (Charleston, 1858; Spartanburg, 1962), 2:190n; Petitions, ND-3327; 1797–100; 1811–132; 1812–88, General Assembly Papers; Robert Mills, *Statistics of South Carolina* (Charleston, 1826), 362.

41. Michael Williams, "Products of the Forest: Mapping the Census of 1840," *Journal of Forest History* 24 (January 1980): 7, 22–23; Manuscript Census Returns, Seventh Census of the United States, 1850, Barnwell and Edgefield districts, South Carolina, Schedule 5, Industry, 549–53, 589–99, SCDAH; William M. Mathew, ed., *Agriculture, Geology, and Society in Antebellum South Car-*

The degree of individual involvement in the timber trade varied, but the motivation was obvious. As early as 1788, planter Thomas Galphin noted the sale of local lumber was a quick and dependable means of obtaining hard money in a typically cash-starved local economy. Some focused their lumber trade on local buyers. Planter Lewis Malone Ayer operated a custom sawmill on the Salkehatchie River, filling plank orders placed by nearby residents for uses ranging from house construction to slats for Venetian blinds. Others set their sights on urban centers. James Myers focused the operations of his Horse Creek sawmill on the Savannah market, keeping in close contact with city merchants for information on which cuts of timber enjoyed the highest demand, a practice later continued by his widow when she inherited the mill. The journal of another Barnwell planter recorded his timber production for both markets, putting his slaves to work cutting rails for the South Carolina Railroad passing near his lands, while also hauling ranging timber overland to the Edisto River, whence he rafted it to the Charleston market.[42]

Individual sawmills ranged widely in size and the value of their product. Barnwell planter William Peyton's mill represented a modest investment of only $400. On the other end of the scale, Edgefield planter C. J. Glover and Barnwell senator Angus Patterson invested $12,000 and $10,000 in their respective sawmill establishments. The annual value of production also varied, from only a few hundred dollars to George Kelly's steam-powered behemoth that cut and sold lumber worth $18,000 annually. Between these extremes, however, the typical sawmill was a more modest but not inconsequential enterprise. The average Edgefield or Barnwell sawmill was valued at between $2,000 to $3,000, and typically cut and rafted $1,500 to $2,000 worth of lumber to local and urban markets. When totaled together, this myriad of sawmills represented a total capital investment of $371,550 by 1850, with a combined annual production of $267,500.[43]

The typical mill was also the product of individual enterprise—only 13 were

olina: *The Private Diary of Edmund Ruffin, 1843* (Athens, Ga., 1992), 236; Barnwell, *Palmetto Sentinel,* June 23, 1852.

42. Letter from Thomas Galphin, April 30, 1788, SCL; L. P. Wade to Lewis Malone Ayer, August 22, 1821, James D. Erwin to Lewis Malone Ayer, [1823], Lewis Malone Ayer Papers, SCL; Taylor, Davies, & Taylor to James Myers, November 26, 1816, A. S. Somers to Mrs. J. J. Myers, October 6, 1829; both in Iveson L. Brookes Papers, SCL; Plantation Journal, Barnwell District, 1843–44, *passim,* SCL.

43. 1850 U.S. Census, Barnwell and Edgefield districts, S.C., Industry, 549–53, 589–99, SCDAH.

owned in partnership—and owners overwhelmingly participated in the region's dominant economic and social systems: agriculture and slavery. At least 106 of 138 persons identified as sawmill operators represented themselves to census takers as planters or farmers. An even larger number owned slaves, with the percentage of slaveholding mill owners approaching 90 percent (122) of all sawmill operators. A handful were among the wealthiest residents of their respective districts. Barnwell and Edgefield sawyers included 6 men who possessed more than 100 slaves, such as James Henry Hammond (235 slaves, $100,000 in real estate) and Edgefield planter-lawyer-politician John Bauskett (221 slaves, $45,000 in real estate). On average, however, Edgefield and Barnwell sawmillers were men of lesser, but hardly inconsiderable means. Slightly over two-fifths (58 of 138) owned from one to 20 slaves, while 42 sawmillers held from 21 to 50 slaves.[44]

Thus sawmill operators were men of property, who primarily sought advancement through the South's traditional avenues of wealth and status, land and slaves. Their sawmilling activities underlined an important entrepreneurial aspect of their mentality, but one that remained closely tied to the agrarian landscape. They were market oriented, and often aggressive in their pursuit of those markets, but still grounded in the state's traditional republican political economy of individual producers, combining the Jeffersonian belief in the virtue of rural life with the Hamiltonian desire to squeeze as much profit from the land as possible. It was a political economy well protected by the legislative and court pronouncements over riparian rights. Entrepreneurship among sawyers was encouraged, but regulated. No riparian proprietor obtained license to undermine others by bending the local political economy to grant exclusive possession of a resource traditionally held in common.[45]

But that didn't prevent some sawyers from trying. During the decades between the Revolution and Civil War, mill owners repeatedly challenged each other over competing claims to waterways in Edgefield and Barnwell districts.

44. Statistical information on sawmills and their owners was gleaned from the industry schedules from the 1850 Census for Edgefield and Barnwell districts. From this source, 128 sawmills or combination saw and grist mills were listed and 138 sawmill owners identified. Information on sawmill owners was found by cross-referencing names from the above industry schedules with the 1850 Census population returns and slave schedules. Not every sawmill owner was located in this additional census data.

45. Ford, *Origins of Southern Radicalism*, 49–51; J. William Harris, *Plain Folk and Gentry in a Slave Society: White Liberty and Black Slavery in Augusta's Hinterlands* (Baton Rouge, 1985), 18–32.

New mill operators demanded recognition of navigability for newly opened streams, enabling them to join the ranks of sawyer entrepreneurs. Established mill owners claimed the prerogatives of private property and fought to exclude interlopers seeking to profit off the fruits of another man's labor. But of all the waterways in the two districts, Horse Creek, a Savannah River tributary in the extreme southern portion of Edgefield, was perhaps the earliest and most frequent site of clashes among mill owners over navigation rights. Sawyers faced off repeatedly over conflicting claims to the waterway as a power source and a transportation route, both vital to the success of any milling enterprise.[46]

In 1792 Abraham Richardson, with the support of fifty-eight nearby residents, petitioned the state senate, protesting the actions of Thomas Lamar. Richardson asserted that he and others "have been at Great Expence in Building & Setting to work Various Valuable sawmills" on Horse Creek, "with prospects of the Great advantage of rafting their Lumber" down the creek and to the Savannah River. Richardson claimed to have personally paid to clear the channel for some twenty miles of logs and other obstructions in order to provide an unobstructed path to raft his lumber. However, Lamar erected his own mill on the same creek, within one mile of its mouth, which included a mill dam that "Extended Intirely Across" Horse Creek. Lamar's action blocked the lumber rafts of upstream mill owners, "all who Conceive themselves Greatly damaged by the said Thomas Lamar's stoping the Channel." The General Assembly responded in 1796, passing an act declaring "no person shall obstruct Horse creek . . . so as to prevent rafts or boats from passing through it." It further stipulated that "every person now owning, or hereafter holding, owning or possessing any mill, mill-dam, or other dam or obstruction" on Horse Creek to "have and keep a good and sufficient floodgate, lock or other passage" of at least thirteen feet in width. The passage was to be opened for every person who wished to send "any raft, boat, lumber or other thing" through the dam. Owners refusing to grant access were liable to indictment or lawsuit.[47]

In 1807 conflict again arose between mill owners on Horse Creek over access to the waterway, with the General Assembly continuing to uphold the

46. For examples of conflicts over water rights, see Petitions, ND-1134, ND-3022, ND-3417, 1839–62, 1851–22; all in General Assembly Papers, SCDAH.

47. "Petition of Sundry Citizens Residing on Horse Creek," Petition, 1792–47; "Report of the Committee on the Petition of Sundry Inhabitants Residing on Horse Creek," Report, 1793–84; both in General Assembly Papers, SCDAH; *Statutes at Large*, IX: 375.

rights of navigation. Mill owner Jesse Roundtree petitioned against "the great expense and inconvenience to which he [was] subjected" by the stipulations of the 1796 act, asserting that the force of water through a thirteen-foot floodgate would "intirely ruin the foundation where his mill [stood]." The assembly offered Roundtree some relief, amending the stipulations of the 1796 act to require dam owners to construct "a good and sufficient slope" ten feet wide and three feet deep instead of a more expensive floodgate or lock. The right of others to pass through the dam, however, remained.[48]

Even this small concession was overturned in 1820 after a petition of "owners and occupiers of Mills, Millseats, and Lands" along Horse Creek complained that the slope through Roundtree's dam, now owned by James Myers, was an inadequate means of passage. The petitioners asserted they were "considerably injured in their business and occupations by reason of the obstruction," and prayed that the legislature require Myers "to errect Locks, or otherwise so to open the main sluice of said creek that your memorialists and others may freely pass with their lumber or produce." Myers offered a counterpetition, maintaining that the present slope was adequate for the passage of lumber rafts, and believing the installation of a lock in his dam would be "dangerous experiment & Expence." In the end, however, the General Assembly sided against Myers. Deeming the present passage through Myers's dam as "insufficient and destructive to the rafts that are now floated down Horse Creek," the assembly rejected Myers's petition. The 1807 act was repealed and the original stipulations of the 1796 statute reinstated, requiring the construction of a flood gate or lock through all present and future dams on Horse Creek. The new act further sought to expedite the resolution of future conflicts by appointing five area inhabitants to superintend the opening of Horse Creek and oversee the removal of existing obstructions.[49]

Whereas, in the case of Horse Creek, the law provided one bulwark against the monopolization of water resources, custom supplied another in contests over other waterways. In the fall of 1842, James Henry Hammond entered into an extended conflict over a dam on his property. Ten years earlier, Hammond

48. "Petition of Jesse Roundtree," Petition, 1807–119, General Assembly Papers; *Statutes at Large* V: 542–43.

49. "Petition of Sundry Inhabitants of Edgefield District," Petition, ND-1083; "Memorial of James Myers," Petition, ND-3342; both in General Assembly Papers; *Statutes at Large*, VI: 143–44.

had agreed to let a neighbor, John Ransey, dig a canal around the dam to raft his lumber to the Savannah River. Now Hammond wished to shut up the canal, an action that drew a scathing protest from Ransey, who claimed a prescriptive right to the canal and refused to recognize Hammond's privilege to close it. Ransey asserted that his ten-year use of the canal prohibited any such action, "converting into a right," Hammond noted, "what had long [been] got of me as a favour." The claim hurt Hammond, who felt it an ungrateful response to his "kindness & indulgence to a neighbor." Although he was within his rights to close the canal on his land (the stream was not declared public or worked on by public levy), Hammond hesitated in pursuing legal action against Ransey. While irked by the infringement on his property, Hammond also harbored ambitions for the governor's office that fall. He could ill afford to appear as a haughty aristocrat attempting to lord it over his neighbors. He attempted a compromise, but Ransey refused to yield his claim and even threatened an indictment, something Hammond dearly wished to avoid while a candidate for governor. Should that occur, Hammond mused, "a great handle will be made of it." No resident could expect a successful public career by displaying a flagrant disregard for customary rights or by placing self-interests above those of his neighbors. Hammond backed down and continued to permit use of the canal gratis until Ransey completed a river landing of his own. As a public figure with higher ambitions, Hammond could do little else. Not even the district's wealthiest planter could violate common rights claimed by his neighbors.[50]

Hammond's dilemma, and its resolution, further highlighted the social compact that governed economic development in the agrarian landscape of Edgefield and Barnwell. Little of the entrepreneurship outside of agriculture escaped the purview of established habits or common law notions of reciprocity and communal rights. Like the layout of public roads or the granting of ferry and bridge franchises, riparian law and custom channeled economic development into a spectrum beyond that of private gain. Likewise, while sawmilling

50. James Henry Hammond to Capt. John Ransey, September 8, 1842, James Henry Hammond Papers, SCL; Hammond Diary, 1841–46, September 10, 17, 30, October 6, 9, November 16, 1842, James Henry Hammond Papers, Library of Congress; Drew Gilpin Faust, *James Henry Hammond and the Old South: A Design for Mastery* (Baton Rouge, 1982), 133; Stephanie McCurry, *Masters of Small Worlds: Yeoman Households, Gender Relations, & the Political Culture of the Antebellum South Carolina Low Country* (New York and Oxford, 1995), 112–15.

contributed to the general prosperity, the theory and practice of water rights limited the prerogatives of private property and entrepreneurship when they sought to exclude themselves from societal notions of the common good.

Furthermore, the above analysis illustrates the degree to which economic development was delegated to the community itself and regulated by its representatives. Roads were laid out at the behest of local demand, with their creation or closure almost entirely left to popular consensus. Toll ferries and bridges were owned and operated by local entrepreneurs, carrying on their operations as both a private enterprise and a public service, but under charters which ensured that the latter purpose was not usurped by the former. The planter-sawyers along Horse Creek and other district waterways counted themselves among the wealthiest land- and slaveholders in their respective neighborhoods, but remained subject to the legal and prescriptive riparian rights claimed by their neighbors and other sawyers as well. Thus, government, law, and custom combined to create an interrelation among citizens and society in the economic realm of Edgefield and Barnwell, blurring the line between private and public, between individual and community, and between self-interest and reciprocity.

The relative homogeneity of economic interests in the two districts helped maintain this compact. Edgefield and Barnwell entered the post-Revolution years with a population dominated by planters and small farmers. Agriculturists all, they shared similar needs and desires from the development of their respective communities. Farmland would be worthless without convenient means of ingress and egress for persons and produce via highways, ferries, and bridges. Likewise, even agricultural adjuncts like a sawmill were influenced by the agrarian landscape, operating seasonally during slack times in the farmer's year and forming a remunerative adjunct to the ongoing activity of clearing virgin lands for planting. As long as this uniformity of economic interests and activities prevailed, the established political economy they oversaw prevailed, albeit not always with good grace.

But by the second quarter of the nineteenth century, multiple challenges to this economic order arose from a series of newcomers to the two districts. Many of these sought to make their mark as merchants and speculators, enhancing their economic position not by planting cotton but by providing goods and services to those that did. By the later stages of the antebellum era, the number of merchants in Edgefield and Barnwell had grown large enough to coalesce into a nascent entrepreneurial class, with goals and attitudes that frequently diverged from those held by their agricultural neighbors. Of even greater significance, the most disruptive of these new interlopers came not from new residents in Edgefield and Barnwell, but from pools of incorporated urban capital in the forms of a railroad and a manufacturing village called Graniteville.

CHAPTER THREE

"AN INDUCEMENT TO CAPITALISTS"

THE RISE OF THE MERCHANT CLASS

The business of the planter is not like that of the merchant; it does not bring him in money all the year round . . . Thus it is that his property is so often at the mercy of reckless creditors, while merchants, as soon as they get into a tight place, may fly to a bank for assistance.

"WINTON," *Remarks on Barnwell District*, 1839

AMONG THE ACCOUNTS OF Edgefield District included by Robert Mills in his 1826 work, *Statistics of South Carolina*, the acclaimed architect and engineer offered a comparison of the district's two principal towns—indeed, the district's *only* two towns. Mills described Edgefield Court House, the seat of district justice, as a "neat little village" of forty to fifty scattered houses which, as a rule, were "neat, commodious, and generally painted." Thirty-eight families resided in the respectable hamlet and enjoyed a "remarkably healthy" situation. This quaint, bucolic depiction came in sharp contrast with the pulsing new town of Hamburg on the Savannah River opposite Augusta, founded barely five years before. Here, Mills wrote, twelve hundred inhabitants occupied two hundred houses. More than fifty stores were in operation and carrying on "a vast deal of business." The town annually received cotton bags numbering in the tens of thousands, as well as "tobacco, flour, and other productions, engrossing nearly all Carolina produce, which before was carried to Augusta." Steamships plying the Savannah River gave Hamburg a direct transportation link to Charleston, with each vessel carrying passengers and cotton

Epigraph from "Winton," *Remarks on Barnwell District, South Carolina* (n.p., 1839), 33.

to the city and "returning with proportionable cargoes of goods." With "its superior advantages of celerity and cheapness of transportation," Mills contended that Hamburg stood poised to capture the lion's share of South Carolina's upcountry trade, as well as a fair portion of Georgia's commerce to boot.[1]

The appearance of Hamburg signaled a new development in the evolution of Edgefield and Barnwell. It was the first commercial town in a region where merchants and tradesmen previously exerted a negligible influence, both demographically and economically. Outside of a few crossroads general stores and a handful of trade establishments clustering about district court houses, commercial activity was infrequent at best and largely confined to specific periods of the agricultural calendar. The autumn harvest saw planters and yeomen trundle wagons or ply rafts to Charleston via the Saluda and Edisto rivers, or down the Savannah River to Augusta or Savannah in Georgia. Once there, they sold their harvest, settled their accounts, and exchanged the remainder for the few necessities they could not produce for themselves before heading back to kith and kin. But Hamburg's emergence in the early 1820s marked a growing commercial presence within their own community. Not only did Hamburg create a convenient new market for district agriculturists, but it also made urban merchants a more salient feature in the agrarian landscape. Furthermore, the growing prevalence of the merchant in Edgefield and Barnwell would not be confined just to Hamburg, but expand to include a number of rural locations, the district court houses, and—after the construction of the South Carolina Railroad—other new commercial towns.[2]

1. Robert Mills, *Statistics of South Carolina, Including a View of its Natural, Civil, and Military History, General and Particular* (Charleston, 1826), 522–23.

2. On the merchant in the antebellum South, see Lewis E. Atherton, *The Southern Country Store 1800–1860* (Baton Rouge, 1949). On the merchant's involvement in marketing and financing cotton, see Harold D. Woodman, *King Cotton and His Retainers: Financing and Marketing the Cotton Crop of the South, 1800–1925* (Lexington, Ky., 1968; reprint, Columbia, S.C., 1990), 76–83. Brief, but useful, local discussions of antebellum merchant activity in the South can be found in Michael Wayne, *The Reshaping of Plantation Society: The Natchez District, 1860–80* (Baton Rouge, 1983; reprint, Urbana, Ill., 1990), 163–65; Peter A. Coclanis, "Retailing in Early South Carolina," in *Retailing: Theory and Practice for the 21st Century*, ed. Robert L. King (Charleston, 1986), 1–5; Lacy K. Ford Jr., *Origins of Southern Radicalism: The South Carolina Upcountry, 1800–1860* (New York, 1988), 88–91, 235–43; Christopher Morris, *Becoming Southern: The Evolution of a Way of Life, Warren County and Vicksburg, Mississippi, 1770–1860* (New York, 1995), 103–13; and Stephanie McCurry, *Masters of Small Worlds: Yeoman Households, Gender Relations, & the Political Culture of the Antebellum South Carolina Low Country* (New York, 1995), 96–104. Charleston's merchant community is

In its initial stage, the parallel rise of Hamburg and a resident merchant class did not seem particularly disruptive to the agriculturists of Edgefield and Barnwell. As suppliers and distributors for district farms, merchants certainly had an obvious fiscal stake in the continuation of the region's plantation economy. However, resentment began to grow over the increasingly visible hand that the General Assembly wielded in Hamburg's development. While government played a largely regulatory role in the local economy in previous times, Hamburg became the beneficiary of unprecedented largesse from the state, which bestowed upon this nascent hub of merchant capital fiscal and legislative favors that raised eyebrows among district inhabitants as well as those residing elsewhere in the state. Despite personal and philosophical misgivings about the activities and ideals that merchants brought to their districts, agrarian ideologues in Edgefield and Barnwell remained confident in their ability to withstand the challenges brought by these intruders into their rural political economy. Their agrarian philosophy had enough elasticity to allow for degrees of nonagricultural activity, as long as it supported agriculture in its role as the proper foundation of civilized society. For the first decades of the nineteenth century at least, merchant capitalists in Edgefield and Barnwell only hinted at the challenges they would bring to the course of political economy charted and sailed in the districts for generations.[3]

The frame of the first building in Hamburg went up on July 2, 1821. Additional houses and stores followed in quick succession. By the end of the year, the building total reached 84. The following year, the number of buildings reached 140, including 2 warehouses and 35 stores. The population grew at a similarly

---

analyzed in Leila Sellers, *Charleston Business on the Eve of the American Revolution* (Chapel Hill, 1934; reprint, New York, 1970), and Gregory Allen Greb, "Charleston, South Carolina, Merchants, 1815–1860: Urban Leadership in the Antebellum South" (Ph.D. diss., University of California, San Diego, 1978). On the influence of merchants in early southern economic development, see Peter A. Colclanis, "The Hydra Head of Merchant Capital: Markets and Merchants in Early South Carolina," in *The Meaning of South Carolina History: Essays in Honor of George C. Rogers, Jr.*, ed. David R. Chestnutt and Clyde N. Wilson (Columbia, 1991), 1–18, and Mark M. Smith, *Mastered by the Clock: Time, Slavery, and Freedom in the American South* (Chapel Hill, 1997), 63–67.

3. On the influence of planters over southern cities and towns, see Eugene D. Genovese, *The Political Economy of Slavery: Studies in the Economy and Society of the Slave South,* 2nd ed. (Middletown, Conn., 1989), 157–73; Michele Gillespie, *Free Labor in an Unfree World: White Artisans in Slaveholding Georgia, 1789–1860* (Athens and London, 2000), 66–93.

impressive rate. Beginning as an unimproved lot of land, Hamburg claimed a population of 200 white inhabitants within 6 months. By the end of 1822, the figure had doubled. Perhaps most impressive, however, was the speed with which the newborn town attracted the lucrative upcountry cotton trade. The first cotton bags arrived in Hamburg in late October 1821. In just 6 weeks, almost 4,800 bags of the staple passed through the Hamburg warehouse. At the conclusion of its first full season, Hamburg speculators purchased some 18,000 bags of cotton. The booming prosperity promptly became manifest in a cocksure attitude among Hamburg residents. "The people here are very important," observed a visitor in 1824, "& seem to imagine themselves, inhabitants of a *Great City*."[4]

The catalyst sparking this commercial El Dorado was an eccentric, driven, and shamelessly self-promoting German immigrant by the name of Henry Shultz. His background was mysterious. One romantic account claimed he was a prisoner of Bonaparte, but escaped and fled to America. Whatever the motive for his emigration, Shultz arrived in Georgia around 1806, without money, connections, or command of the language. Undeterred, he took work as a boatman on the Savannah River. Within three years, Shultz saved enough to purchase a tobacco flat of his own, which he successfully plied on the river between Augusta and Savannah over the next several years. His arrival as an influential local entrepreneur came with the construction of the Augusta Bridge. In partnership with Lewis Cooper, and later with Augusta merchant John McKinne, Shultz secured charters from both the South Carolina and Georgia legislatures to build a toll bridge over the Savannah River at Augusta. Completed in 1814, the bridge was an immediate financial success. Shultz and McKinne soon applied their substantial earnings to other Augusta ventures, including a wharf and a steamship line. Most ambitious, however, was the Bridge Company of Augusta (generally referred to as the "Bridge Bank") organized by the two men in 1816. Backed by the value of their bridge and other Augusta properties, Shultz and his partners issued several hundred thousand dollars' worth of "bridge bills" to finance their ventures. Unfortunately, their speculative bubble fell victim to the Panic of 1819, forcing the Bridge Bank to suspend redemp-

4. "Memorial of Henry Shultz, to the Legislature at the Session of 1821," Petition, 1821–29; Memorial of Henry Shultz, Petition, 1822–50; both in General Assembly Papers, SCDAH; James A. Padgett, ed., "Journal of Daniel Walker Lord, Kept While on a Southern Trip," *Georgia Historical Quarterly* 26 (June 1942): 189.

tion of its bills. Aggravating matters was an attempt by Shultz's partners to extricate themselves from their financial embarrassments by mortgaging the bridge and other assets to the Bank of the State of Georgia, apparently without the consent or knowledge of Shultz. Foreclosing on the mortgage, the bank took control of the bridge and the bulk of Shultz's Augusta property as well. However, the Dutchman refused to admit the bank's right to take "his" bridge, which touched off thirty years of lawsuits that culminated with no less of a tribunal than the U.S. Supreme Court. More immediately, by 1820 Shultz found himself financially ruined and persona non grata in the city of Augusta. Deeply embittered over his treatment at the hands of the "monied aristocrats of Augusta," Shultz set out to recoup his losses and exact his revenge. Hamburg was the result.[5]

The focus of his plan fell upon a 330-acre tract of land on the Savannah River in the extreme southern corner of Edgefield District, directly opposite Augusta. In June 1821, Shultz acquired use of the tract for six years in return for an annual rent to the property's owner. During the term of agreement, Shultz was to lay out a town and erect improvements. At the conclusion of the term, Shultz would be entitled to one-quarter of the tract, plus all its improvements, in return for one-fourth part of the current value of the entire tract, or $1,750. Shultz went to work immediately to fulfill his end of the agreement. By the beginning of 1822, the tract of Savannah River bottom land possessed a 300-foot by 50-foot brick and plank warehouse, three smaller storehouses, a substantial two-story brick public house, and several dozen completed houses and shops, with many more under construction, upon which appraisers placed a value of $69,000.[6]

In spite of his efforts, however, Shultz lacked the resources needed to complete his vision of Hamburg, which included wharves and a steamship line to Charleston. Still reeling from the destruction of his own finances in the Panic of 1819, he gained some aid from private sources, but not enough to complete

5. John A. Chapman, *History of Edgefield County: From the Earliest Settlements to 1897* (Newberry, 1897), 238–39; Rosser H. Taylor, "Hamburg: An Experiment in Town Promotion," *North Carolina Historical Review* 11 (January 1934): 20–21; Charles G. Cordle, "Henry Shultz and the Founding of Hamburg, South Carolina," in *Studies in Georgia History and Government,* ed. James C. Banner and Lucien E. Roberts (Athens, 1940), 79–82; Edwin J. Scott, *Random Recollections of a Long Life, 1806 to 1876* (Columbia, 1969), 25–28.

6. "Report of the Solicitor of the Western Circuit concerning the Town of Hamburg," Miscellaneous Communications, 1830–4, General Assembly Papers, SCDAH; "Assessment of Hamburg Estate," January 19, 1822, Henry Shultz Papers, SCL.

the job. Ever resourceful, however, and ever bold, Shultz turned to the institution he believed would be the most likely ally in his high-stakes rivalry with Augusta: the South Carolina General Assembly. In December 1821, Shultz sent the state legislature a carefully worded petition, praying for a loan of $50,000 to complete construction of Hamburg and build a steamship to open a water communication with Charleston. In addition, he sought a six-year tax exemption on all stock in trade, buildings, and professions in Hamburg, a tobacco inspection station, and permission to establish a bank to protect Hamburg inhabitants "against the rivalry and oppression of those institutions in Augusta, and . . . supply the upper districts with the more valuable currency of our own banks."[7]

The loss of South Carolina commerce to Georgia was a theme Shultz particularly emphasized. The Savannah River would continue to attract an extensive upcountry trade, Shultz pointed out, "which must be lost to South-Carolina, unless arrested by some town on that river." Shultz claimed $2 million in South Carolina commerce had contributed to the wealth of Augusta and Savannah instead of remaining in its native state. It was Shultz's avowed purpose to redirect this stream of produce to Charleston. Given this stated goal, he asked the legislature, "Can you doubt then, that [Augusta and Savannah] are hostile, and will combine their powers to crush me if possible?" It was up to the General Assembly to act and support his plan, or, Shultz predicted, Hamburg would revert to the cornfield it had been before his arrival. Seeking additional aid from the legislature the following year, Shultz was even more direct in asserting the role Hamburg was destined to play in securing for South Carolina "all the benefits of the commerce arising from its own productions." By the end of 1822, Shultz claimed 35,000 bags of cotton had been shipped from Hamburg to Charleston, all of which previously would have gone to Savannah. He asked for river improvements, new roads and bridges to Hamburg, and a bank to sever the interior's financial peonage to Georgia. Why, asked Shultz of the legislature, would they "suffer the paper of the Georgia Banks" to inundate the middle and upper districts of South Carolina, when a bank at Hamburg would ensure a better medium of exchange and "give that advantage to the citizens of your own state, which is now enjoyed by those of another."[8]

7. Taylor, "Hamburg," 22; "Memorial of Henry Shultz," Petition, 1821–29, General Assembly Papers, SCDAH.

8. "Memorial of Henry Shultz," Petition, 1821–29; Memorial of Henry Shultz, Petition, 1822–50; both in General Assembly Papers, SCDAH.

While much of Shultz's rhetoric was undoubtedly inspired by his desire to exact emolument and revenge, the patriotic aspect of his petitions struck a deep-seated chord with the solons of the South Carolina General Assembly. A cardinal tenet of republican ideology and agrarian rhetoric held that economic sovereignty was the necessary precursor to political sovereignty. Yeomen and planters represented the ideal republican citizen in large part because, as landowners, they theoretically controlled their own economic destinies. Those reliant on others for their livelihood, either as tenants or employees, crippled their political independence and rendered themselves subject to manipulation by those who controlled their livelihood. Writ large, the same canon was applied at a state level. South Carolina saw its status in the Union as directly proportional to its economic clout within the same. Thus, the more South Carolina rendered itself independent of other states for its produce and merchandise, while retaining control over the commerce emanating from within its own borders, the less the state would be subjected to outside, or "foreign," forces beyond its control. Concomitantly, as one legislative committee opined, by retaining its own commerce and increasing its foreign exports, South Carolina would "enhance its weight in the scale of the union." Commerce, then, benefited the state the most when it remained largely an intrastate affair.[9]

The earliest and most consistent nemesis to South Carolina's desired economic sovereignty was not the North but the neighboring state of Georgia. Since colonial times, South Carolina and Georgia made mutual accusations of unwarranted efforts by each to control or subvert the economic affairs of the other. In the 1760s, Georgians cried loudly over South Carolina's resolution to grant lands south of the Altamaha River, complaining to the British crown that such actions threatened to place vast tracts of Georgia land into the hands of speculating Carolinians, rather than "persons who will actually improve them and reside in the Province." In the 1780s, the two states sparred over territory claimed by both between the Keowee-Seneca and Tugaloo-Chattooga rivers, as each asserted a right to grant the land to settlers and develop the area's economic resources for their own respective benefit. Even after a 1787 convention established the Savannah and Tugaloo rivers as the fixed boundary between the two states, South Carolina bristled at efforts by Georgians to deny them free navigation of the Savannah. After an overzealous Georgia official in Savannah

9. "Report of Special Committee of Senate for Joint Committee with the Com. of the House on the petition of Henry Shultz," Reports, ND-153 [ca. 1823], General Assembly Papers, SCDAH.

seized a Carolina vessel for its failure to clear customs, an angry Governor Thomas Pinckney decried to his Georgia counterpart that the action was "a violation of the Law of Nations," and "repugnant to the Spirit of the Confederation." Even if Georgia actually possessed exclusive right to the Savannah River, "the attempt to enforce such a Right would rather be expected from a hostile nation," Pinckney declared, than from a sister state.[10]

Interstate commercial disputes continued into the antebellum era. In 1811 Edgefield residents objected to an extension of the court term in order to hasten settlement of the excessive suits for debt incurred during the recent embargo. The protesters claimed a large part of these cases emanated from neighboring Georgia, "whose Legislature, at this moment," they pointed out, "are engaged in passing a Law for *again* extending the time for the payment of debts," many of which were presumably owed to Carolinians. To expedite the operation of the Edgefield court while Georgia solons were "impeding the wheels of Justice" against South Carolinians "would be particularly Hard and oppressive." Nineteenth-century proposals for a joint effort to improve the Savannah River generally foundered, as each state feared the commerce of the other would derive greater benefit from their own public expense. An 1804 attempt to improve the upper Savannah "between two Sovereign and Independent States" failed as South Carolina commissioners noted that "local jealousies" had created too many "obstacles" for the project to succeed. Almost a quarter of a century later, the South Carolina Senate refused to support another joint attempt to improve the river, deeming the proposal to be "inexpedient." The Charleston business community concurred. "All the money expended by South Carolina on the Savannah River," they believed, "will result in benefit which can only be reaped by the Commercial Capital of Georgia."[11]

10. Lilla M. Hawes, ed., "Letters to the Georgia Colonial Agent, July 1762 to January 1771," *Georgia Historical Quarterly* 36 (September 1952): 257; Thomas Pinckney to George Mathews, September 5, 1787, Governor's Messages, No. 448, General Assembly Papers, SCDAH. For more detail on the South Carolina-Georgia border disputes of the 1780s, see correspondence of Gov. Benjamin Guerard in Governor's Messages, No. 306, 53, 55–56, 58, 291–92, 297–98, and correspondence of Gov. Thomas Pinckney, Governor's Messages, No. 448; all in General Assembly Papers, SCDAH; "Georgia-South Carolina Territorial Disputes," *Georgia Historical Quarterly* 12 (March 1928): 53–61; E. Merton Coulter, "The Georgia-Tennessee Boundary Line," *Georgia Historical Quarterly* 35 (December 1951): 270–74.

11. "Petition of Sundry Inhabitants of Edgefield District," Petitions, 1811–32; "Report of Commissioners appointed to examine the practicability of opening and improving navigation on the

The city of Augusta, in particular, became the primary focus of South Carolina concerns over "foreign" influence in upcountry commercial affairs. Situated at the falls of the Savannah River, Augusta became the natural inland market for upcountry commerce from both states, whence it inevitably found its way to the river's mouth at the Georgia port of Savannah. Arresting the flow of South Carolina tobacco, corn, cotton, and other produce into the Georgia city became a serious concern of the state legislature. Several schemes for backcountry development were undertaken with an avowed purpose of retaining upcountry commerce within South Carolina's borders and channeling it to its own port of Charleston. Post-Revolution efforts to relocate the state capital inland were spurred in part by the possibility of attracting upcountry commerce away from Augusta. Judge Henry Pendleton argued in favor of an inland seat of government to augment Charleston's commercial presence in the backcountry:

> The State of Georgia, by means of the town of Augusta, would rival South-Carolina by furnishing our back-countries with necessaries; but if the seat of government was removed to the Congarees, it would take that trade to itself by means of a communication with Charlestown, which still should be considered as the grand emporium of the State. This communication might be kept up by means of traders being fixed at the new settlement.[12]

A 1784 petition supported by almost two hundred backcountry residents sought to establish a town opposite Augusta, with the promise that it would promote settlement and save South Carolinians the trouble of carrying their produce over the river to Georgia, "which is very troublesome and Expensive,

---

Savannah River," August 17, 1804, Governor's Messages, No. 896; "Resolution appointing Commissioners to meet Commissioners of the State of Georgia on the Savannah River," Resolution, 1820–20; "Report of the Commee on Internal Improvements on the 6th claim of the Govr Message No 1 as relating to the navigation of the Savanna River," Reports, 1828–86; "Memorial of the Inhabitants of the Parishes of St. Philips & St. Michael," Petition, ND-1643 [1827]; all in General Assembly Papers, SCDAH. U. B. Phillips also noted the negative impact of the interstate rivalry on efforts to improve navigation on the Savannah River. Phillips, *A History of Transportation in the Eastern Cotton Belt to 1860* (New York, 1908; New York, 1968), 116–19. For an excellent overview of how persistent localism undermined national internal improvement schemes, see John Lauritz Larson, *Internal Improvement: National Public Works and the Promise of Popular Government in the Early United States* (Chapel Hill, 2001).

12. Charleston, *South Carolina Weekly Advertiser,* February 19, 1783.

and at Once Carries a great part of the produce of our back country out of the State." Another set of inland residents asserted that the lack of public roads between the interior and Charleston meant that twenty thousand bales of South Carolina cotton traveled instead to Augusta, where they were "converted to the advantage of the State of Georgia." They believed that a series of turnpikes would remedy the situation and put an end to "the heavy expenditures made in another State for transportation, commissions and profits, on our own commodities and the foreign merchandize consumed in our State."[13]

Thus, when Henry Shultz petitioned for legislative aid for Hamburg, he tapped into an established mistrust of the commercial sway wielded by Augusta in the South Carolina interior, and, more broadly, a nagging fear of interstate influence upon intrastate commercial affairs. As a result, Hamburg became the beneficiary of unprecedented legislative largesse. In its December 1821 session, the General Assembly overwhelmingly approved a $50,000 loan to Shultz and exempted all property from taxation within the limits of Hamburg for the next five years. In the following session, a committee recommended an appropriation of $20,000 to improve inland navigation between Hamburg and Charleston and another $5,000 for a bridge over Steven's Creek, and authorized the incorporation of a private bank. Two years later, a pair of new roads laid out by Shultz (which he asserted were "of great public utility as [they] diverts much of the trade from Augusta to Hamburg") were declared public highways, making them subject to maintenance by public levy. In addition, a special joint legislative committee recommended exempting Hamburg lots from taxation for an additional three years, in order to encourage "permanent settlers and capitalists in Hamburgh." These actions by the South Carolina assembly went far beyond its customary roles of authorizing local improvements and regulating economic activity. Whereas previous efforts sought to increase access to markets, the legislature's support of Hamburg sought to create a marketplace itself.[14]

13. "Petition of Sundry Inhabitants of 96 District for a Town opposite to Augusta," Petitions, 1784–50; "Petition of sundry citizens praying the establishment of turn pike roads and other internal Improvements," Petitions, ND-1470; both in General Assembly Papers, SCDAH; Theodora J. Thompson and Rosa S. Lumpkin, eds., *Journals of the House of Representatives, 1783–1784* (Columbia, S.C., 1977), 444. Also see Chapman, *History of Edgefield*, 239–40.

14. "Report of the Memorial of Henry Shultz," Reports, 1821–147; "Report of the Special Committee on the Memorial of Henry Shultz," Reports, ND-154; "Recommendation of the Commissioners of Roads of the battalion in which Hamburg is situated, for the establishment of a public

The legislative favor shown Shultz and Hamburg did not go unnoticed outside of Edgefield and Barnwell. A Laurens District grand jury presented a grievance against the tax exemptions granted to Hamburg, "deeming it contrary to the spirit of our government to exemt any particular portion of the inhabitants of the state from the payment of their general Tax," and particularly granting such privilege to "any incorporated town, Borough, or city." Even among Hamburg residents, the seemingly narrow number of persons reaping fiscal benefit from the state's favoritism raised eyebrows. "You will, no doubt, think hard of being taxed for the benefit of an individual or more properly, individuals," an angry Hamburg inhabitant told his neighbors, "but you ought to think hard of the prodigality of your Representatives who gave the money."[15]

The General Assembly offered no apologies for its actions. Like the establishment of a new road or ferry, legislators deemed its encouragement of Hamburg fostered the public good. One had only to cite a litany of commercial statistics to see how South Carolina had prospered from Shultz's vision. In 1821 water communication from western South Carolina to Charleston was all but unknown. Three years later, seven steamships plied the Savannah River and coastal waterways between Hamburg and Charleston. Almost 54,000 bales of cotton had traveled from the new town to Charleston in that time. "Our exports," legislator Andrew Pickens Butler claimed, "by which, the importance of this State is estimated abroad, have been increased and that of Georgia decreased to this amount." As Augusta was considered the cotton conduit of Savannah, Butler declared "Hamburgh may now be regarded as entirely a place of deposit for Charleston." But the permanence of this condition had yet to be secured. "There is now, and no doubt will continue to be," legislators warned, "a great competition between South Carolina and Georgia for this trade, which has thus been secured." Without continued legislative succor, the interior might fall back into its old dependency on Augusta, with the commerce of Charleston and the state suffering in proportion. Placing Hamburg's importance in such a public light, the General Assembly confidently asserted it should act to protect the town from falling prey to persons "whose interest in

road to Hamburg," Petition, 1824–157; "Petition of Henry Shultz—praying the establishment of certain Roads," Petitions, ND-1252; "Report of the special committee on Henry Shultz petition relative to Hamburg," Petitions, 1824–76; all in General Assembly Papers, SCDAH; *Statutes at Large*, VI: 175, 203–4; VIII: 40–44; IX: 542.

15. "Laurens District. Presentment of the Grand Jury, April Term 1822," Presentments, 1822–8, General Assembly Papers, SCDAH; Edgefield, *Carolinian*, November 21, 1829.

it may be either to obstruct its further improvement, or make it subservient to commercial views directly contrary to the intentions of its founder and the interests of the State."[16]

The legislature's dedication to fostering the growth of Hamburg was sorely put to the test. By 1824, Bridge Bill creditors placed liens on Shultz's Hamburg property totaling $50,000, which threatened some or all of the town with foreclosure. Shultz quickly pointed out the ominous consequences to the state if Hamburg was sold at auction. The trade of Hamburg would be regained by Georgia "if suitable exertions are not made on the part of the State to counteract her present extraordinary efforts again to seize it." If the legislature would relieve the "incumbrances" upon Hamburg, Shultz announced his willingness to yield up the town to the state to "sell and appropriate the lots in such manner as will best advance the interests of the state in securing a most important branch of commerce." Or, if the legislature wished to advance $50,000 directly to Shultz, he would clear the liens himself and sell town lots for repayment.[17]

The General Assembly was predictably impressed with Shultz's forebodings, if not his plans for preventing them. "Considering the importance of Hamburg in a public point of view," reported the Senate committee deliberating on the petition, "it is obvious that the State should not let it pass into hands, which might direct its commerce from its present direction." To protect the town from Shultz's creditors, the assembly passed resolutions directing the comptroller general to pay the judgments against Shultz and ordered the sale of town lots in Hamburg, the profits of which were to be applied to the state treasury to repay its loan to Shultz. In addition, legislators also directed the comptroller and state solicitor to attend the sale of Hamburg lots, "and if in their opinion the interest of the State may be endangered by such sale," the officials were authorized to bid on behalf of the state "to such ammount as they in their discretion may deem necessary to secure the interest of the State."[18]

16. "Report of the special committee on Henry Shultz petition relative to Hamburg," Reports, 1824–76; "Report of the Committee of the Senate on the petition of Henry Shultz," Reports, 1824–78; both in General Assembly Papers, SCDAH.

17. "Petition of Henry Shultz relative to Hamburg," Petitions, 1824–48, General Assembly Papers, SCDAH.

18. "Report of Senate Committee," Reports, 1824–78; [Resolution concerning judgments against Henry Shultz], Resolutions, ND-289; "Resolution concerning the sale of lots in Hamburg," Resolutions, 1824–10; all in General Assembly Papers, SCDAH.

But the $37,370 cleared by the sale of fifty Hamburg lots was not enough to unsnarl the financial entanglements between Shultz and the state of South Carolina. Even with the respite he received from this additional state largesse, Shultz soon became overwhelmed by an avalanche of creditors, liens, judgments, and mortgages, from which he found it impossible to liberate himself. In 1828 Shultz spent nine months imprisoned for debt in the Edgefield District jail, as creditors demanded an assignment of his assets and the settlement of outstanding accounts. The following year, the state foreclosed the mortgage on Hamburg made by Shultz as collateral for the $50,000 loan granted in 1821, taking possession of most of the town and ordering the sale of additional lots to satisfy the debt. But the General Assembly had little interest in becoming the new landlord of Hamburg. To extricate the state, a joint committee recommended forgiving the interest on Shultz's loan and, upon receiving payment for the last portion of the principal still due to the state, returning the remainder of the town lots to Shultz. By the end of 1833, Shultz had paid the remaining $16,225 due to the state, who, in turn, reconveyed the unsold remainder of Hamburg back to the town's founder. By the account of one legislative committee, the aggregate expenditure made by the state to promote and protect Hamburg and the commerce of the upcountry totaled $110,000, of which only a fraction was ever repaid.[19]

But the state's efforts to liberate itself from the fiscal support and administration of Hamburg did little to dampen the legislature's overall enthusiasm for the town. Despite the legal and fiscal embarrassments that Shultz's vision caused the state, the General Assembly remained pleased with Hamburg and its success. "The establishment of the Town of Hamburg has already been of essential value to the State," declared representative James S. Deas. Hamburg's future seemed secure by the 1830s, with the town well placed to continue its rivalry with Augusta for control of upcountry trade. Shultz was also duly lauded for his efforts in erecting "a mart, for the sale of the produce of our own Citizens in our own State." But the town was entering a new epoch, one in which

19. The above gives only a brief sketch of the legal and fiscal wrangling over Hamburg between the state and Henry Shultz. For more detailed accounts, see Cordle, "Shultz and the Founding of Hamburg," 90–93; Taylor, "Hamburg," 26–27; Petitions, 1828–25 and 1829–29; Reports, 1829–59, 1830–51, 1831–286, and 1832–80; and Miscellaneous Communications, 1828–18, 1830–4, 1833–3 and ND-392 [ca. 1838]; all in General Assembly Papers, SCDAH. Public announcements for the sale of Hamburg town lots are printed in the Pottersville, *Edgefield Hive—Extra,* September 3, 1830; Broadside [1835], Henry Shultz Papers, SCL; and the *Edgefield Advertiser,* March 8, 1838.

Hamburg needed direction not from its founder or the General Assembly, but from its own citizens. "It is high time for the State to close her interests in the Town of Hamburgh," reported the Committee on Ways and Means in December 1832. "Private enterprize is the best stimulus to all improvements," the committee asserted, "and the sooner this Town falls into the hands of the Citizens of this Country, the sooner and better will those objects be accomplished for which the State has made such sacrifices." With the town seemingly secure, legislators no longer felt the need to remain a partner in directing the town and its inhabitants. Hamburg and its capitalists would hereafter be left to administer the town as they saw fit.[20]

Besides increasing the exports of Charleston and helping to retain the commerce of South Carolina within its borders, the rise of Hamburg also signaled a growing commercial presence in Edgefield and Barnwell. State legislators foresaw this role for the town in addition to serving as a cotton conduit between inland districts and the coast:

> That since [Hamburg's] establishment the inhabitants of an important and large section of this State are enabled to sell their produce and purchase necessaries on much better terms than before—In short, it has brought the commerce of Charleston, comparatively speaking, to the doors of the upper Country planters.

Merchants were the catalyst in this transformation, being precisely the type of "permanent settlers and capitalists" Shultz and the legislature hoped to attract to Hamburg. Not all of the newly arrived merchants were interested merely in grabbing quick profits from Hamburg's speculative boom and then moving on. Many were eager to settle permanently in the promising new market town, anticipating that the commercial tide rising in Hamburg would lift their boats as well. Within a few years of the town's founding, sizable firms such as Addams & Thew, Tully F. Sullivan & Co., Robert McDonald & Co., and John Sale & Co. had leased or purchased lots in Hamburg. By 1825, local newspapers identified no fewer than fourteen "principal Wholesale Merchants" in the growing town, while the Charleston press estimated "two hundred shop-keepers and

20. "Report of the Special Joint Comme on the Town of Hamburgh," Report, 1830–51; "Report of the Committee of Ways & Means upon the Report of the Commissioners of Hamburgh," Report, 1832–80; both in General Assembly Papers, SCDAH.

traders" had taken up residence in Hamburg. Many of these ambitious new arrivals worked quickly to fulfill the legislature's prophecy of bringing urban commerce closer to the rural population of the interior. The wholesale firm of Rodgers & Latimer soon found itself supplying merchandise to planters as far away as Pendleton in the extreme northwest of the state, while Hamburg factorage houses, like Watt & Bowie and Holmes & Gray, quickly gained the patronage of inland planters by marketing their cotton and other produce.[21]

A similar growth in trade could be found in the rest of Edgefield and Barnwell as well. Between the 1810s and 1820s, the amount of stock in trade almost tripled in Barnwell, while that in Edgefield more than quadrupled, thanks in large part to the presence of Hamburg. In the 1830s, Barnwell's mercantile activities jumped again following the completion of the South Carolina Railroad through the district. The total volume of trade transacted by merchants in both districts continued to post significant gains throughout the latter decades of the antebellum era (table 3).

While the merchants' ascent was most obvious in district towns, country merchants remained a fixture in both Edgefield and Barnwell, dispersed among crossroads, bridges, mills, river forks, muster grounds, and other prominent points in the agrarian landscape. A few rural operators demonstrated a decided flair for retailing and succeeded in establishing quite substantial mercantile concerns. Cousins Hampton and Josiah J. Brabham operated a dry goods and grocery store for almost two decades at Buford's Bridge in southern Barnwell District, earning reputations as trusted businessmen and carrying on one of the largest volumes of trade in the entire district. J. G. Sheppard invested $15,000 in his Edgefield District store at Liberty Hill, which sold as much as $10,000 worth of merchandise annually. James M. Richardson's general store gained such local prominence that the crossroads where it was located came to be known as "Richardsonville."[22]

21. "Report on Petition of Henry Shultz," Report, 1824–78, General Assembly Papers, SCDAH; Edgefield Deeds, Book 40, 184–85, 323–324; Book 41, 375–76, SCDAH; Pottersville, *South-Carolina Republican*, October 22, 1825; Cordle, "Shultz and the Founding of Hamburg," 91; Receipt, B. M. Rodgers and A. R. Latimer to James Thompson, April 27, 1824; Receipt, "Cotton Sold D.L. Addams, Hamburg," November 15, 1825; Watt & Bowie to Capt. James Thompson, May 21, 1826; Receipt for cotton sold by Holmes & Gray, Hamburg, October 15, 1827; G. S. Symmes to Jas. Thompson & Son, October 13, 1828; all in Norris and Thompson Family Papers, SCL; Account of "Mr. Mitchell" with Rodgers & Latimer, Hamburg, November 22, 1825, SCL.

22. Credit Reports, South Carolina, vol. 3 (Barnwell), 80; vol. 9a (Edgefield), 55, 58, R. G. Dun

TABLE 3. Value of Stock in Trade

YEAR	BARNWELL	EDGEFIELD
1801	$4,379	$11,700
1811	$7,667	$12,300
1821	$19,221	$51,150
1831	$20,923	$29,250[a]
1841	$60,750	$114,120
1851	$74,600	$192,225

SOURCE: "Report of the Comptroller General of South Carolina," *Reports and Resolutions* (1801–51).

NOTE: The comptroller general collected the above figures to assess an annual inventory tax on stock in trade, which was levied upon all articles of trade, barter, or exchange in a merchant's possession on January 1. Since the tax on inventories was assessed only at that time, it seems likely that merchants kept inventories low in January to avoid higher tax assessments. Thus, stock in trade was probably higher at other times of the year. Ford, *Origins of Southern Radicalism,* 237n.

[a]The decline in value for Edgefield in 1831 reflects a tax exemption upon stock in trade in the town of Hamburg. "Report of the Committee to whom was Recommitted the Memorial of Henry Shultz," Reports, 1829–59, General Assembly Papers, SCDAH.

However, most country stores operated on a much smaller scale, with capitalizations of only $1,000 or $2,000 (sometimes even less), and conducting trade, as described by an R. G. Dun credit agent, "embracing a little of everything for which there is a sale." Few owners ran their mercantile investments as their primary undertaking. Bennet Perry operated his crossroads store in Edgefield District as a secondary concern to his planting interests. A credit report complimented Edward Furse on the talent he demonstrated in the operation of his small country business, but noted he nevertheless remained "more a farmer than a merch[ant]." Even highly successful rural store owners like the Brabham cousins, J. G. Sheppard, and James Richardson operated their stores as lucrative sidebars to even larger investments in land and slaves.[23]

& Co. Collection, Baker Library, Harvard Business School; M. M. Brabham, *A Family Sketch, and Else, or Buford's Bridge and its People* (Columbia, S.C., 1923), 83–84.

23. Credit Reports, South Carolina, vol. 3 (Barnwell), 80, 108; vol. 9a (Edgefield), 55, 56, 58, R. G. Dun & Co. Collection, Baker Library, Harvard Business School. Michael Wayne and Lacy Ford

Fewer still were the number of rural store operators who considered merchandising to be their life's calling. Many used retailing as a stepping stone to planting. Running a store frequently served as a temporary career choice for rural merchants, helping to augment limited means or providing useful employment until a planting concern could be established, either from store profits or through a fortunate inheritance. Partners O. G. and R. G. Hay quit a remunerative mercantile business in Barnwell District after several years to concentrate their energies on their growing planting interests. John Sale owned successful investments in both planting and merchandising, but sold his share in a crossroads store in preference to his agricultural pursuits. R. M. Fuller opened his tailor shop outside of Hamburg with the backing of wealthy planter John Rainsford. But after several profitable years of business and an advantageous marriage, Fuller retired from his tailor's trade to a newly acquired plantation, investing some of his cotton profits as a silent partner in a Hamburg dry goods store. After P. B. Weaver received a substantial inheritance and dowry, he quit his rural Edgefield store and set up as a farmer on land purchased in Georgia.[24]

Whereas a blurred line often divided planter from merchant in the rural sections of Edgefield and Barnwell, such was seldom the case in Hamburg. There, stores, factorage houses, and warehouses were owned and operated by men whose interests strayed but infrequently beyond their mercantile and commercial concerns. Merchant, factor, or agent was their calling and rarely did they exchange their commercial avocation for one in agriculture. Their backgrounds varied. Some were local in origin, like grocer Robert McDonald of Edgefield District who took a lease on a Hamburg lot in 1823 with a Charleston partner, John McGrath. Others, like dry goods merchant Hays B. Jackson, emigrated across the Savannah River from Augusta, believing the boomtown of Hamburg offered promising opportunities for an ambitious merchant in search of the main chance. Still others arrived from more distant lo-

---

have also noted the interest of planters in rural stores. See Wayne, *Reshaping of Plantation Society,* 164; Ford, *Origins of Southern Radicalism,* 88–89.

24. Credit Reports, South Carolina, vol. 3 (Barnwell), 84; vol. 9a (Edgefield), 54, 55, 63, R. G. Dun & Co. Collection, Baker Library, Harvard Business School. Other historians of the antebellum South have also noted the frequent involvement of planters in the ownership and operation of country stores. Wayne, *Reshaping of Plantation Society,* 163–65; Morris, *Becoming Southern,* 107–8; Jonathan M. Bryant, *How Curious a Land: Conflict and Change in Greene County, Georgia, 1850–1885* (Chapel Hill, 1996), 41.

cales. Alfred B. Church came to Hamburg from the North in the 1830s as a tin peddler. With capital supplied by a brother in New York City, Church established the hardware firm of A. B. Church & Co. and earned a reputation as "a shrewd kind of Yankee." Even more cosmopolitan was the Hamburg house of Henkell & Robinson, whose partners hailed from Canada and imported hardware and cutlery directly from English factories at Sheffield and Birmingham.[25]

Hamburg's emergence as an inland cotton market, however, provided the sharpest distinction between the behavior of its commercial population and that of their country neighbors. "Mostly all the Hamburg merch[an]ts speculate in cotton," observed an R. G. Dun agent, with particularly aggressive traders earning reputations for "buying cotton from wagons." B. S. Dunbar came to Hamburg as a new partner in an established grocery business. However, the store gradually became subsidiary to his growing interest in cotton speculation, causing his fortunes to rise and fall annually at the dizzy pace only the hardiest entrepreneur could stomach. In one year, Dunbar cleared $25,000, lost half that amount in the next, then earned $20,000 in the year after that. Dunbar continued his career as a "wild speculator," making and losing fortunes in Hamburg annually for almost two decades. Andrew Burnside served as an agent for the Bank of Charleston in Hamburg and a director of the South Carolina Railroad. He sold no merchandise but amassed tens of thousands of dollars through his cotton speculations. Ability and good fortune eventually carried Burnside to the status of a leading citizen and businessman in Hamburg, but his cotton trading also gave him a reckless air shared by others of his avocation. "Speculates largely in cotton," read a R. G. Dun report on Burnside, "may be perfectly safe one time & insolv[an]t in a few days."[26]

Large and respected traders, such as Henry L. Jeffers, Thomas Kernaghan, Josiah Sibley, Jeremiah W. Stokes, and Golithan Walker, dominated the cotton business of Hamburg, but never completely monopolized the trade. Smaller speculators mingled among larger operators, hoping to augment their mercantile businesses through a fortuitous advance in cotton prices. Those who

25. Edgefield Deeds, Book 40, 323–24, SCDAH; Credit Reports, South Carolina, vol. 9a (Edgefield), 37, 39, 41, 43, R. G. Dun & Co. Collection, Baker Library, Harvard Business School; *Edgefield Advertiser,* November 4, 1841; November 12, 1845.

26. Credit Reports, South Carolina, vol. 9a (Edgefield), 38, R. G. Dun & Co. Collection, Baker Library, Harvard Business School.

gambled wrong, however, paid dearly. Lacking the means, connections, and reputation of the large cotton dealers in Hamburg, small speculators failed and fled the town with alarming frequency. Elihu Hodges and Isaac Smith wrecked their small grocery and liquor establishment through an unfortunate gamble on the cotton market. An unexpected drop in cotton prices likewise ruined grocer William Miller, as his small business collapsed under the weight of a $20,000 debt. By 1840, leading Hamburg merchants tried in vain to rein in maverick speculators by moving to forbid cotton purchases east of Centre Street and fining those who engaged cotton sellers beyond the town limits. The effort did nothing to civilize the trade. The unending stream of merchants, traders, and speculators arriving in and departing from Hamburg led an exasperated R. G. Dun reporter to declare, "Almost all the Hamburg people change ab[ou]t once a quarter . . . *easy come, easy go!*"[27]

The rapid emergence of the merchant class in Edgefield and Barnwell did not escape the notice of local observers, nor was their assessment particularly favorable. Many saw the trend as bordering on a mania. "Every boy in the land is turning rampant to get into a store," noted the *Edgefield Advertiser.* "Cannot something practical be done to choke off this mawkish love of *polish*," the paper asked, which seemed to manifest itself as "a dread of dirt, a scorn of work, and a passion for professional life?" Even William Gregg, the leading voice of economic diversification in the districts, felt the aggressive commercial attitude of the merchant population had gotten out of hand, "infusing speculation into the minds of those men whom nature had fitted for productive laborers."[28]

"Merchants love nobody," Thomas Jefferson is alleged to have once opined, although the historian Peter Colclanis observed that a transposition of the same phrase would be equally true. Nobody, it seemed, loved merchants, particularly the agrarian population of Edgefield and Barnwell. "Avoid much intercourse with the Taverns and Stores," Orsamus D. Allen advised his son, "and you will save many a dollar." While riding in a crowded stage coach to Columbia, an English traveler was stunned by the blunt epithets offered by his

27. Credit Reports, South Carolina, vol. 9a (Edgefield), 37–38, 40–42, 58, 66, R. G. Dun & Co. Collection, Baker Library, Harvard Business School; *Edgefield Advertiser,* September 17, 1840. On the role of antebellum storekeepers in the marketing of cotton, see Woodman, *King Cotton and His Retainers,* 76–83.

28. *Edgefield Advertiser,* October 14, 1857; William Gregg, *Speech of William Gregg, Member from Edgefield District, in the Legislature of South Carolina, December, 1857, on the Bank Question* (Columbia, 1857), 37–38.

fellow passengers against "the prevailing immorality and dishonesty of the mercantile classes," which they accused of "maintaining themselves by defrauding others." A planter visiting Hamburg in 1849 considered the town a great business locale, but also a place where "decency and good living they are Strangers." Sawyers on the Upper Three Runs in Barnwell District were convinced that they were regularly swindled by lumber merchants in Savannah. In retaliation, mill owners determined to establish their own agency rather than submit to the high charges "exacted of them by the Lumber Factors." Similarly, the Farmers Society of Barnwell District called for the erection of a public livestock market in Charleston, claiming it would end price collusion by city butchers and subject transactions between stock drivers and butchers "to the control of public opinion." Under current arrangements, the society complained, beef prices "do not remunerate the planter, while the Butcher's realize enourmous profits."[29]

Predictably, the barbed pen of James Henry Hammond offered the most pointed statement of the disdain with which many district planters held the mercantile profession:

> The *only safe* business for us is planting, & that in this country is the only independent and really honorable occupation. The planters here are essentially what the nobility are in other countries. They stand at the head of Society & politics. Lawyers & professed politicians come next, then Doctor's, merchants &c. . . . Those who argue & perhaps think that money is the thing no matter how gotten are low minded scoundrels. I would never for the sake of money embark in *any* thing calculated to lower me in my own esteem or the esteem of others. Yet I hardly know a man about Augusta or Hamburg who would not & that is what makes those places so much despised by *gentlemen*.

In no uncertain terms, Hammond advised his younger brother against a merchant career, believing it to be "everywhere the most hazardous that can be em-

29. Colclanis, "The Hydra Head of Merchant Capital," 1; Orsamus D. Allen to Joseph Allen, January 18, 1843, Orsamus D. Allen Letterbook, SCL; J. S. Buckingham, *The Slave States of America,* 2 vols. (London and Paris, 1842), 2:3; Elijah Webb to Rosa H. Webb, April 4, 1849, SCL; William Bush to James Henry Hammond, October 26, 1834, James Henry Hammond Papers, SCL; "Petition of the Farmers Society of Barnwell District Praying for the Establishment of a publick Market for the Sale of livestock in or near the City of Charleston," Petition, ND-3754 [ca. 1829], General Assembly Papers, SCDAH.

barked in." Another English tourist to South Carolina in the 1830s found a similar disposition held by the slaveholders he encountered. "The leading planters of South Carolina . . . consider themselves, not without some reason, *the gentlemen of America*," the traveler observed, noting that they "always cherish when they are placed in competition with men engaged in mercantile pursuits, whom they consider to be, by the nature of their avocations, incapable of rising to their level." Nor were such opinions confined to parvenus like Hammond. Lewis Malone Ayer Jr., a second-generation Barnwell District planter, likewise believed that the merchant's avocation was no place for an agrarian gentleman. "Indeed I have always thought a Planter's business was to make and prepare his produce for market, and not to speculate on it when it is in market," Ayer declared. A planter might withhold his crop for a time, but once sent to market, Ayer felt the planter "ought to take the market price. If anything is to be made by speculation, let it be made by that class of persons to whom the business legitimately belongs."[30]

To the agrarian ideologues of the districts, too many aspects of the merchant's profession appeared rather seamy and disreputable. While planters held few qualms over their own pursuit of economic advancement and material progress, the blatant speculation of cotton traders and storekeepers seemed to be mere materialism and avarice. That the merchant's sphere of economic activity was largely outside the more socially acceptable realm of agriculture placed them even lower in the eyes of agrarian aristocrats. "Speculation in every form & degree, beyond a moderate one as to the selling of ones own produce, is detestable," Hammond once declared. As sectional divisions grew in the aftermath of nullification and proslavery spokesmen worked to dichotomize northern and southern society, business ability and the aggressive pursuit of commerce began to be tainted as "Yankee" characteristics and a successful merchant might find himself dubbed—sometimes in jest, sometimes in contempt—"a shrewd kind of a Yankee." Not only were individual merchants frequently tagged as "Yankees," but the adjective was habitually applied by area planters to the entire merchant communities of Hamburg and Augusta. Ed-

30. James Henry Hammond to M. C. M. Hammond, May 9, 1848 (first quotation), James Henry Hammond Papers, Library of Congress; James Henry Hammond to M. C. M. Hammond, January 20, 1839, James Henry Hammond Papers, SCL; G. W. Featherstonhaugh, *Excursion Through the Slave States, from Washington on the Potomac to the Frontier of Mexico; with Sketches of Popular Manners and Geological Notices* (1844; reprint, New York, 1968), 155–56; Lewis Malone Ayer Jr. to unknown, September 29, 1852, Lewis Malone Ayer Papers, SCL.

ward Spann Hammond sneeringly called Augusta "a Southern Yankee town" and "the meanest city South." His father held a like opinion, lamenting "the place . . . is completely filled with Yankees." Although Augusta was Hammond's adolescent home, the place held no attraction to him as an adult and his affection for it extended "not farther than the soil."[31]

Stereotypes of merchants and the merchant class held by the rural residents of Edgefield and Barnwell were not entirely without foundation. Many tradesmen in the region actually were natives of the North, with northern business and familial ties that sometimes made full acceptance into the local southern community difficult, though not impossible. Marcella Holmes, a visitor from Maine, found little to distinguish Augusta from northern cities. Northerners were so prevalent in the population, she observed, that some locals took to calling Augusta "the Conn[ecticut] reserve." Other merchants, like F. Miller and B. Schwartz of Barnwell village, were true foreigners—immigrants to America from the German palatines. The presence of a number of Jews among these émigrés only added to the alien image of the local merchant class, as epithets like "Jew shop" and "Hebrew peddler" directed equal doses of snobbery, xenophobia, and anti-Semitism at their merchant targets.[32]

Nor was the sometimes unsavory reputation of district merchants entirely without merit. While most storekeepers worked hard to earn a reputation for honesty and fair business practices, a handful acquired justifiable notoriety. Shoemaker Gideon Hull boldly continued to solicit business for his trade despite his temporary residence in the Edgefield district jail. Hamburg grocer Ferdinand Schroder defrauded creditors of several thousand dollars, then escaped punishment by cutting a hole through the ceiling of his jail cell and fleeing to parts unknown. R. G. Dun credit ledgers frequently employed terms like

31. Genovese, *Political Economy of Slavery*, 28–29; Ford, *Origins of South Radicalism*, 277; Credit Reports, South Carolina, vol. 9a (Edgefield), 41, R. G. Dun & Co. Collection, Baker Library, Harvard Business School; Edward Spann Hammond Diary, January 2, 1852, Edward Spann Hammond Collection, SCL; James Henry Hammond to M. C. M. Hammond, February 16, 1847; James Henry Hammond to M. C. M. Hammond, February 9, 1833; both in James Henry Hammond Papers, SCL. Despite occasional adverse judgments made against merchants, Lewis Atherton argues they were generally accepted in southern society. See Atherton, *Southern Country Store*, 184–215.

32. Marcella Fayette Holmes to Sarah Carter, December 5, 1858, Holmes Family Papers, Massachusetts Historical Society; Credit Reports, South Carolina, vol. 3 (Barnwell), 77–78 and *passim;* vol. 9a (Edgefield), *passim,* R. G. Dun & Co. Collection, Baker Library, Harvard Business School.

unsavory, tricky, or *slippery* to characterize merchants with dubious reputations. Liquor dealer William Johnson was described as a "careless" and "doubtful" businessman, with his "reputation for virtue and honesty to be measured by the character of his calling." R. S. Roberts abandoned his general store in Edgefield Court House, leaving behind his paltry stock of goods to satisfy sundry writs and legal attachments against him. For several years, grocer William B. Beazley made his living "by filling the hands & Stomachs of his patrons with the most abominable frauds of the day," before fleeing Barnwell District insolvent and deeply in debt. James H. Willis "swindled every one who has been so unfortunate as to be in league with him" before his business finally succumbed to a dozen bail writs issued against him by angry creditors.[33]

Even worse, local storekeepers at times exercised a corrupting influence on slaves in the districts. W. Havird was jailed for selling liquor to slaves, as was grocer W. F. Phillips. Merchant John Platt amused members of the Barnwell District court by "reap[ing] where he had not sowed," that is, trading with slaves for produce stolen from their masters. In 1851 a number of Savannah River planters in Edgefield formed the Beech Island Agricultural and Police Society to enforce the laws preventing the unsupervised movement of the local slave population, with a particular emphasis on curtailing "the free and unrestricted intercourse they have with the cities of Augusta and Hamburg." The mercantile career of grocer and liquor dealer Jesse Peacock ended with a conviction for slave stealing and an appointment with the gallows.[34]

The majority of merchants in Edgefield and Barnwell were cut from finer cloth than Jesse Peacock, but rural residents had other reasons for resenting the

33. Edgefield, *Carolinian,* June 6, 1829; *Smith, Mowry & Son v. Ferdinand A. Schroder and Segesmund C. Schroder,* Court of Equity, Edgefield District, Spring Term 1849, in Benjamin Cudworth Yancey Papers, Southern Historical Collection, University of North Carolina, Chapel Hill; *Edgefield Advertiser,* September 13, 1848; Credit Reports, South Carolina, vol. 3 (Barnwell) 76, 79, 103 and *passim;* vol. 9a (Edgefield), 62 and *passim,* R. G. Dun & Co. Collection, Baker Library, Harvard Business School.

34. Credit Reports, South Carolina, vol. 3 (Barnwell), 84, 89, 94; vol. 9a (Edgefield), 66, R. G. Dun & Co. Collection, Baker Library, Harvard Business School; "Rules of the Beech Island Agricultural and Police Society," June 28, 1851, Beech Island Farmers Club Records, 1846–1934, SCL. Orville Vernon Burton also noted that planter mistrust of slaves in towns and cities around Edgefield also made such places unreceptive to free blacks as well. See Burton, "Anatomy of an Antebellum Rural Free Black Community: Social Structure and Social Interaction in Edgefield District, South Carolina, 1850–1860," *Southern Studies* 21 (fall 1982): 298–300.

commercial class in their midst. Nothing provided a clearer or more omnipresent reminder to planters and yeomen of their tenuous independence than their reliance on the credit supplied by a merchant or factor. Despite the oft-recited platitudes about the virtue of a debt-free existence, few—if any—planters or yeomen managed to attain the ideal. Cotton and slavery made many Edgefield and Barnwell agriculturists property-rich, but perpetually cash-poor. With most farm profits reinvested in additional land and slaves, advances in the form of short-term credit were essential to planter and yeoman alike in order to prepare the next year's crop and meet contingent expenses until the harvest could be sold. But the very act of asking for credit admitted a degree of dependence upon another. Southern nationalists and economic reformers alike decried the unseemly willingness of planters and yeomen to jeopardize their independence with self-inflicted debt. But no viable alternatives existed. While slavery became the positive good of southern society, credit remained the necessary evil. And no one wielded a more prevalent control over this lifeblood of the antebellum southern economy than the merchant and factor.[35]

George McDuffie considered indebted planters to be "the mere stewards of their creditors," and even members of the planter elite all too often found themselves under obligations to neighborhood merchants, most of whom possessed a social and economic standing far beneath their own. English visitor George W. Featherstonhaugh recorded a perceptive account of this foundation of planter animosity toward the merchant class:

> The planter, although his crops of cotton and rice often produce him an annual income far exceeding that of the cultivator of the North . . . yet is frequently less independent than the opulent merchant or farmer he undervalues, his annual expenditures being large and certain whilst his returns are somewhat precarious. He had perhaps to feed and clothe several hundred slaves, and it is not convenient for him to reduce his style of living; so that not unfrequently the merchant at the north, who is his agent, and to whom he consigns his productions for sale, sends him an account current, where, instead of small charges being deducted from large returns, he finds the advances made to him in money, the bills for feeding and clothing his slaves, his wines and luxuries, and other charges, swelled to an amount far exceeding the sum-total that his crops have sold for; perceiving himself

35. Woodman, *King Cotton and His Retainers*, 132–64; Ford, *Origins of Southern Radicalism*, 320–24.

therefore the debtor and quasi slave of the man he despises, his pride, his interest, and his passions, all combine to rouse indignation: at such moments the agitated planter is easily led to follow in the wake of any politicians who flatter him with the prospect of redress.[36]

Consider the example of the relationship between James Edward Calhoun and Alfred B. Church. Calhoun was a well-known planter and scion of a leading South Carolina family, who claimed as a brother-in-law no less a personage than John C. Calhoun. Church was a recent arrival to Hamburg from New York, only a few years removed from life as a peddler and now operating a small hardware store in Hamburg. In early 1842, Church sold Calhoun a supply of goods on credit, but at cash prices with a promise that Calhoun would "pay in a short time." Calhoun, however, was slow to settle the account, leaving Church to write several letters to remind him of the debt. The humble merchant was initially hesitant to dun Calhoun on the embarrassing subject, displaying not only courtesy to a customer but also a deferential sign of respect for a prominent planter, asking a favor rather than demanding payment of an overdue account. "I take the liberty to address you on the subject," he wrote, trusting that Calhoun would not hesitate to pay his bill and "help along a fellow mortal in this troublesome world." But as Calhoun continued to delay payment, Church became more curt and direct, losing his respectful tone and eventually making clear to Calhoun the potential ramifications that a debtor could expect by ignoring his creditors. Calhoun could either pay Church or "pay Lawyers, & officers of the Law." "Unless you pay me before many weeks, I shall certainly take such course to get my dues," warned Church.[37]

Like planters elsewhere in the South, Calhoun was accustomed to being a creditor in his neighborhood, through loans of food or cash to distressed friends or neighbors, which served as a means of both social and economic exchange between plain folk and gentry. Repayment of such debts was often deferred, sometimes indefinitely, as planters gained authority—and interest—by

36. George McDuffie, "Anniversary Oration of the State Agricultural Society of South Carolina . . . the 26th November 1840," in State Agricultural Society, *The Proceedings of the Agricultural Convention and of the State Agricultural Society of South Carolina, From 1839–1845—Inclusive* (Columbia, 1846), 105; Featherstonhaugh, *Excursion Through the Slave States*, 156.

37. A. B. Church to James Edward Calhoun, July 28, 1842 (first quotation); A. B. Church to James Edward Calhoun, December 28, 1842; A. B. Church to James Edward Calhoun, April 3, 1843 (second and third quotations); all in James Edward Calhoun Papers, SCL.

keeping their social inferiors indebted to them. Giving credit displayed both paternalism and power. For a tradesman like Church to wield a measure of that same power over a prominent member of the planter elite threatened to invert the relationship. As a result, planters like Calhoun often delayed, or even refused, to pay their debts to merchants, even if able to do so. "A gaming debt is a debt of honour," the writer and planter William J. Grayson once explained, "but a debt due a tradesman is not." Merchants, like Church, however, drew no such distinctions among debts, and local lawyers earned their bread and butter by forcing payment of similar obligations, underlining a purely economic purpose for debt in Edgefield and Barnwell's increasingly commercial society.[38]

But despite their personal and philosophical misgivings about the merchant class in their midst, most planters grudgingly admitted the necessity of their presence. Agriculture may be the proper foundation for civilized society, but it could never be its sole support. Merchants, factors, forwarding agents, and the commerce they fostered were needed as well. No community made up entirely of farmers could ever be great, not even one as amply blessed as that of Edgefield and Barnwell. Put simply, the southern economy could not survive by agriculture alone. Some commerce was necessary, particularly in the collection and distribution of goods and produce—precisely the type of services proffered by merchants in the districts. "An agricultural people may be happy *if not trampled upon as they always are*," Hammond once observed. But whether in the Union or out of it, he understood that a degree of commerce and manufacturing was necessary in the agrarian landscape. "They give us strength and independence," Hammond admitted, "which cannot be derived from any other sources." Lowcountry planter Elias Horry espoused similar sentiments on this necessary synergy between agriculture and commerce. "Commerce is founded through the medium of Agriculture," Horry told the State Agricultural Society in 1828, and the nations that attained the highest degree of wisdom and civilization were those "which have brought their Agriculture to the greatest improvement, and have most successfully combined it with Commerce."[39]

38. [William J. Grayson], "The Character of the Gentleman," *Southern Quarterly Review*, new series, 7 (January 1853): 59. On the social role of debt among antebellum planters, see Harris, *Plain Folk and Gentry*, 95–100; Bertram Wyatt-Brown, *Honor and Violence in the Old South* (New York and Oxford, 1986), 136–38; Bryant, *How Curious a Land*, 48–52.

39. James Henry Hammond to H. W. Conner, July 17, 1850, James Henry Hammond Papers, Library of Congress; Elias Horry, *An Address Delivered in Charleston, Before the Agricultural Soci-*

Thus, local planters saw commerce, in the form of merchants and tradesmen, in a necessary but subordinate role in their political economy. Agriculture was to remain dominant. "Trade," declared Charleston patriot Christopher Gadsden in the aftermath of the Revolution, "was only the handmaid to *her mistress*, agriculture." Mistress agriculture could survive without her handmaid commerce, Gadsden argued, "but the maid is Nothing At All *without* her mistress." It was a sentiment that still imbued the agrarians of Edgefield and Barnwell. Angus Patterson admitted to his fellow Barnwell planters that trade and manufacturing had their place in society, but in a civilized state, agriculture "has been and must continue to be in all ages, the primary source of public as well as of individual prosperity." Likewise, Francis Pickens declared that agriculture remained "the basis of progressive civilization," whence also sprung commerce and manufacturing. Combined, this economic trinity "constitute[s] the bones, and the muscles, and the veins of a great people." All parts had importance, but Pickens still held that agriculture was and continued to be "the centre upon which rests the whole structure of society."[40]

For the time being, disciples of the agrarian gospel in Edgefield and Barnwell comforted themselves with the belief that agriculture remained the unchallenged foundation of their society. Although they relied on merchants for credit and marketing services, planters still seemed settled in a comforting hegemony. After all, most economic activity in the district towns revolved around the surrounding farms and plantations, providing the rural economy with shipping and marketing services as well as supplying the limited consumer demands of the districts' planters, yeomen, and slaves. Towns, and to a greater extent merchants, seemed more dependent on farmers than the reverse, or so area planters persuaded themselves. Like planters across the South, agrarians

ety of South Carolina, at its Anniversary Meeting, on Tuesday, the 19th August, 1828 (Charleston, 1828), 3–4. Robert Weir noted that the awareness of a shared economic interest between planters and merchants in colonial South Carolina "helped to bind together potentially disparate segments of society." Weir, "'The Harmony We Were Famous For': An Interpretation of Pre-Revolutionary South Carolina Politics," *William and Mary Quarterly*, 3rd series, 26 (October 1969): 481.

40. Richard Walsh, ed., *The Writings of Christopher Gadsden, 1746–1805* (Columbia, 1966), 236–37; Angus Patterson, *An Address to the Farmers' Society of Barnwell District, Delivered on the Second Day of January, 1826* (Charleston, 1826), 4; Francis W. Pickens, *An Address Delivered Before the State Agricultural Society of South Carolina, In the Hall of the House of Representatives, November 29, 1849* (Columbia, 1849), 4.

in Edgefield and Barnwell remained convinced that trade and industry around the world revolved on an axis of southern cotton.[41]

Thus, despite some uneasiness, little serious apprehension developed over the initial rise of the merchant class in Edgefield and Barnwell. Merchants appeared thoroughly subservient to the plantation economy and displayed seemingly scant potential for becoming a catalyst for deeper transformations of the agrarian landscape. The commerce fostered by district tradesmen fit rather neatly into established rural ideologies. It also served more immediate and tangible purposes. The founding of Hamburg enhanced the economic sovereignty of Edgefield and Barnwell, as well as South Carolina, not only in relation to its traditional rival of Georgia, but, more and more proslavery ideologues saw commercial development and economic sovereignty as a necessary precursor to maintaining South Carolina's political sovereignty within the Union.

But as the antebellum period progressed, merchants in general—and town merchants in particular—would turn planter fears over security and independence to their advantage and undertake a concerted effort to alter the agrarian landscape to better suit the needs of commercial capital in Edgefield and Barnwell. To outsiders, the changes would seem inconsequential, even nonexistent, as they did to most of the historians who examined the Old South with the benefit of over a century of hindsight. But while cotton remained king and slaves grew more prominent with each passing decade, so too would the influence of the merchant class in shaping the political economy in antebellum Edgefield and Barnwell. Nor would they do so by themselves. Like moths to a flame, many of the new merchant establishments would be attracted to the most conspicuous engine of change to appear in the districts: the railroad.

41. David R. Goldfield argued that the influence of staple agriculture pervaded the form and function of cities and towns across the antebellum South, with most of the economic activities carried out in urban places dependent upon the success or failure of the year's cotton crop. See *Cotton Fields and Skyscrapers: Southern City and Region, 1607–1980* (Baton Rouge, 1982), 28–44.

CHAPTER FOUR

"THE GREAT AVENUE OF INTERCOURSE AND COMMON CHANNEL OF COMMERCE"

THE RAILROAD

The success which has attended the establishment of Rail Ways, with the application of steam as a motive power, has created a new era in the history of mechanical science: promising in the novelty and vast utility of its results, to effect a great change in the physical and social condition of the country.

ANONYMOUS, Barnwell District, 1833

IT WAS A DAY OF great excitement for "M." Just before dawn, the correspondent for the *Edgefield Advertiser* mounted a passenger car at Hamburg and began his first railroad journey to Charleston. As a youth, he recalled traipsing for days by foot with his father to reach the great Carolina entrepôt. Now, with the railroad, the journey from Hamburg to Charleston could be made between dawn and dusk of just a single day. As his train emerged from Hamburg, the writer thrilled as the steam locomotive "puffed and snorted with a fiery fury, sublime and terrible, scarce equalled by the volcanic explosions of an Ætna." Times had indeed changed. While speeding toward the coast at a pace "determined on outstripping the lightning in velocity," the writer could not help but rejoice "that my lot was cast in an age so glorious." Some of his bemused fellow travelers, however, were more skeptical about this alleged glory of their time. Looking out their car, they wondered whether the stone

Epigraph from "To the Friends of Internal Improvement in the Southern States, July 24, 1833" (n. p., 1833).

markers they saw recorded the passing miles or the graves of those killed by the railroad.[1]

Aside from occasional acerbic comments by local wits, the residents of Edgefield and Barnwell rapidly embraced the iron "Ætna" and its concomitant rolling stock. Few would disagree that railroads were the engineering marvels of their day and plain folk and planters alike soon incorporated them into their daily existence. Farmers and factors sent cotton bales to Charleston by rail in ever larger amounts, while returning trains reciprocated with a steady bounty of goods and merchandise to satiate consumer appetites in interior districts. Among the more well-to-do, rail travel became a liberating and increasingly common experience. Planters, merchants, and their respective families passed along the line on missions of business and pleasure with growing regularity. Nothing provided a more tangible sign of modernity. By combining power, speed, innovation, and precision, the railroad quickly became the physical definition of "progress" in Edgefield and Barnwell.

Partnered with the embrace of the railroad as a technological marvel, however, was an uncertainty over the railroad as a business and a corporate body. More than just an advance in mechanical science, the railroad also introduced Edgefield and Barnwell to the modern business corporation. At first, this innovation seemed significantly less revolutionary than the union of steam locomotion and iron rails. Corporations were hardly new and even their application to business enterprise was not without precedent in South Carolina. State government and local residents saw little initial difference between a corporation in the shape of the railroad and more traditional forms of vested entrepreneurship, such as bridges and ferries. Both received special privilege, but both were also seen as servants of the common good and agents of the social compact between public and private interests.

But this perception of the business corporation in Edgefield and Barnwell was about to cross into what the legal historian Morton Horwitz described as a "twilight zone" in the eyes of the district inhabitants, "sometimes conceived of as a public instrumentality, at other times regarded as a private entity." The bestowal of the power of eminent domain on the railroad heightened the public aspect of the enterprise, in both the minds of residents and the rhetoric of company officials. However, other actions by company directors soon chal-

1. *Edgefield Advertiser,* February 11, 1836.

lenged the perceived harmony of interests between the public and the railroad. In particular, the politically embarrassing effort by railroad management to fulfill their unprecedented capital requirements with federal aid created public doubt as to whether the railroad was primarily a servant of the common good or a means of advancing private interests at public expense.[2]

The railroad under discussion was the 136-mile line of the South Carolina Canal and Railroad Company (SCC&RR). Completed in 1833 at a total cost of almost $1 million, the road traveled between Charleston and Hamburg in the approximate shape of an inverted fishhook. Running northwest from Charleston, the road crossed into Barnwell District just below the confluence of the Edisto River forks, then proceeded along a ridge between the south fork and the Savannah River until it reached the sandhills of the Barnwell-Edgefield boundary, whence it arched southwest and descended into the town of Hamburg. The accomplishment of the SCC&RR was not only a pioneering effort in the history of railroading in South Carolina, but in the United States and beyond. Upon completion, the Charleston-to-Hamburg line was the longest stretch of railroad in the world under a single management. In 1834 chief engineer Horatio Allen proudly boasted to a New York correspondent that his road conveyed passengers between termini in just eleven hours, "which for an overland conveyance is I believe unequalled *on the Globe*."[3]

In its original layout and operation, the Charleston and Hamburg road was an awkward affair, reflecting both the inexperience of SCC&RR management and the nascent state of railroad technology. In an effort to provide a uniform surface for the cars at an economical cost, most of the line consisted of a sys-

2. Morton J. Horwitz, *The Transformation of American Law, 1780–1860* (Cambridge, Mass., 1977), 113–14.

3. Horatio Allen to Messrs. J. & J. Townsend, April 2, 1834, Horatio Allen Papers, SCL. The history of the SCC&RR is thoroughly detailed in Samuel M. Derrick, *Centennial History of South Carolina Railroad* (Columbia, 1930). The SCC&RR also received extended attention from Ulrich B. Phillips in *A History of Transportation in the Eastern Cotton Belt, to 1860* (New York, 1908; reprint, New York, 1968), 132–67, and William H. Pease and Jane H. Pease, *The Web of Progress: Private Values and Public Styles in Boston and Charleston, 1828–1843* (New York and Oxford, 1984), 56–62. On railroad development in antebellum South Carolina, see Alfred G. Smith Jr., *Economic Readjustment of an Old Cotton State: South Carolina, 1820–1860* (Columbia, 1958), 156–92, and Lacy K. Ford Jr., *Origins of Southern Radicalism: The South Carolina Upcountry, 1800–1860* (New York and Oxford, 1988), 219–43.

tem of vertical wooden piles driven into the ground, elevating the line into a single, almost continuous trestle. If a car derailed—not an uncommon occurrence—it might fall as much as twenty feet before hitting the earth below. One disconcerted early SCC&RR passenger observed a steady stream of car parts and even the remains of entire cars lining the route. Another rider found that "looking over on each side [of the cars] affected the passengers disagreeably." The rails—iron straps affixed to wooden stringers—provided an additional source of unwanted thrills for passengers. The thin bands wore quickly and occasionally worked loose, whipping up at one end as a train passed, causing derailments or piercing the underside of cars to the peril of passengers inside. As a result, the company spent most of its first decade of operations rebuilding the line, replacing wood piles with earth embankments and iron straps with heavier "T" rails, at an expenditure only slightly less than the original cost of the road.[4]

The paltry horsepower generated by the first generation of steam locomotives provided further peculiarities. Although the highest point on the route was only 515 feet above sea level, much of this elevation had to be climbed during the short stretch passing through the sandhills. Available locomotives proved incapable of pulling trains over the steeper grade. To fix the problem, railroad engineers placed a stationary steam engine at the summit, which raised or lowered trains along an inclined plane. The annoying bottleneck created by the inclined plane was partially offset by laying double-tracks so trains could be raised and lowered simultaneously. The remainder of the Charleston and Hamburg line was single-tracked, with turnouts placed every eight to ten miles to permit the passing of trains.[5]

Though clumsy and hazardous in hindsight, this eccentric engineering feat soon demonstrated advantages over traditional modes of overland transportation. As the route matured beyond its predictable growing pains, the railroad

4. Albert Fishlow, *American Railroads and the Transformation of the Ante-Bellum Economy* (Cambridge, Mass., 1965), 5; Derrick, *Centennial History*, 39–127; Amos A. Lawrence Diaries, vol. 2A, January 16 [1837], Massachusetts Historical Society; J. S. Buckingham, *The Slave States of America*, 2 vols. (London and Paris, 1842), 1:548. For a concise discussion of the "teething problems" experienced by the first generation of southern railroads, see Mark M. Smith, *Mastered by the Clock: Time, Slavery, and Freedom in the American South* (Chapel Hill, 1997), 79–85. For more on the construction of the Charleston and Hamburg line, see Donald A. Grinde Jr., "Building the South Carolina Railroad," *SCHM* 77 (April 1976): 84–96.

5. Derrick, *Centennial History*, 32–33, 59, 104–5.

slowly but surely gained patronage in Edgefield and Barnwell. By 1835, the editors of the Edgefield *Carolinian* urged their readers to conduct all their travels via the SCC&RR. "The truth is," the newspaper declared, "we think it in bad taste, to travel now in the old fashioned way." Why would one trudge on foot, bestride a four-footed beast, or in a cumbersome wagon, "when he can mount a Rail Road or a Balloon, and move with the rapidity of light?" Why, indeed? As the railroad improved in speed and reliability, passengers increasingly took advantage of the new opportunities created by rail travel. Young Edward Spann Hammond used the railroad to enhance his social life with frequent overnight jaunts to friends and family along the line. The railroad allowed the Reverend Abiah Cartledge to expand his spiritual ministries into two separate locales. Residing in Aiken, he rode the line to Hamburg on Saturday evenings to spend the weekend making pastoral visits before returning to his home congregation. Another local divine believed the railroad offered even greater spiritual benefit by providing a literal fulfillment of the biblical prophecy of Isaiah: "The crooked places shall be made straight, and the rough places smooth."[6]

Other, more material, blessings emanated from the railroad as well. Many local landowners and residents along the route enhanced their income by selling railroad ties and firewood to the SCC&RR. One Barnwell planter earned $2.75 for every hundred feet of eight-inch by ten-inch railroad timber his slaves cut for the company. Company president Tristram Tupper claimed his railroad's constant demand for wood gave "employment to hundreds of inhabitants on the line." If the families of those engaged by the road were added as well, Tupper asserted, there were "*thousands* who have support from this institution." Stockholders congratulated themselves on this fact, which Tupper anticipated would likewise serve to "enlist the good feelings of the community towards the Company."[7]

Property values in Edgefield and Barnwell benefited from their proximity to the railroad as well. Pine barrens that had sold for less than fifty cents per

6. Edgefield, *Carolinian,* May 9, 1835; Day Book, Edward Spann Hammond Collection, SCL; Rev. Abiah Morgan Cartledge, unpublished autobiography, 1893, SCL; Anonymous travel journal, "Trip to Aiken with sister Wilder in the Spring of 1849," SCL. The good Reverend quotes Isaiah 40:4.

7. Entry for October 4, 1843, Plantation Journal, Barnwell District, 1838–44, SCL; *Semi-Annual Report of the Direction of the South Carolina Rail Road Company, July 10, 1837* (Charleston, 1837), quotation 8.

acre vaulted to between $1 and $5 per acre after completion of the Charleston-to-Hamburg line. By 1837, Tupper claimed the total advance in land values within one mile of the road, excluding the termini, equaled the original construction cost of the entire line. While most of the increase was the passive consequence of the railroad's construction, other more deliberate speculations surrounded the undertaking as well. Georgia resident John Fox swapped four acres of his property in Edgefield to the SCC&RR for two shares of company stock. Hamburg factor Beverly M. Rogers granted the company his interest in several tracts of land along the route in exchange for a railroad turnout, which was to run by the site of his factorage business. The most ambitious speculation, however, focused on the land surrounding the inclined plane in Barnwell District. In February 1832, local landowner William W. Williams and the SCC&RR agreed to an equal moiety in a 350-acre tract surrounding the company's stationary engine at the head of the plane. The two partners proceeded to lay off streets and a sizable quantity of 60-foot by 150-foot lots, which Williams and the company then divided equally between themselves. The new town was named Aiken after the first president of the SCC&RR, William Aiken. Speculation in Aiken town lots drew many participants (including future SCC&RR president Tristram Tupper, who bought twenty-nine lots from his company) and lot prices quickly rose to as high as $100 apiece. By 1837, a visitor to Aiken could find a population of 750, four hotels, two churches, an academy, a bank agency, a public market, "and a goodly number of stores and houses."[8]

Local slaveholders enjoyed additional opportunities for remuneration by hiring out their surplus labor to the railroad. By 1840, the SCC&RR had 238 slaves on its payroll at wages averaging between $14 and $15 per month plus subsistence, with some Barnwell slaves hiring at times for as much as $19 per month. At such rates, slaveholders in Edgefield and Barnwell found hiring out to the railroad to be a lucrative enterprise, especially during slack seasons of the agricultural calendar or times of low cotton prices. When upcountry railroad construction expanded in the latter decades of the antebellum period, local slaveholders found even greater opportunity to profit from the boom. Francis Pickens hired out forty of his Edgewood slaves to a nearby railroad project at $15 per month plus food and clothing. "Go & hire yours immediately," he

8. *Charleston Courier*, July 18, 1837; July 19, 1837; Barnwell County Deeds, Book S, 305–10; Book T, 146–49, 346–49; Book U, 163–64, SCDAH.

advised a fellow planter. "This year, when provisions are so high it is a fine business."[9]

The most visible consequence of the railroad's arrival, however, was its role in strengthening the fealty of Edgefield and Barnwell to King Cotton. Even during the decade-long slump in cotton prices that followed the Panic of 1837, the SCC&RR carried an increasing overall volume of cotton from local depots to Charleston. Especially in Barnwell District, where agricultural development had generally lagged behind that of neighboring Edgefield, cotton production posted notable gains in the years after the railroad's completion. The new railroad town of Aiken soon began to attract a significant cotton trade from eastern Edgefield District as well as parts of neighboring Lexington and Newberry districts. By the time Edmund Ruffin journeyed through Barnwell in 1843, the agricultural reformer discovered farms and small plantations "very thickly placed" around the railroad depot at Midway, an area of the district formerly derided for its omnipresent pine barrens.[10]

However, it was Hamburg that stood poised to reap the lion's share of the economic bounty sown by the SCC&RR. Once the western terminus of the line reached the town, the flow of Carolina cotton from Hamburg to Charleston promised to turn into a deluge. Henry Shultz worked to hasten the

9. Entry for June 27, 1838, and *passim,* Plantation Journal, Barnwell District, 1838–44, SCL; *Semi-Annual Report of the South Carolina Canal and Rail Road Company, Accepted January 18th, 1840* (Charleston, 1840), 5–7, 12; Francis W. Pickens to J. Edward Calhoun, December 1 [no year], Francis W. Pickens Papers, SCL. The wages paid for slave labor by the SCC&RR compared favorably with those received by unskilled labor on other internal improvement projects. In the years immediately before the Panic of 1837, Irish laborers on the C&O canal earned from $14 to $16 per month, with day labor wages reaching as high as $1.25. See Peter Way, *Common Labour: Workers and the Digging of the North American Canals, 1780–1860* (Cambridge, 1993), 106–7. On railroad construction in the South Carolina upcountry during the late antebellum era, see Phillips, *History of Transportation,* 335–49, and Ford, *Origins of Southern Radicalism,* 219–43.

10. For statistics on increasing cotton production in Barnwell after 1830, see table 1. "Petition of Sundry Citizens of Barnwell District," Petition 1836–23, General Assembly Papers, SCDAH; William M. Mathew, ed., *Agriculture, Geology, and Society in Antebellum South Carolina: The Private Diary of Edmund Ruffin, 1843* (Athens and London, 1992), 237–38. David Weiman and Lacy Ford have also noted the railroad's role in stimulating cotton production among upcountry farmers in the antebellum era. See Weiman, "Farmers and the Market in Antebellum America: A View from the Georgia Upcountry," *Journal of Economic History* 47 (September 1987): 627–47; and Ford, "Yeoman Farmers in the South Carolina Upcountry: Changing Production Patterns in the Late Antebellum Period," *Agricultural History* 60 (fall 1986): 17–37, esp. 30–32.

forthcoming bonanza through the donation of several Hamburg lots to the railroad for a depository and other buildings—a "generous and liberal donation" that garnered the cordial thanks of SCC&RR directors. (After the line was completed, the cash-strapped Shultz sold the railroad nine additional lots for $2,000.) Not only would a rail connection with Charleston bolster Hamburg in its border war with Augusta, but it also held the promise of furthering the economic sovereignty of Edgefield and Barnwell, as well as the state at large. If the line failed to develop, local doomsayers predicted Hamburg would dwindle into insignificance and compel the surrounding population "to trade in a foreign port, with foreign people." With a railroad in their midst, however, residents could "effect all their purposes at home, and keep amongst them the profits of that trade which would be diffused amongst her citizens, and render them comfortable and happy" (table 4).[11]

By erecting a quick, convenient, and reliable means of transporting cotton and other produce to Charleston, the SCC&RR was welcomed as a valued confederate in the agrarian landscape of Edgefield and Barnwell. Cotton production increased, land values rose (and sometimes soared), and the influence of "foreign" commerce was further mitigated. Other boosters saw railroad technology as enhancing the agrarian landscape in political as well as economic terms. "It is not too much to say that [in addition] to the important political measure of repealing the Tariff, and restraining the wasteful expenditures of the general government upon pensions and internal improvements," the *Carolinian* declared nothing would contribute more to the prosperity of South Carolina "than the success of the rail roads now projected." When a thousand local patriots offered their toasts in celebration of the Fourth of July 1835, the railroad found itself conspicuous among the objects of praise and patriotic pride. Amid jeers for the tariff and federal patronage and cheers for states' rights and the "yeomen of Barnwell district," a toast was offered to the Charleston and Hamburg railroad: "Long may it continue as it now is, the pride and ornament of South Carolina."[12]

11. Elias Horry, *An Address Respecting the Charleston & Hamburg Railroad, and on the Railroad System as regards a Large portion of the Southern and Western States of the North American Union* (Charleston, 1833), 27; Edgefield Deeds, Book 47, 242–43, SCDAH; Edgefield, *Carolinian*, December 24, 1829.

12. Edgefield, *Carolinian*, December 24, 1829; *Aiken Telegraph and Commercial Advertiser*, July 8, 1835. Several influential works have maintained that antebellum southern railroads reinforced dependence on agriculture, particularly cotton production, rather than serving as a means of eco-

TABLE 4. Bales of Cotton Received by the SCC&RR in Edgefield and Barnwell Districts

YEAR	HAMBURG	AIKEN	BLACKVILLE	MIDWAY	TOTAL
1835 (Jul–Dec)	15,156	1,862	1,166	1,525	19,709
1836	17,630	4,920	1,559	2,249	26,358
1837	19,663	6,599	1,744	2,856	30,862
1838	21,329	5,676	1,338	2,972	31,315
1839	32,580	9,861	1,443	2,037	45,921
1840	43,865	7,650	1,211	2,176	54,902
1841	41,672	3,559	1,345	2,526	49,102
1842	48,982	3,304	1,761	1,592	55,639
1843 (Jan–Jun)	27,208	897	986	517	29,608
1844 (Jan–Jun)	34,070	271	947	211	35,499
1845	107,328	783	3,080	1,764	112,955
1846	94,853	346	2,949	1,679	99,302
1847	73,149	227	1,869	1,034	76,279
1848	130,993	231	3,862	1,667	136,753
1849	132,003	125	4,101	1,423	137,652

SOURCES: Semiannual reports of the South Carolina Canal & Railroad Company, 1836–44, and the semiannual and annual reports of the South Carolina Railroad Company, 1845–50.

The steam locomotive quickly altered habits of transportation and the duration of travel in Edgefield and Barnwell, but did little to change the basic contours of the established political economy. As a technology, railroads only seemed to heighten the devotion of district agriculturists to cotton production, spurring growth but accomplishing little in the way of change. But the railroad introduced other innovations besides steam locomotion and a reliable, year-

nomic diversification. See Phillips, *History of Transportation*, 19–20, 387–90; Eugene D. Genovese, *The Political Economy of Slavery: Studies in the Economy and Society of the Slave South*, 2nd ed. (Middletown, Conn., 1989), 164, 308; David R. Goldfield, *Cotton Fields and Skyscrapers: Southern City and Region, 1607–1980* (Baton Rouge and London, 1982), 64–65.

round means of conveyance. The SCC&RR also marked the rise of the business corporation in South Carolina, a feature of railroad development that held the potential to impart far deeper transformations in the local society. Indeed, Morton Horwitz has held that altering conceptions of the corporation marked "one of the fundamental transitions" in the United States between the eighteenth and nineteenth centuries. While residents of Edgefield and Barnwell rapidly embraced the railroad, they would experience a far more problematic relationship with the railroad corporation.[13]

As a legal entity, a corporation is essentially an artificial person, providing a unified identity to a collective enterprise. South Carolinians utilized the form before the arrival of the railroad, but confined it almost entirely to the public sphere, with only limited application to private undertakings. Following common law precedents, the state legislature granted corporate charters to any "public body charged with carrying out public functions," thus bestowing a means to serve the commonweal in ways beyond the ability of an individual to perform. The advantages of corporate status were several. Corporate bodies held the potential for perpetual existence, or at least beyond the death or succession of individual members. In addition, scattered property and assets could be held in common under a single legal entity, with members permitted to enact rules and by-laws for governing the association and its combined assets.[14]

The most prominent use of the corporate form was by cities and towns through the formation of municipal corporations, by which local officials received the right of taxation, police powers, and generally whatever other au-

---

13. Horwitz, *Transformation of American Law*, 111–12. On the simultaneous development of the railroad as a technology and a corporate enterprise in antebellum America, see John Lauritz Larson, *Internal Improvement: National Public Works and the Promise of Popular Government in the Early United States* (Chapel Hill, 2001), 225–55.

14. The evolution of the American business corporation has been the subject of several fine studies. See especially Oscar Handlin and Mary F. Handlin, "Origins of the American Business Corporation," *Journal of Economic History* 5 (May 1945): 1–23; Ronald E. Seavoy, "The Public Service Origins of the American Business Corporation," *Business History Review* 52 (spring 1978): 30–60; and idem, *The Origins of the American Business Corporation, 1784–1855* (Westport, Conn., and London, 1982); Lawrence M. Friedman, *A History of American Law,* 2nd ed. (New York, 1985), 188–97; Pauline Maier, "The Revolutionary Origins of the American Corporation," *William and Mary Quarterly,* 3rd series, 50 (January 1993): 51–84. On the corporation in the antebellum South, see Milton Sydney Heath, *Constructive Liberalism: The Role of the State in Economic Development in Georgia to 1860* (Cambridge, Mass., 1954), 293–335.

thority was deemed necessary for the proper regulation of corporate members, that is, town residents. Charleston led the way in 1783, becoming the first incorporated city in South Carolina. But the state's overwhelmingly rural population kept the number of municipalities extremely low. By 1820, only five other towns possessed corporate status.[15]

More frequently, corporate bodies appeared as benevolent or fraternal societies, such as churches, charities, and educational institutions. Corporations of this type had long dotted the landscape of Edgefield and Barnwell. When district residents had contact with a corporation prior to the SCC&RR, it typically came in the shape of entities such as the Barnwell Baptist Church of Christ, Edgefield Farmer's Society, Mechanic's Society of Hamburg, Edgefield Academy, Republican Circulating Library of Barnwell District, or some similar combination of civic-minded individuals whose primary concern was the moral and intellectual advance of the community, not the monetary emolument of the corporation's membership.[16]

Before the SCC&RR, South Carolinians had little experience with large-scale, business corporations. Aside from a handful of Charleston-based banking institutions, the only other significant appearance of the corporation in the economic sphere came in the 1780s, shortly after the Revolutionary War. In an effort to extend the commercial hinterlands of Charleston, several groups of lowcountry investors requested and received corporate charters from the General Assembly to clear piedmont rivers and construct canals to connect the Edisto and Ashley rivers and the Santee River with the Cooper. Deeming each project to be of "great public utility," the legislative charters spelled out the purpose, privileges, and restrictions under which each company would operate. But despite the scale of these corporate undertakings, the stipulations in their charters differed little from those that regulated the operation of toll bridges, ferries, or other public franchises. The legislature described the scope of each project, set limits on rates of toll, vested exclusive rights of operation, and obliged each company to maintain and operate its respective franchise "in good and sufficient order."[17]

15. The five other incorporated towns in South Carolina were Camden (1791), Beaufort (1803), Columbia (1805), Georgetown (1805), and Cheraw (1820). *Statutes at Large*, VII: 97, 165, 218, 227; VIII: 235–37, 313.

16. *Statutes at Large*, VIII: 223–24, 296, 326, 336, 346.

17. Bray Hammond, *Banks and Politics in America: From the Revolution to the Civil War* (Princeton, 1957), 168; George C. Rogers Jr., *Evolution of a Federalist: William Loughton Smith of Charleston*

Even with such generous charters, these private corporations produced results well short of expectations. Indeed, results in most cases were largely nonexistent. With the exception of the Santee Canal, the improvement companies accomplished practically nothing. Subscriptions to the Edisto and Ashley canal company never filled, leaving embarrassed investors to ask the state to purchase the remaining shares. By 1807, frustrated Barnwell residents demanded that the company's charter be revoked and that the Edisto improvement effort be replaced by "a portion of that aid of the legislature, which has so laudably and generously been bestowed" upon similar projects. The following year, the legislature considered the charter forfeit since "the said company have wholly neglected the objects of their establishment." Even the apparent success of the Santee Canal proved a disappointment, as its capacity proved too small and profits too few to satisfy either its patrons or stockholders. Given such dismal outcomes, it was hard to view corporations as monopolistic concentrations of economic power. More often, the corporation was looked upon as an impotent means of developing state resources. When efforts to improve inland navigation were renewed early in the nineteenth century, the employment of private corporations for the task garnered little consideration. By 1810, the house Committee on Inland Navigation adamantly declared that "the state ought never to grant charters to companies for opening . . . navigation, where the funds of the state are adequate to the purpose."[18]

When the next major enthusiasm for internal improvement occurred in South Carolina after the War of 1812, the entire scheme was state planned, state

(1758–1812) (Columbia, 1962), 129–34; Rachel Klein, *Unification of a Slave State: The Rise of the Planter Class in the South Carolina Backcountry, 1760–1808* (Chapel Hill and London, 1990), 244–46; *Statutes at Large,* VII: 541–51, 558–60.

18. For the Edisto and Ashley Canal project, see "Petition of Thos. Bennet & als.," Petition, ND-776 [ca. 1801]; "Petition of a number of land holders on Edisto River praying that the Charter for clearing Out & making Navigable the same may be broken," Petition, 1807–106; and [Petition of sundry citizens of Charleston regarding the Edisto and Ashley Canal], Petition, 1809–58; all in General Assembly Papers, SCDAH. For the Santee Canal, see Phillips, *History of Transportation,* 36–43; "Report of the Committee on Inland Navigation," December 10, 1810, Report, 1810–131, General Assembly Papers, SCDAH. For a history of the Santee Canal, see Robert B. Bennett Jr., "The Santee Canal, 1785–1939" (Master's thesis, University of South Carolina, 1988). Georgia's inland navigation corporations fared no better in improving that state's waterways. Heath, *Constructive Liberalism,* 301. For more on the failure of private enterprise to meet the early transportation needs of South Carolinians, see Norman Gasque Raiford, "South Carolina and the Issue of Internal Improvement" (Ph.D. diss., University of Virginia, 1974), 72–74.

funded, and largely state controlled. Beginning in 1818, the General Assembly instigated a statewide plan of internal improvement, appropriating $1 million and creating a Board of Public Works to oversee an ambitious attempt to unite Charleston and the piedmont with a comprehensive system of roads, canals, and other waterway improvements. But ten years and $2 million in public money later, the state had largely abandoned its grand scheme of improvement. Lack of experience, poor planning and execution, and copious bad luck doomed the effort to a humiliating and highly public failure. As expenditures mounted without justifiable benefit, enthusiasm for the project rapidly waned and opponents condemned the undertaking as a corrupt and extravagant means of taxing the many for the benefit of the few. It was an episode not soon forgotten by the generation of Carolinians reared in the era of nullification, who invoked the "folly" and "convulsion" of the state's internal improvement plan of the 1820s as a vivid reminder of the consequences of government run amok.[19]

The impetus behind the SCC&RR came from neither the state nor planting interests in Edgefield and Barnwell, but from the business community of Charleston. Suffering through a decade of economic depression following the Panic of 1819, Charleston's merchants and factors became keenly interested in developing a means to revive their flagging commercial trade. Hamburg's founding held great initial promise in achieving this end, but the expense of steam boat navigation and several consecutive years of low water in the Savannah River kept the percentage of upcountry cotton flowing into Charleston far below expectations. More than one observer noted with alarm that too many bales of South Carolina cotton were still winding up in Augusta and Savannah and "contributing to build up our rival[s] in another State." Invoking economic sovereignty, Charleston boosters tied the revival of their trade to the enhancement of the entire state. "When Charleston was in a flourishing condition," the *Charleston Courier* recalled, "it added weight and character to South-Carolina, in our own country and in Europe." But as another commentator noted, the current state of communication between Charleston and the interior left many upcountry Carolinians paying "commercial tribute to an outside market." While some sources revived the idea of connecting the Ash-

19. Smith, *Economic Readjustment*, 135–55; Daniel W. Hollis, "Costly Delusion: Inland Navigation in the South Carolina Piedmont," *Proceedings of the South Carolina Historical Association, 1968* (Columbia, 1968), 29–44; Ford, *Origins of Southern Radicalism*, 15–19.

ley River to the Edisto or Savannah by canal, others made a more convincing argument for employing the new technology of the railroad. After a series of enthusiastic public meetings in Charleston in late 1827 and early 1828, a fund was raised to survey a route between Charleston and Hamburg and judge the feasibility of a railroad. Shortly thereafter, the surveyor reported, "I can unhesitatingly pronounce, that *such a road is perfectly practicable.*"[20]

In December 1827, the state legislature granted a charter authorizing the creation of the SCC&RR. But while the scale and novelty of the enterprise were far beyond those typical of a private undertaking, the General Assembly still made little distinction between the railroad and traditional improvement projects. Aside from naming the company and dividing its capital stock into seven thousand shares, nothing in the brief charter deviated from the stipulations traditionally applied to other franchise projects. Indeed, the legislature specifically declared that the company would be organized and operated on the same terms that governed bridges, ferries, and turnpike roads. The railroad was granted the exclusive right of building a railroad or canal between Charleston and Hamburg. Rates of toll were set for cargo and passengers and annual profits were not permitted to exceed total expenses by more than 25 percent. The rights and privileges were to remain in effect for a term of thirty-six years.[21]

While the actions of the legislature displayed neither blatant enthusiasm nor hostility toward the project, railroad organizers in Charleston felt their charter was defective, even burdensome. They had hoped that the legislature would provide special inducements for encouraging "persons of capital" to invest in a project "so nearly and essentially connected with the prosperity of this city, and of the State." But as the charter currently stood, company promoters doubted "whether a single share will ever be taken on the present terms." The privileges granted may have been fine for establishing a bridge, ferry, or turnpike, but in order to encourage subscriptions to railroad stock, company pro-

20. "Memorial of the Inhabitants of the Parishes of St. Philips & St. Michael," Petitions, ND-1643 [1827], General Assembly Papers, SCDAH; *Suggestions for the Improvement of the Commerce of the State of South-Carolina, As Originally Published in the Charleston Courier, the 27th October, 1827* (Charleston, 1827), 7 (first quotation), 5 (second quotation); Derrick, *Centennial History,* 1–19 (third quotation, 6); Report of Abraham Blanding, March 15, 1828, Miscellaneous Communications, 1828–16, General Assembly Papers, SCDAH.

21. *Statutes at Large,* VIII: 354–55. In the same session that it granted a charter to the SCC&RR, the state legislature also passed a general act for the formation of bridge, ferry, and turnpike companies. *Statutes at Large,* VI: 302–15.

moters deemed it better to have a charter "single and distinct" from other improvement franchises. Too many restrictions, particularly on profits, would be placed on the company if the current charter were accepted. If the project was merely "a common speculation," the railroad men agreed that the legislature would understandably wish to grant as few privileges as possible. However, not only was the railroad a work "worth encouraging on public grounds," but one that also needed fiscal inducements to spur private investment. As a result, railroad organizers pressured the legislature for a new charter, one possessing "a greater degree of liberality" toward the company and its potential stockholders.[22]

The General Assembly responded with a revised charter, one that recognized the claim of company spokesmen that the railroad was a "single and distinct" improvement franchise. Indeed, the new charter specifically exempted the SCC&RR from the general act governing bridge, ferry, and turnpike companies. Most of the articles in the new charter merely provided greater detail on how shares were to be purchased and how the company was to be organized. But new inducements to attract private capital were present as well. Restrictions on the amount of annual profit were removed, although the legislature still set rates of toll. And, after overcoming considerable opposition in the state senate, company stock and real estate were exempted from taxation for the thirty-six years of its charter.[23]

However, the article in the SCC&RR's charter with the greatest potential for controversy involved the acquisition of land required by the company to carry out its defined mission. If an agreement with a property owner could not be reached regarding the purchase of land needed by the company, the General Assembly authorized that "the same may be taken at a valuation, to be made by commissioners . . . appointed by the court of common pleas of the district where any part of the land or right of way may be situated." Landowners could challenge the valuation set by the commissioners, but no stipulations were offered by the legislature to challenge the taking of land. For all intents and purposes, the SCC&RR received the right of eminent domain.[24]

The apparent devolution of eminent domain by the legislature to a private undertaking had precedent. Post-Revolution canal companies received similar

22. *Charleston Courier,* January 3, 1828.
23. *Statutes at Large,* VIII: 355–63; *Charleston Courier,* February 1, 1828.
24. *Statutes at Large,* VIII: 359–60.

powers and the general act governing bridge, ferry, and turnpike charters also included the right to take lands at a valuation set by court-appointed commissioners. But while these provisions held the potential for heated confrontations between charter holders and local residents, the meager accomplishments of these projects precluded opportunities for serious conflict. Except for the short Santee Canal, no private canal project advanced beyond the planning stage and no private turnpike was ever constructed. Bridges and ferries only required a landing, which was usually already in the possession of the franchise holder. The taking of private land by the state for public purpose still underwent periodic challenge, but state courts continued to uphold the state's power of eminent domain. As late as 1836, South Carolina jurist John S. Richardson again reiterated the government's right of eminent domain "for the public safety and general convenience." But Richardson also identified the basis for future debate by maintaining that the privilege resided exclusively with the general government. Eminent domain, he argued, "belongs only to that tribunal which exercises, practically the sovereign power of the whole civil society, and should be restricted to it alone, and never confided to other hands." Thus, every clause in a corporate charter that permitted the taking of private land seemed a direct contradiction of this legal tenet. Such corporations, it appeared, were seizing private property for private use. It was not until the development of railroads in the 1830s, however, that the corporate exercise of eminent domain underwent serious public challenge.[25]

The challenge met a swift and decisive response from state jurists. What confused the issue, they explained, was the ability of the state to name an agent, a road commissioner, for example, to carry out a specific exercise of eminent domain, such as opening a public highway. The commissioner became the means of carrying out the action specified by the legislature, but the actual power to take private land for public purpose remained with the sovereign, that is, the legislature, not its agent. Thus, by receiving a charter of incorporation, the SCC&RR was perceived, in essence, to be an authorized agent of the state carrying out a great public improvement, not a private corporation seeking private emolument. Implicit in this assumption was the categorization of the railroad as a public highway, practically identical to any public road ordered

25. *State v. Thomas Dawson*, 3 Hill (21 S.C.L.), 107 (1836). Morton Horwitz considered the right of eminent domain to be "the one truly explosive legal 'time bomb' in all antebellum law." *Transformation of American Law*, 259.

opened by the legislature. By classifying the railroad as a public road, the state legislature claimed the right to appropriate private land for a right of way, or more accurately, to authorize the SCC&RR to appropriate private land in the name of the legislature. The only significant distinction in the charter between the exercise of eminent domain by the state and its agent (the SCC&RR) was the requirement that the agent provide compensation for lands taken. This concept of the railroad as public agent acquired the legal benediction of the state Court of Errors in 1838:

> The whole use of the eminent domain . . . is to be found in the enactment, that a rail road shall be constructed between specific termini: and the land essential for its track and construction, shall be released, for the purpose of the road, upon full compensation, be such land whose it may. Surely this is an intelligible and plain exercise of their high privilege by the legislature itself, and not by the company. The provisions, that the precise track of the road, preserving the termini, shall be marked out, and the road constructed by the company, are mere executive or mechanical processes; like the ordinary administrative offices of overseers, surveyors, and operatives, to lay out and open a public road, or erect a public building, upon land before designated, and appropriated to such public use.[26]

Thus, regardless of the fact that the Charleston and Hamburg railroad was privately conceived, organized, and operated with an expectation of earning substantial dividends for its stockholders, the receipt of eminent domain powers in its charter led to a tacit—essentially explicit—understanding that the SCC&RR was *publici juris* and carrying out a valuable public service.[27]

Such legal arguments merely confirmed perceptions already prevalent in

26. *L.C.&C.R.R. Company v. J. J. Chappell; The Same v. Dr. Reese and Mrs. Reese,* 1 Rice (24 S.C.L.), 383–400 (quotation 390–91). This 1838 case involved the Louisville, Cincinnati, & Charleston Railroad Company, the second major railroad project chartered by the South Carolina General Assembly.

27. The parameters of the legal debate in South Carolina over the application of eminent domain powers to railroad corporations is discussed in John Steven Benfield, "Judge John Belton O'Neall: The Law of Eminent Domain, Railroads, and Internal Improvements" (Master's thesis, University of South Carolina, 1982), 24–44. See also Seavoy, "Public Service Origins," 49; Heath, *Constructive Liberalism,* 323–25; Harry N. Scheiber, "The Road to *Munn:* Eminent Domain and the Concept of Public Purpose in the State Courts," *Perspectives in American History* 5 (1971): 360–76.

Edgefield and Barnwell, which likewise understood the SCC&RR to be a quasi-public institution and the railroad a great public improvement. Residents in both districts held sanguine expectations of the great benefits to emanate from the SCC&RR, to both themselves and their community. The widespread presence of such feeling made any potential controversy over the privilege of eminent domain a moot point, as the railroad acquired the necessary rights-of-way through the districts for next to nothing. Hundreds of Barnwell land-owners eagerly offered the SCC&RR passage through their property, seeking no compensation other than the presence of the railroad itself. Inhabitants in and around Barnwell Court House tried to woo the company with offers of free land and timber if the railroad located its line through the town, even promising to assist with a survey and to clear the route themselves should any serious obstacles become present. Along the ridge route eventually selected by the company, landed proprietors displayed the same generosity toward the rail-road. Although the route passed through the premises of several hundred in-dividual landowners, SCC&RR superintendent Alexander Black reported that no more than five or six cases arose in which "terms of accommodation" had to be arranged. In all other instances, "the Land and very generally the Timber has been yielded gratuitously." The generosity of property holders along the route saved the SCC&RR tens of thousands of dollars in additional construc-tion costs. Of the almost $1 million spent in building the railroad, the company only expended $2,212.18 in obtaining its right-of-way.[28]

Company officials were quick to acknowledge the collective liberality of Edgefield and Barnwell as an act of reciprocity. "These acts were generous as to the Company," said SCC&RR president Elias Horry, "and patriotic as re-gards the State." Such manifestations of public support lent credence to re-peated assertions by company directors that their railroad was to be the servant of the common welfare. "The fact must be acknowledged," Horry told his backers, "and the stockholders of the [SCC&RR] . . . must feel that delight in a very eminent degree, when they reflect on the public good they have rendered the State." Railroad boosters trumpeted an endless litany of economic and so-

---

28. Barnwell Deeds, Book S, 411–12, 481–88, SCDAH; *First Semi-Annual Report, to the President and Directors of the South-Carolina Canal and Rail-Road Company, by their Committee of Inquiry* (Charleston, 1828), 21–22; *Annual Report of the South-Carolina Canal and Rail Road Company, by the Direction. Submitted and Adopted May 2, 1831* (Charleston, 1831), 15–16; Derrick, *Centennial His-tory*, 68–69.

cial benefits the project would produce: convenient travel, increased commerce, enhancement of the cotton trade "that diffuses a general benefit throughout all classes of society," new markets for Charleston commodities, a speedy means of retreat during time of yellow fever, the development of inland towns and villages, a further impetus to develop mill seats in Barnwell District, rapid troop movement to the interior in times of war, and easy access to the country for travelers seeking to escape the rigors of northern winters. Only the most hardened cynic could deny, declared company directors, "that the enterprize grew out of, and is sustained by a spirit of pure devotion to the public good."[29]

In hindsight, such mutual declarations of patriotism and public servitude are easy to dismiss as self-serving and even hypocritical. Railroad stockholders certainly expected their investment in the "public good" would produce a steady flow of annual dividends. Likewise, the "patriotic" generosity of planters and yeomen along the route through Barnwell and Edgefield was undoubtedly inspired in part by the expectation of a sizable increase in the value of their land bordering the railroad's path. But while neither side could claim a completely selfless interest in the railroad, a harmony of public and private interests still seemed to prevail—a harmony not unlike that which prevailed between local entrepreneurs and their surrounding community. If SCC&RR stockholders expected a handsome return on their investment, the local community through which the railroad passed had no reason to begrudge them a profit as long as the enterprise served their needs as well. And during the SCC&RR's first decade, the public seemed quite satisfied with the results. Like a ferry or bridge franchise, the railroad seemed quite capable of masking private entrepreneurship with the guise of public service. It was a dual role that the agriculturists of Edgefield and Barnwell expected. Indeed, they would accept no less.

But good will and a gratis right-of-way only went so far in constructing a railroad between Charleston and Hamburg. To complete their grand design, company directors needed capital, and lots of it. Initial construction estimates reached $600,000 while the SCC&RR's charter specified an initial capitalization of $700,000, with the privilege of increasing the amount if directors

29. Horry, *Address Respecting the Charleston & Hamburg Railroad*, 10, 27; *Report of a Special Committee Appointed by the Chamber of Commerce, to Inquire into the Cost, Revenue and Advantages of a Rail Road Communication Between the City of Charleston and the Towns of Hamburg & Augusta* (Charleston, 1828), 18–21; *First Semi-Annual Report, 1828*, 23.

deemed it necessary. The voracious financial demands of the SCC&RR quickly provoked a heated confrontation between company directors and the sectional doctrines of South Carolina's increasingly belligerent political leadership. It was a showdown that the railroad was destined to lose, but one that provided a vivid demonstration of the potential friction between railroad entrepreneurs and the community in which they operated, particularly when the financial interests of the SCC&RR failed to coincide with expectations of public service and political loyalty.

Despite the liberal terms granted in its revised charter, the SCC&RR struggled to attract private investors. When subscription books were first opened in 1828, only half of the authorized stock was subscribed, with all but fifty shares taken by Charleston investors. Interior residents took a few shares when the books reopened, "but not to a very large amount," lamented the company's president. Inland newspapers were no less embarrassed by this lack of fiscal enthusiasm. "Will South Carolina permit her enterprising citizens, who seek to effect such noble purposes, to sink," asked the Edgefield *Carolinian,* "when her aid alone, will bear them safely to the wished for port?"[30]

The initial disappointment in raising private funds forced company boosters to seek other means of fulfilling their capital requirements. The city of Charleston became an early source of public support for the SCC&RR, taking two hundred shares of company stock. However, city officials soon went beyond mere financial aid. Since South Carolina had yet to share in the federal patronage for internal improvements, the Charleston city council assumed that an application to Congress for aid would be favorably received. In April 1828, the council petitioned Congress to exempt the SCC&RR from all import duties on iron and machinery required to construct their railroad. It was a carefully worded prayer, displaying a proper respect for the antitariff and states' rights sentiment mounting in South Carolina. Since railroads were still a novelty in the United States, the council deemed it "safest and best" that the SCC&RR procure the necessary iron from England, "where it can be worked up in the proper manner, so as to ensure greater certainty in the execution of the projected roads." However, the council pointed out that federal import duties constituted "a very large portion of the expense of procuring such iron." While Congress had authorized subscriptions to similar undertakings, the

30. Derrick, *Centennial History,* 22–23, 71; *Statutes at Large,* VIII: 355–56; Horry, *Address Respecting the Charleston & Hamburg Railroad,* 8; Edgefield, *Carolinian,* December 24, 1829.

Charleston council made it clear that the SCC&RR sought no such direct federal aid. It merely asked permission "to act for ourselves" and acquire necessary articles from the best possible source, which the company would do "if we are not trammelled by the operation of laws, which . . . will act, if permitted to act, a public as well as a private injury."[31]

The petition attained only partial success. Congress rejected an outright exemption from import duties, but the treasury department was authorized to reduce the iron duties in Charleston from $30 per ton to an *ad valorum* duty of 25 percent, saving the SCC&RR $17 per ton. But while the tariff reduction saved the company a considerable sum in construction costs, it did nothing to overcome its immediate shortage of capital. Private subscriptions continued to be slow in coming and SCC&RR president William Aiken began to seriously fear that these "portentous circumstances" might force the "termination of this important and patriotic enterprize" before it even got started. In May 1829, Aiken promised SCC&RR directors and stockholders that the company would continue its exertions for private subscriptions, but also suggested the possibility of seeking federal patronage as well, but "only under such an emergency, as may involve the existence" of the company itself.[32]

Evidently, "such an emergency" was already present, for Aiken and superintendent Alexander Black had already been to Washington in an unsuccessful attempt to secure a federal subscription to SCC&RR stock. In February 1829, Senator Robert Y. Hayne of South Carolina presented the company's petition to the Senate, while Representative William Drayton of Charleston offered the same to the House. The object of the memorial quickly drew fire from the South Carolina delegation, who immediately worked to distance their state from the actions of the SCC&RR. Representative James Hamilton disclaimed South Carolina from any part of the bill presented to grant the requested subscription, forcefully declaring that his state "did not ask or desire to share in the bounty intended by the bill." Drayton explained that his presentation of the company's petition was never intended to bring the interests

---

31. *By-Laws of the South Carolina Canal and Rail Road Company, adopted by the Stockholders, May 13, 1828, together with The Act of Incorporation Granted by the State Legislature* (Charleston, 1828), 6; *Report of A Special Committee,* 15; City Council of Charleston, S.C., *Memorial of the Canal and Rail Road Company,* Doc. No. 246, House of Representatives, 20th Cong., 1st sess. (Washington, D.C., 1828).

32. Derrick, *Centennial History,* 72–73; *Semi-Annual Report of the Board of Directors, of the South-Carolina Canal and Rail Road Company* (Charleston, 1829), 6.

of the SCC&RR "into collision with the interest of the state." Hayne expressed mortification that the memorial died in committee before he had an "opportunity of vindicating my own course, as well as that of the State" before the full Senate. With the bill castigated by their own congressional delegation, Aiken and Black returned to Charleston disheartened, but not defeated. Rebuked in Congress, the SCC&RR next turned to the South Carolina General Assembly in December 1829, with a request that the state take a subscription of 2,500 shares ($250,000) of company stock. Although approved by the house, the bill failed to pass in the senate. Memories of the millions misspent on state internal improvement projects and the SCC&RR's recent embarrassing application for federal funds hardened the resolve of the General Assembly against generous grants of public money. A counteroffer was made, however, of a $100,000 loan to the company, at 5 percent interest, to be repaid within seven years. If accepted, the offer further required the SCC&RR to mortgage all its property to the state, or at least as much as was demanded for security. The SCC&RR, however, balked at the offer. Not only was the amount of the loan insufficient to company needs, but it also appeared "likely to embarrass the Company in any other arrangement that may be found practicable and necessary." How could the company secure additional credit if its collateral was already mortgaged to the state? With private subscriptions still not up to the task at hand, Aiken decided to return to Washington in a reinvigorated effort to acquire federal aid.[33]

Results of the renewed effort were even less auspicious than the previous attempt. William Drayton again presented the SCC&RR's memorial to the House—a request for a $250,000 federal subscription to company stock—but told Aiken that he could offer no support of the measure "without a departure from opinions which I have frequently expressed." In January 1830, Aiken asked Senator Hayne to again introduce his company's memorial to the Senate. But Hayne likewise balked at the petition's object, which he bluntly contended was "at variance, with *the principles* for which the State of South Carolina was contending, in relation to the powers of the federal government." Furthermore, he informed Aiken that if he presented the petition to the Senate, Hayne would

33. *Charleston Courier*, March 2 and 3, 1829; Columbia, *Southern Times*, February 8, 1830; Derrick, *Centennial History*, 76; Phillips, *History of Transportation*, 141; "Petition of the SCC&RR Co. praying for a Loan," Petitions, ND-3495 [ca. 1832], General Assembly Papers, SCDAH; Edgefield, *Carolinian*, December 24, 1829.

immediately accompany it "with *such explanations,* as would prevent the compromitment of my own principles, or those of the State." Aiken rejected Hayne's terms and instead turned to the man rapidly emerging as the premier advocate of federal support to internal improvements and national sovereignty: Daniel Webster of Massachusetts. On the very eve of his legendary debate with South Carolina Senator Robert Y. Hayne, Webster was approached by Aiken for assistance, since his own senate delegation opposed "the object of our petition" on constitutional grounds. Aiken assured Webster, however, that he did not hold the views of his fellow Carolinians. Rather, he shared Webster's belief that "the General Government do legitimately possess the power to aid such works." He went on to emphasize the broad importance of the SCC&RR project, not only in supplying "certainty and confidence" to commercial intercourse between Charleston and the interior, but in serving national interests as well by providing convenient access to the U.S. Arsenal at Augusta and a facility for "transporting troops from . . . the interior to the Atlantic border" of South Carolina. Webster approved of the project and obliged Aiken by presenting the SCC&RR's memorial to the Senate on January 18, announcing that the enterprise was "of a very laudable nature" and that he believed the proposed Charleston-to-Hamburg railroad to be of "sufficient magnitude and importance to be properly called national." It was a nationalist gesture that Webster underscored the following week in his immortal "Reply" to the states' rights declarations of Senator Hayne: "Sir, if a railroad or canal beginning in South Carolina and ending in South Carolina, appeared to me to be of national importance . . . [and] if I were to stand up here and ask, What interest had Massachusetts in a railroad in South Carolina? I should not be willing to face my constituents."[34]

Back in South Carolina, public opinion excoriated the actions of the SCC&RR and many undoubtedly breathed a sigh of relief when the railroad's memorial died in committee. A public meeting in Colleton District denounced the petition as "destitute of propriety and expediency" and "unworthy the countenance of the citizens of South Carolina." The meeting maintained their sup-

34. Derrick, *Centennial History,* 74–76; *Charleston Mercury,* January 8, 1830; Charles M. Wiltse et al., eds., *The Papers of Daniel Webster,* 14 vols. (Hanover, N.H., 1974–89), Correspondence, 3:9; William Aiken to Daniel Webster, January 9, 1830, William Aiken Papers, SCL; 21st Cong., 1st sess., *Register of Debates in Congress* (Washington, D.C., 1830), VI, pt. 1, 21–22; Merrill D. Peterson, *The Great Triumvirate: Webster, Clay, and Calhoun* (Oxford and New York, 1987), 172, 176–77.

port of the railroad (part of which would pass through their own district), but not if it compromised the state's political principles. If the Charleston-to-Hamburg line was built with federal support, "it will form one of those strange instances in which the end is entirely overlooked in seeking the means, or where commercial cupidity has swallowed up every principle of patriotism." The editors of the *Southern Times* in Columbia heartily approved of the rebuke and lauded Colleton's defense of "the great principles of Constitutional Republicanism . . . with promptness and unanimity sacrifice their own private interests for their country's good." Similar sentiment held sway in Edgefield and Barnwell. Local agriculturists may have supported a railroad, particularly if it passed through their districts, but they could not support the course pursued by the SCC&RR. "It manifested an indifference to the great principles involved in our present controversy," wrote the Edgefield *Carolinian,* "and furnished our adversaries, with supposed evidence of a fatal division in the State." The company's selection of Daniel Webster, a nationalist and tariff advocate who "has never shown himself to be our friend," was singled out as particularly obnoxious.[35]

It was a scathing public rebuke of an obvious political blunder by SCC&RR management and its Charleston backers. Subdued, the company quit all efforts to acquire federal aid and soon after accepted the state's offer of a $100,000 loan with all its attendant provisions. But the SCC&RR's exertions in Washington were not entirely in vain. Spurred by fears that the railroad might not be completed, and that South Carolina might be accused of lacking the daring and determination to bring the project to fruition, private subscriptions for the remaining shares of company stock gradually came forward. By late summer 1830, six thousand shares of SCC&RR stock had been taken. The rift between the SCC&RR and the South Carolina public over the issue of federal aid closed quickly and was soon forgotten. Never would the divergence of public and private interest over the railroad appear as stark as it did in the winter of 1830. Nor would the hegemony of public opinion over the actions of the SCC&RR carry such force again in the antebellum era. Despite the inconveniences sectional politics visited upon the SCC&RR, the railroad quickly yielded to the ideological climate spawned by South Carolina's political leadership and its agrarian electorate.

35. Edgefield, *Carolinian,* February 6 and 27, 1830; Columbia, *Southern Times,* February 18, 1830. Also see the *Charleston Mercury,* January 27 and February 10, 1830.

However, even in the midst of the aid debacle, the SCC&RR did not bear the entire brunt of public disapprobation. As the Edgefield *Carolinian* observed, a little less fiscal parsimony on the part of the South Carolina legislature "would have prevented the necessity of applying to any other power for assistance." Another scribe made the point with even greater force, placing the blame for the railroad's actions squarely on the shoulders of the General Assembly and the state's political leaders. The writer accused the legislature of backing the railroad with only "a paper charter and a closed fist," while the state's grandiloquent orators in Congress failed to take a single share in support of an enterprise upon which "the *honor* and *dignity* of the State of South Carolina hang suspended." The author closed with an astute and slightly ominous observation: "When *State* governments fail to answer the ends of government to the encouragement of domestic industry, it is time for men to look to their individual rights and interests: and that government is best, which best secures them."[36]

The declaration would prove prophetic. Despite the comeuppance suffered by the SCC&RR, confrontations between the railroad and the public soon reappeared on the horizon in Edgefield and Barnwell. But the political atmosphere in which they would take place manifested a much greater willingness to work for "the encouragement of domestic industry." The SCC&RR never again offered so dramatic a challenge to the political hegemony of South Carolina slaveholders as it did in 1830. But the final stages of the antebellum era would witness a different set of challenges to the agrarian landscape, as the capital interests of the SCC&RR again diverged from the interests of the community in which it operated. In the ensuing decades, the evolution of the business corporation would be a lesson in trial and error for railroad officials, state government, and local residents alike, but one in which the various participants would take away very different experiences. Railroad boosters in Edgefield and Barnwell quickly discovered the growing importance of incorporated capital to modern internal improvements, while SCC&RR directors found that corporate capital chafed under the narrowly intrastate outlook of agrarian ideologues. And, as the economic development of South Carolina took on increasingly political overtones, members of the General Assembly found it harder and harder to maintain a proper Jeffersonian separation between gov-

---

36. Derrick, *Centennial History*, 76–77; Edgefield, *Carolinian*, January 9, 1830; *Charleston Courier*, March 5, 1830.

ernment and private enterprise. Nor was the SCC&RR the only corporate intruder to challenge the status quo in Edgefield and Barnwell. Near the passing engines and cars of the SCC&RR emerged a more stationary corporate presence along the banks of Horse Creek: the textile mills at Vaucluse and Graniteville. And while dissimilar in operation, cotton factories like railroads would paradoxically both strengthen and undermine the agrarian landscape of the two districts.

CHAPTER FIVE

"A CHANGE IN OUR
INDUSTRIAL PURSUITS"

VAUCLUSE AND GRANITEVILLE

Surely there is nothing in cotton spinning that can poison the atmosphere of South-
Carolina. Why not spin as well as plant cotton?

WILLIAM GREGG, *Essays on Domestic Industry*, 1845

IN THE SUMMER OF 1842, several young gentlemen of Barnwell District
formed the Demosthenian Debating Society. Meeting every other week, the
society gave members an opportunity to hone their proficiency in debate and
oratory, skills essential to one's standing in proper South Carolina society. The
questions discussed at their meetings covered a spectrum of topics, from the
virtues of novel reading to the susceptibility of females to mental improvement.
But at their gathering of June 23, 1843, members debated what they considered
a somewhat weightier question: "Is Agriculture or Manufactures of more benefit to Society?" A spirited rhetorical contest quickly ensued. Indeed, debate
was so fervent that the sides deadlocked, with neither contestant able to claim
victory or admit defeat. Unable to select a victor, the membership proposed
"that the President decide the question." After giving careful consideration to
the merits of each side, the society minutes recorded that "the President decided in favor of agriculture."[1]

Epigraph from William Gregg, *Essays on Domestic Industry: or, An Inquiry into the Expediency of
Establishing Cotton Manufactures in South Carolina* (Charleston, 1845), 21.

1. Minutes of the Demosthenian Debating Society, June 17, 1842, to July 21, 1843, SCL.

In hindsight, the outcome of the dispute seems predictable. A victory by "Agriculture" over "Manufactures" was hardly shocking in a debating club composed of planters and the sons of planters. But the spirit and tenacity of the rhetorical contest further suggests that the victory was hardly a foregone conclusion, even in the overwhelmingly agrarian society of Barnwell District. The relationship of manufacturing, both foreign and domestic, to southern agriculture remained a topic of frequent discussion throughout the antebellum period. The subject became particularly volatile in the nullification era when South Carolina leaders—and those they led—seldom passed up an opportunity to rail against the malignant influence of northern manufacturing interests in national government. Even in nullification's aftermath, the subject of manufactures remained prevalent, as the agricultural depression of the 1840s prompted endless calls for industrial development in order to diversify the southern economy. But all this eloquence produced rather schizophrenic results. Slaveholders maintained deep suspicions and animosities toward industrial society—particularly where it existed in New England and Great Britain—but simultaneously decried the lack of a domestic industrial sector that left the South as an economic, and therefore political, vassal of the North. Slaveholders sought manufacturing. They did not seek a manufacturing society.[2]

In the middle decades of the antebellum era, Edgefield and Barnwell confronted the reality of manufacturing head-on in the form of cotton mills at Vaucluse and Graniteville. Straddling the bold running waters of Horse Creek near the districts' common boundary, the factories became two of the most successful and best-known industrial efforts of the Old South. As they did with their rising merchant class and the arrival of the Charleston and Hamburg railroad, Edgefield and Barnwell appeared willing, even eager, to accept the intrusion of large-scale manufacturing into the agrarian landscape. Vaucluse and Graniteville would be touted as sterling examples of southern economic diversification, as well as prime political symbols of the South's determination to break its reliance on foreign manufacturing and strike back at northern tariff advocates. But while district agrarians proved deft at adapting their theories

2. Chauncey Samuel Boucher, "The Ante-Bellum Attitude of South Carolina Towards Manufacturing and Agriculture," *Washington University Studies* 3 (April 1916): 243–70; Laurence Shore, *Southern Capitalists: The Ideological Leadership of an Elite, 1832–1885* (Chapel Hill, 1986), 31–40; Eugene D. Genovese, *The Political Economy of Slavery: Studies in the Economy and Society of the Slave South,* 2nd ed. (Middletown, Conn., 1989), 180–85; Lacy K. Ford Jr., *Origins of Southern Radicalism: The South Carolina Upcountry, 1800–1860* (New York and Oxford, 1988), 263–64.

on manufactures to fit their changing reality, Vaucluse and Graniteville would likewise prove adept by not only thriving in a theoretically uninviting environment, but in altering it to their advantage, particularly as control of these new features passed from district agrarians into the hands of outside men of capital.

To be sure, manufacturing was not entirely foreign to the agrarian landscape of Edgefield and Barnwell. A wide array of processing activities had long claimed the time and effort of district agriculturists, while household production continued to be an important source of clothing and other sundries for district inhabitants. By the second decade of the nineteenth century, some manufacturing activities even began to betray decidedly entrepreneurial overtones. Since colonial times, settlers and travelers knew of high-quality clay deposits in Edgefield, especially in the central and southern sections of the district. In the 1810s, physician and newspaper editor Abner Landrum established a pottery works just north of Edgefield Court House, employing both slave and free artisans to produce a wide variety of stoneware crockery that found a reliable market in the district. Landrum's establishment spawned the village of Pottersville, which attracted an artisan population that briefly vied with the nearby court house as the center of district trade. A number of artisans and entrepreneurs who apprenticed at Pottersville went on to found other stoneware "factories" in the district, expanding the market for Edgefield pottery beyond district borders. In 1840 the Phoenix Factory established itself near the SCC&RR depot at Aiken, offering to deliver its wares "any distance under one hundred and fifty miles," particularly to the merchants of Charleston. By 1860, Edgefield claimed two-thirds of South Carolina's pottery works, employing not only slave artisans, but 80 percent of the state's free potters as well.[3]

But by and large, manufacturing continued as a decided adjunct to agriculture in Edgefield and Barnwell as well as the rest of the state. It was a relationship that seemed just and proper to Carolina planters. Like commerce, manufacturing was bound to agriculture, observed Elias Horry, "since the pro-

3. Robert Mills, *Statistics of South Carolina, Including a View of its Natural, Civil, and Military History, General and Particular* (Charleston, 1826), 523–24; *Edgefield Advertiser*, May 7, 1840; May 11, 1859; Orville Vernon Burton, *In My Father's House Are Many Mansions: Family & Community in Edgefield, South Carolina* (Chapel Hill, 1985), 34; Cynthia Elyce Rubin, "The Edgefield Pottery Tradition," *Early American Life* 18 (1987): 24–29; Cinda K. Baldwin, *Great & Noble Jar: Traditional Stoneware of South Carolina* (Athens and London, 1993), chaps. 2 and 3.

ductions of nature are the materials of Art." That every plantation and farm should produce all its own needs was a cardinal tenet of the agrarian ideal. The products made by households and local artisans were the natural allies of republican agriculture, keeping resident freemen and slaves alike supplied with the basic material necessities of their daily lives. An occasional indulgence on a foreign-made finery or two might be a well-deserved deviation from the path of self-sacrifice, but encouraging the accumulation and production of such frippery was hardly considered a virtue. The manufacture of such indulgences meant expanding production beyond the household to large-scale factories, which in turn led to excessive luxury, wage labor, propertyless dependence, and poverty—in short, all those social ills that agrarian society sought to keep at bay.[4]

In South Carolina, large-scale manufacturing gained special infamy in the 1820s, with antipathy reaching a fevered pitch during the nullification crisis, as a maturing industrial North consistently sought and received tariff protection from the federal government. A rising chorus of Carolinians denounced the federal favoritism of manufacturing over agriculture, which grew particularly shrill in backcountry districts suffering from years of disappointing cotton prices. A public meeting in Barnwell District resolutely expressed their opposition to the Woolens Bill of 1827, condemning it as operating "injuriously and oppressively on the interests of agriculture, already depressed, for the benefit of manufactures." Edgefieldians, in typical style, voiced their consternation in more flamboyant terms. "We want no set of manufacturers to *force* from us a certain portion of our income, for their own use," they exclaimed to Congress. Protective tariffs only profited "*the moneyed monopolists of the North and East,*" while fostering a system "which naturally . . . brings down the lofty independence of *a man,* and converts him into a mere mechanical engine administering cotton to a spinning jenny." With the enactment of the "Tariff of Abominations" the following year, the reputation of large-scale manufacturing sank to an all-time low in South Carolina, as the moniker *manufacturer* came to be virtually indistinguishable from that of *tariff advocate.* Mere accusations of

4. Elias Horry, *An Address Delivered in Charleston, Before the Agricultural Society of South Carolina, At Its Anniversary Meeting, on Tuesday, the 19th August, 1828* (Charleston, 1828), 3. On the place of manufacturing in the classical republican thought of early America, see Drew R. McCoy, *The Elusive Republic: Political Economy in Jeffersonian America* (Chapel Hill, 1980; New York, 1982), 105–19, 223–35, and Walter Licht, *Industrializing America: The Nineteenth Century* (Baltimore and London, 1995), 13–20.

support for a manufacturing concern resulted in public brawls. When George McDuffie returned to Edgefield in the summer of 1828, the only ticket required to a dinner in his honor was a suit of homespun clothes as a visible embrace of McDuffie's call to shun the tariff-protected broadcloth of New England.[5]

Paradoxically, while vilifying northern industrialists, nullification simultaneously provided the impetus to expand manufacturing in South Carolina. As part of what the historian William Freehling dubbed "The Great Reaction," Carolinians entered the postnullification era recognizing the need for a more diversified economy, particularly a domestic industrial sector, to wean the state from cotton monoculture and diminish its embarrassing reliance on the North for its manufactured necessities. "It was at last becoming patriotic rather than degrading," Freehling observed, "for chivalric gentlemen to take part in manufacturing and mercantile enterprises." Among others, James Henry Hammond hoped to encourage this trend. "It makes an immense difference in the prosperity of any people, and especially an agricultural people, whether their workshops are at home or in other countries," he observed. Not only would domestic manufactures omit "heavy taxations" in the form of tariffs, commissions, and freight, but agriculturists would also enjoy an increased demand for their produce by "the mechanic classes." If manufacturers could be "united in the same community with a class of industrious and enlightened agriculturists," Hammond believed the two classes would "mutually enrich and strengthen one another." Capital was already beginning to find its way into cotton factories in South Carolina, and Hammond argued that "our citizens, and especially our planters, ought to encourage such investments." Enthusiasm for industrial pursuits was not universal, however, even if its economic and political necessity were increasingly obvious. Abner Landrum's Unionist newspaper, the *Edgefield Hive,* looked upon this embryonic industrial impulse and lamented, "Thus we see the South has been most reluctantly driven to the manufacturing business which they would most anxiously have avoided, but which now in self-defence they are compelled to pursue."[6]

Edgefield District would loom large in this guarded enthusiasm for man-

5. House Doc. No. 20, 20th Cong., 1st sess., *Memorial of the Inhabitants of Barnwell District, in S.C. Remonstrated Against Any Additional Duties on Imported Woollen Goods* (Washington, 1827), 4; House Doc. No. 24, 20th Cong., 1st sess., *Memorial of The Citizens of Edgefield, Against the Woollens Bill* (Washington, 1827), 4–6; Boucher, "Antebellum Attitude of South Carolina Towards Manufacturing," 243–44, 245; Edwin L. Green, *George McDuffie* (Columbia, 1936), 102–3.

6. William W. Freehling, *Prelude to Civil War: The Nullification Controversy in South Carolina,*

ufacturing, particularly along the banks and tributaries of Horse Creek. It was here, at Vaucluse, that manufacturing in western South Carolina took its first tentative steps beyond the household hearth and village workshop. It would not be an immediate break from the past. As one scholar aptly wrote, "The plantation master would also be a factory master" in the South's initial experiments in industrial development, particularly planter-nullifiers like George McDuffie and John Bauskett. But while politics and political rhetoric colored the mill a defender of southern rights and society, Vaucluse would also point out a new direction in Edgefield and Barnwell's "alternate route to modernity," one that would invoke changes not just in manufacturing methods, but in the relationship between manufacturing and the agrarian landscape as well.[7]

In its initial manifestation, Vaucluse was the primitive but impressive progeny of a local immigrant-planter by the name of Christian Breithaupt. Like Henry Shultz, Breithaupt was a European native who came to South Carolina in search of fortune. Unlike Shultz, however, Breithaupt chose the South's more traveled road to wealth, becoming a successful planter in Edgefield District and acquiring no fewer than eighty slaves by 1830. Aside from his ability and ambition, we cannot be sure of Breithaupt's motivations for building a cotton factory. Whatever the source of his inspiration, his Vaucluse mill launched the initial stage of the Horse Creek Valley's transformation from a bucolic haven for grist and saw mills into the South's cradle of industrialization.[8]

The original Vaucluse mill had a brief existence and surviving details of its operation are spotty. Sometime in the late 1820s, Breithaupt and a handful of partners began to construct a factory, sawmill, gristmill, and operative housing on a 1,200-acre site near the source of Horse Creek in Edgefield District. By

1816–1836 (New York and London, 1965), 303–6; James Henry Hammond, "Anniversary Oration, of the State Agricultural Society of South Carolina; read Before the Society, on the 25th November, 1841," in *Proceedings of the Agricultural Convention and of the State Agricultural Society of South Carolina, from 1839–1845—Inclusive* (Columbia, 1846), 189–90; Pottersville, *Edgefield Hive*, March 19, 1830.

7. Allen Heath Stokes Jr., "Black and White Labor and the Development of the Southern Textile Industry, 1800–1920" (Ph.D. diss., University of South Carolina, 1977), 5; Eugene D. Genovese, *The Slaveholders' Dilemma: Freedom and Progress in Southern Conservative Thought, 1820–1860* (Columbia, 1992), 13.

8. Ernest McPherson Lander Jr., *The Textile Industry in Antebellum South Carolina* (Baton Rouge, 1969), 35–36; Manuscript Census Returns, Edgefield District, 1830, SCDAH.

1830, the men had filled a four-story wooden building with carding machines, drawing frames, mule and throstle spindles, looms, and a host of other machinery with which they produced cotton bagging and a variety of coarse wool and cotton fabrics. Local buyers were impressed with the quality of Vaucluse products. One enthusiast asserted that the factory's cotton bagging "appears to be strong, well made, and of good width," and had no doubt that it could compete successfully with the hemp bagging traditionally used by Edgefield planters. But Breithaupt and his associates were evidently dissatisfied with their concern, or perhaps with each other. They dissolved their partnership at the beginning of 1831 and sold the factory to a Massachusetts firm for $15,000. But Vaucluse never had a chance to prove itself as a "Yankee concern." In July 1831, a fire—allegedly set by a slave operative—destroyed the wooden factory and the northerners soon after exhausted their capital in an attempt to rebuild.[9]

Breithaupt reacquired Vaucluse in 1833, purchasing a half-built factory, a sawmill, and a completed set of dams and races for the bargain price of $7,000, and rapidly set about to resurrect his cotton mill. The second incarnation of the Vaucluse factory displayed definite signs of industrial maturation. First, there was the impressive size and appearance of the resurrected mill. Built upon the site of the original ("in the Midst of Woods 16 miles from any Town," remarked a site foreman), the new Vaucluse factory presented a memorable spectacle for visitors to the Edgefield sandhills. Five stories in height (including an attic) and constructed of granite taken from an adjacent quarry, the new Vaucluse mill conjured up the image of "an old feudal castle" in the imagination of one scribe. The machinery grew to include more than 1,500 spindles and between twenty-five and thirty-five looms. Commencing operations in 1834, within two years Vaucluse was turning out goods worth $250 to $300 daily, making the mill one of the largest textile factories in South Carolina. Vaucluse products could be found on store shelves in Hamburg, Edgefield Court House, and Aiken, as well as across the Savannah River in Augusta. Perhaps an even greater innovation was the decision to incorporate the manufacturing establishment. In December 1833, the General Assembly granted Breithaupt and his

9. Lander, *Textile Industry*, 35–36; *Charleston Courier*, July 9, 1830; November 22, 1830; January 7, 1831; January 6, 1860. The identity of Breithaupt's partners is uncertain. Ernest Lander identifies them as Richard Cunningham of Abbeville District and Paul Fitzsimons (probably the brother-in-law of James Henry Hammond). Lander, *Textile Industry*, 35. However, a later newspaper account claims Breithaupt established the Vaucluse factory "together with several gentlemen of Columbia." *Charleston Courier*, January 6, 1860.

associates a charter for "The Vaucluse Manufacturing Company," with an authorized capitalization of $100,000. It was only the second charter of incorporation ever granted to a textile factory in South Carolina.[10]

But while an incorporated factory filled with the latest machinery exuded a modern industrial appearance, an agrarian mentality still pervaded operations at Vaucluse. Planters predominated among Vaucluse owners during the first two decades of its existence; the same "men of property" that owned and operated most of the manufacturing establishments in Edgefield and Barnwell since time immemorial. Besides Breithaupt, planters George McDuffie (thirty-four slaves in 1830), Paul Fitzsimons (thirty slaves in 1830), and James G. O. Wilkinson (twenty-one slaves in 1830) were among the early Vaucluse investors. William Gregg later asserted that a scion of the Seabrook family of Edisto Island planters was also among the early Vaucluse stockholders. By the time John Bauskett purchased the factory in the late 1830s, he was well on his way toward becoming one of the largest slaveholders in Edgefield (112 slaves in 1840; 221 slaves in 1850), besides possessing one of the most lucrative legal practices in the district.[11]

Despite an impressive productive capacity, Vaucluse nevertheless geared its output toward local demand. Analyzing the early history of Vaucluse, *De Bow's Review* observed that the original proprietors clung to the notion that their factory would sell only in its immediate neighborhood and thereby assumed "that all the cotton fabrics constituting the stock in trade of a country store, from muslin to cotton bagging, should be manufactured by it." In consequence, by attempting "to get machinery to make *everything*, they got that which could make *nothing* well or profitably." The factory first concentrated on cotton bagging, then later added other coarse fabrics to its production. Both yarn and

---

10. Lander, *Textile Industry*, 35; William Gregg, "Report of the President of the Graniteville Manufacturing Company, April, 1849," 2, Gregg-Graniteville Collection, Gregg-Graniteville Library, University of South Carolina-Aiken; John Munro to James Spears, May 5, 1834, SCL; *Charleston Courier*, September 5, 1837; January 6, 1860; *Edgefield Advertiser*, November 10, 1836; *Statutes at Large*, VIII: 381–82. For advertisements for the sale of Vaucluse products, see *Edgefield Advertiser*, April 7, 1836; August 25, 1836; May 18, 1837; November 16, 1837; April 12, 1838; April 17, 1838.

11. Manuscript Census Returns, Abbeville and Edgefield Districts, 1830; Edgefield District, 1840, SCDAH; William Gregg, "Southern Patronage to Southern Imports and Domestic Industry," *De Bow's Review* 29 (October 1860): 494; N. Louise Bailey, Mary L. Morgan, and Carolyn R. Taylor, eds., *Biographical Directory of the South Carolina Senate, 1776–1985*, 3 vols. (Columbia, 1986), 1:109.

cloth were being produced by the mid-1830s. "Negro Shirting" and "Cotton Osnaburgs" were advertised for sale in 1836. That same year, Vaucluse installed woolen machinery and added linsey to its product list. And while the factory boasted a daily output of more than one thousand yards of cloth and two hundred pounds of yarn, the planter-manufacturers at Vaucluse seemed content to dispose of it locally. "Our customers are the planters," McDuffie declared and he urged his partners to drum up business among Carolina agriculturists rather than depending upon "a few Augusta merchants" to dispose of their production.[12]

Vaucluse proprietors also favored the "peculiar institution" to fill their labor requirements. In 1836 almost half of the factory's operatives were slaves, who could be found at work in every department except weaving, where "whites are said to have the advantage" besides being "equally cheap." Some operatives were hired from neighboring slaveholders. Edgefield farmer Lark Swearingen leased one of his slaves, Letty, to John Bauskett at Vaucluse for $100 per annum, besides selling cotton and fodder to the factory. But most slave operatives came to Vaucluse from the factory's owners, who angled to further profit from their manufacturing investment by supplying Vaucluse with a portion of its labor. Paul Fitzsimons hired out slaves to Vaucluse, as did George McDuffie, who employed at least five of his younger male and female slaves at Vaucluse as well as a carpenter, Jesse, and his wife. In return, McDuffie sought a total of $1,000 in annual wages. Likewise, John Bauskett transferred several hands from his plantation to work at Vaucluse. By 1840, Bauskett employed almost one-fourth of his own slaves (27 of 112) in his cotton mill, while a visitor asserted that all the slaves working in the mill belonged to the factory's proprietors.[13]

Even Vaucluse's progressive status as a chartered corporation proved illu-

12. *De Bow's Review* 11 (November 1851): 542–43; *Charleston Courier,* June 9, 1830; November 22, 1830; George McDuffie to John Bauskett, February 3, 1838, George McDuffie Papers, SCL; *Edgefield Advertiser,* February 11, 1836; April 7, 1836; August 25, 1836; September 7, 1837.

13. *Edgefield Advertiser,* November 10, 1836; Accounts of Lark Swearingen with Vaucluse factory, 1838–1840, John Eldred Swearingen Papers, SCL; George McDuffie to John Bauskett, February 3, 1838, George McDuffie Papers, SCL; Thomas P. Martin, ed., "The Advent of William Gregg and the Graniteville Company," *Journal of Southern History* 11 (August 1945): 402; John Bauskett to Thomas Bauskett, April 19, 1839, fiche no. 28–368-d, David Duncan Wallace Papers, SCL; Manuscript Census Returns, Edgefield District, 1840, SCDAH; William Thomson, *A Tradesman's Travels, in the United States and Canada in the Years 1840, 41, & 42* (Edinburgh, 1842), 113–14.

sory. Only fifty-four and a half shares of company stock were subscribed (at a par value of $1,000 each), with forty taken by just seven investors. Meeting shortly after the receipt of their charter, the stockholders chose a president and directors, ordered a plethora of machinery from the North, and contracted for the necessary buildings. However, this was apparently the first and only meeting of the Vaucluse Manufacturing Company directorate for the next two and a half years. After Breithaupt died in 1835, stockholders neglected company affairs and daily operations were left to the care of "an ignorant Englishman" who possessed no prior experience in mill management. In February 1837, McDuffie urged Vaucluse stockholders to meet and "create a government, for there is now none," then simultaneously announced his resignation as president of the company. The result of all this inattention was predictable. By 1837, Vaucluse found itself with a debt of $6,000 and teetering on the verge of bankruptcy. By the end of the year, the shareholders sold out their interest (at a loss) for $33,000 to McDuffie and Bauskett, who proceeded to run Vaucluse in partnership. However, within a year, Bauskett bought out McDuffie's share and became the sole proprietor of the Vaucluse factory.[14]

The financial turmoil surrounding Vaucluse in its first decade of operation underscored a crucial factor that kept the factory from evolving into a more thriving example of industrial capitalism, namely, the unwillingness of the "men of property" who invested in Vaucluse to commit themselves to cotton manufacturing on a permanent basis. After Breithaupt's untimely death, none of the Vaucluse investors stepped forward to give their full-time attention to the factory. George McDuffie took over as company president in 1835, but was far more involved in his gubernatorial duties and new plantation in Abbeville District to give Vaucluse more than passing attention. Both he and John Bauskett held grand expectations for Vaucluse after they bought the mill at the end of 1837, expecting to sell 150,000 yards of osnaburgs to local planters annually. But within a year, McDuffie sold his half of Vaucluse and refocused his energies on establishing direct trade between Carolina planters and English manufacturers rather than encouraging further industrial development at home. After becoming the factory's sole proprietor, Bauskett found Vaucluse earned him more than his plantation, but simultaneously complained that the factory took too much time away from his legal practice and political activities. Rather

14. Gregg, *Essays,* 34; idem, "Southern Patronage," 494; *Charleston Courier,* January 6, 1860; Martin, "Advent of Gregg and Graniteville," 402; Lander, *Textile Industry,* 37.

than remain bound to the confining life of a manufacturer, Bauskett sold a half interest in Vaucluse for $20,000 to James Jones, the former adjutant and inspector general of militia in South Carolina. Jones entered the partnership on the condition that he would manage the factory and release Bauskett from day-to-day responsibilities. But within a short time, Jones too lamented the confines of Vaucluse: "The demand for my attention here is hourly and unceasing and I cannot name any future day as one of leisure, or not imperiously requiring my presence here." The unrelenting application required of a manufacturer also deterred James Henry Hammond from making an investment in the Vaucluse factory, where he briefly considered establishing his brother, Marcellus, as proprietor. "If alone & you did not *take to* the business, but let it go its own way, you would be broke before you knew it," Hammond cautioned his brother. "It requires a little closer watching than planting or drilling."[15]

While unwilling to become manufacturers themselves, planters in Edgefield and Barnwell still manifested enough interest in manufacturing to encourage and support the erection of cotton mills in South Carolina. But planter investment in manufactures quickly proved long on enthusiasm and short on resolve. Indeed, an investment in manufacturing could at times seem like an act of public charity by Carolina planters. James Henry Hammond sank $1,000 into a cotton factory at Limestone Springs, which he quickly found to be a poor investment. He attempted to sell out at a loss, but his close friend and fellow stockholder, Pierce Mason Butler, convinced him to reconsider. Neither man felt an affinity for "the Yankee concern," but Butler felt that abandoning the project "would injure the Stock & create prejudice against you." Better for Hammond to "stick to a bad bargain" and lose his money, Butler advised, than risk being accused of lacking patriotism and faith in southern enterprise. Hammond sold his stock below par the following year and the total losses of the factory reached an estimated $25,000. In 1842 Francis Pickens spent months lobbying an English company to invest part of its substantial capital in creating cotton factories in South Carolina, particularly one contemplated by his friend James Edward Calhoun in neighboring Abbeville District. Despite Pickens's grand expectations, no investment of English capital was forthcom-

15. Lander, *Textile Industry*, 37–38, 74; George McDuffie to John Bauskett, February 3, 1838, George McDuffie Papers, SCL; Martin, "Advent of Gregg and Graniteville," 403; Edgefield Deeds, Book BBB, 510–12; Book CCC, 30–32, SCDAH; James Jones to James Edward Calhoun, March 19, 1845, James Edward Calhoun Papers, SCL; James Henry Hammond to M. C. M. Hammond, November 27, 1847, James Henry Hammond Papers, SCL.

ing and nothing came of his grand scheme. He later invested in one of the Pot-tersville stoneware factories, but gave scant attention to the investment, which earned him barely $1,000 a year and employed a paltry four hands.[16]

Even though Vaucluse struggled through much of the 1830s and 1840s, the fac-tory might have foundered altogether had it not been for the propitious arrival of a new stockholder in 1837, a semiretired Columbia jeweler named William Gregg. According to his own rather immodest account, Gregg entered the Vaucluse picture after purchasing enough shares in the company "to excite some interest." While his fellow stockholders seemed content to abandon the concern in the face of pending debt judgments, Gregg took it upon himself to reverse the declining fortunes of Vaucluse. He took up residence at the factory, dismissed the overseer, and assumed personal charge of the works. He reorga-nized Vaucluse's marketing arrangements, closed agencies at Hamburg and Augusta, and instead sold its production directly from the factory to merchants at fixed prices. In just eight months, Gregg doubled production and trans-formed Vaucluse's $6,000 debt into a $5,000 surplus. After boosting the value of Vaucluse stock to within sight of par, Gregg joined the other owners in sell-ing their company to McDuffie and Bauskett, which likely netted Gregg (who probably bought the stock at depressed levels) a tidy profit while the remain-ing original investors were only able to cut their losses.[17]

Gregg's one-year foray at Vaucluse was the auspicious manufacturing de-but of the individual who was to emerge as the South's leading advocate of in-dustrial development in the antebellum era. His origins were modest and his upbringing practical. Born in Virginia in 1800, Gregg was placed as a child in the care of an uncle, a successful Alexandria watchmaker who also made spin-ning machinery. By 1810, they moved to Georgia, where the uncle constructed a cotton mill that prospered during the War of 1812 but collapsed after peace brought the return of foreign imports. Financially ruined, the uncle appren-ticed his young ward and Gregg undertook to learn the watchmaker's art over

16. Pierce Mason Butler to James Henry Hammond, June 23, 1834; John Felder to James Henry Hammond, November 9, 1846, James Henry Hammond Papers, Library of Congress; Lander, *Tex-tile Industry,* 39; Francis W. Pickens to James Edward Calhoun, April 10, 1842, May 6, 1842, no date [ca. 1842], Francis W. Pickens Papers, SCL; Baldwin, *Great and Noble Jar,* 38–39; 1850 Manuscript Census Returns, Edgefield District, Manufactures, 593, SCDAH.

17. Gregg, *Essays,* 34–35; Lander, *Textile Industry,* 46–47; *Edgefield Advertiser,* September 7, 1837; October 26, 1837.

the next several years in Kentucky and Virginia. By the mid-1820s, Gregg was in South Carolina, where he entered the watch repair and jewelers' trade in Columbia. Within several years, the former apprentice had advanced from artisan to merchant, building a thriving import business by supplying well-to-do Carolinians with a wide assortment of fancy goods, silver, and military regalia. By the time he made his investment in the Vaucluse factory, Gregg was living in retirement with a comfortable fortune but poor health.[18]

After divesting himself of Vaucluse at the end of 1837, Gregg moved to Charleston. Regaining his health, he established himself anew in the jewelry business in partnership with brothers Nathaniel and Hezekiah Sidney Hayden, a pair of Connecticut Yankees with extensive family and business connections in the North. The import firm of Hayden, Gregg, & Company (later renamed Gregg, Hayden, & Company) became Charleston's leading dealer in jewelry and fancy goods and made William Gregg a wealthy and well-connected member of the Charleston business community. He was elected a director of the South Carolina Railroad in 1845, and Gregg, Hayden, & Company soon after became the Charleston agents of the Hartford Insurance Company. By the end of the decade, Gregg's firm was valued at well over $100,000.[19]

Despite his notable success within the Charleston merchant community, Gregg maintained a keen interest in manufacturing. "But for my delicate health when I retired from business in Columbia," he confided to James Henry Ham-

18. Broadus Mitchell, *William Gregg: Factory Master of the Old South* (Chapel Hill, 1928), 2–8; Martin, "Advent of Gregg and Graniteville," 389–90; *De Bow's Review* 10 (1851): 348; Columbia, *South Carolina State Gazette and Columbia Advertiser,* November 10, 1829. Receipts for items purchased by James Henry Hammond from Gregg in Columbia between 1829 and 1833 can be found in Business Papers, James Henry Hammond Papers, SCL.

19. Martin, "Advent of Gregg and Graniteville," 391; *De Bow's Review* 10 (1851): 349; T. C. Fay, *Charleston Directory, and Strangers' Guide for 1840 and 1841* (Charleston, 1840), 36, 40; John H. Honour Jr., *A Directory of the City of Charleston and Neck, for 1849* (Charleston, 1849), 49, 128, 142; J. H. Bagget, *Directory of the City of Charleston, for the Year 1852* (Charleston, 1851), 51, 157, 204; *Edgefield Advertiser,* May 14, 1845; *Proceedings of the South Carolina Rail-Road Company and the South-Western Rail-Road Bank, at their Annual Meeting, in the Hall of the Bank, on the 10th, 11th, and 12th February, 1846* (Charleston, 1846), 17; *Proceedings of the Stockholders of the South-Carolina Rail-Road Company, and of the South-Western Rail-Road Bank, at their Annual Meeting, in the Hall of the Bank, on the 9th, 10th, and 11th February, 1847* (Charleston, 1847), 28; Credit Reports, South Carolina, vol. 6 (Charleston), 35, R. G. Dun & Co. Collection, Baker Library, Harvard Business School.

mond in 1841, "I should have embarked in the manufacturing of cotton." With his constitution revitalized and his fortune on the ascent, Gregg returned to Vaucluse and the Horse Creek Valley in 1843. In league with James Jones (his brother-in-law), Gregg bought Vaucluse from John Bauskett for $25,000, a price that included not only the factory but also 11,000 acres of land on Horse Creek and its tributaries. Deeming Bauskett's machinery and production to be hopelessly complicated, Gregg and Jones rearranged the factory, sold the woolen machinery, and focused exclusive attention on the coarsest cotton goods: osnaburgs and bagging. Buoyed by his success at Vaucluse, Gregg took an extended tour of New England's manufacturing districts and began to develop not only a plan for expanding his personal interest in cotton manufacturing, but a vision of industrial development for the entire South.[20]

In the fall of 1844, Gregg burst forth as a public figure with a twelve-part series of articles in the *Charleston Courier*. Encouraged by the public reaction, he reprinted the series the following year under his own name in a pamphlet entitled *Essays on Domestic Industry*. The piece was a blunt and sometimes scathing critique of southern agriculturists and their failure to cultivate cotton mills along with cotton bolls on their native soil. Reprinted in newspapers and periodicals across the South, Gregg's *Essays* drew both praise and fire, but seldom failed to elicit a reaction from readers. Gregg reiterated and honed his opinions in additional pamphlets and articles throughout the remainder of the antebellum period. These writings, coupled with his achievements at Graniteville, placed William Gregg as the de facto spokesman for industrial development in the Old South.[21]

Gregg's vision for reorganizing South Carolina's industrial pursuits had lit-

20. William Gregg to James Henry Hammond, November 3, 1841, James Henry Hammond Papers, SCL; Edgefield Deeds, Book CCC, 472–75, SCDAH; Gregg, *Essays*, 34–35; *Edgefield Advertiser*, August 9, 1843; November 3, 1845. A specimen of cotton osnaburg produced by Gregg and Jones at Vaucluse won a silver medal from the American Institute of the City of New York in 1845. The judges declared that the cloth was "superior to much the larger proportion made north of the Carolinas." "Register of Premiums, 18th Annual Fair" [1845], No. 423, and "Judges Reports, 18th Annual Fair, Report of the Judges on Cotton Goods"; both in American Institute Collection, New York Historical Society, New York.

21. Mitchell, *William Gregg*, 15–32; Lander, *Textile Industry*, 52–54; Shore, *Southern Capitalists*, 32–33. Postbellum factory booster Daniel A. Tompkins reprinted Gregg's *Essays* in his own work "because it seems to me that his arguments are as good to-day and for our time, as for the time in which they were written and published." Tompkins, *Cotton Mill, Commercial Features* (Charlotte, 1899), 206.

tle room for planter-manufacturers. With innumerable advantages in raw materials, labor costs, and water power, Gregg insisted that the South's industrial deficiencies were the result of nothing but "unpardonable ignorance" and "the grossest mismanagement" on the part of its factory owners. Their cotton mills had been badly undercapitalized. They produced too great a variety for too small of a market. Far too little attention was paid to day-to-day management. And while he lauded South Carolina planters and politicians for the patriotism displayed by their investment, Gregg nonetheless condemned the inattention that led to the failure of their factories, which subsequently deterred others from investing in similar enterprises.[22]

When he looked upon the fluctuating fortunes of Vaucluse during its first decade of operations, Gregg saw every misfortune that resulted from entrusting manufacturing to southern planters. He castigated George McDuffie for allowing Vaucluse to "dwindle, sicken and die" for want of attention. Had McDuffie shown the same zeal toward Vaucluse as he did toward planting and opposing the tariff, Gregg was convinced he would have built up a lucrative establishment that "would have given an impetus to manufacturing, worth millions to our State." Subsequent Vaucluse owners fared no better in Gregg's eyes. Bauskett may have realized enviable profits from the factory, but his public and private affairs were so numerous that "the mill received but little of his attention." Nor did the addition of James Jones as a partner improve matters. Gregg confided to James Henry Hammond that during the "Bauskett & Jones reign" at Vaucluse, the factory yielded no more than eight hundred yards of cloth per day while "Jones slept till 11 O'clock & Bauskett saw the Factory once a month, as one of many of his speculative rambles, or Court attendance afforded an opportunity." Under his own management of Vaucluse with Jones, Gregg took unblushing credit for boosting the daily cloth output at Vaucluse to 2,500 yards as well as several hundred pounds of yarn. "I have the satisfaction of believing," he told Hammond, "that my pushing at [Jones's] back made him a fortune that would not otherwise have been earned."[23]

Besides allowing their factories to suffer from a want of sustained attention, Gregg likewise criticized planter-manufacturers for disregarding the

22. Gregg, *Essays*, 20.

23. Ibid., 8–9, 34; William Gregg to James Henry Hammond, October 30, 1847, James Henry Hammond Papers, SCL.

landless white population in their midst. By giving preference to slave labor in their factories, Gregg accused Carolina planters of ignoring "the thousands of poor, ignorant, degraded white people among us." Tens of thousands of South Carolinians lived in a state of want and illiteracy "because they are neglected by those possessing the capital of our country." Employment in manufacturing villages could prove to be the economic salvation of these forgotten whites. And if proprietors also invested "a small share of philanthropy" in the erection of schools and churches to educate and Christianize, they would simultaneously undertake the moral salvation of a class of citizen "but one step in advance of the Indian of the forest." "These people must be brought into daily contact with the rich and intelligent," Gregg believed, "they must be stimulated to mental action, and taught to appreciate education and the comforts of civilized life." Nothing would bring about this change more effectively than "the introduction of manufactures, for there seems to be no other employment so well calculated to induce them to habits of industry." Not only would this transform poor whites into productive citizens, but Gregg sagely opined that they would also render Carolina agriculturists "independent of our neighbors," and become "a strong arm of defence in case of need." Elevating poor whites to respectability, Gregg implied, would strengthen their attachment to southern "institutions," that is, slavery.[24]

But true progress toward reorganizing South Carolina's industrial pursuits needed to come from a source other than state planters. "Let the present labour and capital engaged in Agriculture remain very much as it is," Gregg told John C. Calhoun in 1845. If South Carolina built cotton mills, Gregg would have them "put in operation and owned by the capitalists now in the state, not engaged in Agriculture." Such men investing their resources in cotton manufacturing would soon "prove the business to be profitable," and stimulate investment in additional factories. A different breed of entrepreneur was required to take up the task of industrial development in South Carolina. "Cotton manufacturing will not probably be speedily introduced into this state," Gregg wrote in his *Essays*, "unless our business men of capital take hold of it." Those involved in "mercantile pursuits" emerged as the prime candidates for manufacturers. Such men, Gregg observed, possessed dispositions that forbade their

24. Gregg, *Essays*, 22, 46–47; idem, "Manufactures in South Carolina and the South," *De Bow's Review* 11 (July 1851): 135–36.

"living in idleness" and the supervision of a well-regulated manufacturing establishment was "best adapted to such a man."[25]

Not only did "men of capital" have the habits of industry essential for managing a cotton factory, but they also possessed the concomitant requirement for industrial development: capital. "The want of this one thing has been the chief obstacle to success with southern establishments," Gregg asserted. Almost every southern factory began work with only a fraction of the capital necessary to build and operate a successful cotton mill. The common result, Gregg noted, was a factory that commenced deeply in debt and quickly suffered fiscal embarrassment and failure. Gregg believed no company should attempt to build a factory with less than $200,000 in hand, which subsequently required pooling capital from a variety of sources into a corporation. "Nearly all the great developments of the present age, have been consummated through the instrumentality of incorporations," Gregg observed, a practice that stimulated enterprise and through which "no undertaking is too great to be consummated." If South Carolina was to develop its industrial potential, associated capital was as essential as an association of capitalists. All that was needed was someone to be an example for others to follow. By 1845, Gregg was ready to assume the part.[26]

In the autumn of 1845, Gregg took the first steps toward establishing his manufacturing city on a hill. After his *Essays* had circulated for a year, Gregg followed up with an anonymous pamphlet on the propriety of granting charters of incorporation for manufacturing purposes. Besides reiterating the legal and organizational advantages of corporate status, Gregg also argued that corporations replaced reckless individual speculators with "cool-headed calculating persons" and "prudent capitalists" whose discretion and foresight would allow their factories to "pass over a time, which would either break down an individual owner, or cause him and the community to suffer severe loss, by suspending the operations of the mill." Furthermore, Gregg downplayed republican fears that such companies tended "to usurp political power and oppress the poor." In his opinion, nothing could be further from the truth. "It is by

25. Gregg, *Essays*, 214, 218, 226; William Gregg to John C. Calhoun, April 1845, in *The Papers of John C. Calhoun*, ed. Clyde N. Wilson, Shirley Bright Cook, and Alexander Moore, 28 vols. (Columbia, 1959–2003), 21:523–24.

26. *Report of the President and Treasurer of the Graniteville Manufacturing Company, for the Year 1854* (Charleston, 1855), 11; [William Gregg], *An Enquiry into the Propriety of Granting Charters of Incorporation for Manufacturing and Other Purposes, in South Carolina* (Charleston, 1845), 5.

means of incorporations," Gregg held, "that every individual in a community, may become a participator in a business, which would otherwise be confined to the rich." Even factory hands could own shares in their company, which in turn would minimize the gulf between owner and operative. If South Carolina was in earnest about manufacturing, the state needed to remove "restrictions on capital" that left the business in the hands of a very wealthy few. Corporations would open the door to the planter, the merchant, "indeed, to every individual, who may have a hundred dollars of spare capital to invest."[27]

Confident his public lobbying had properly influenced state legislators, Gregg and three other investors sought and received a charter from the South Carolina General Assembly in December 1845, creating the Graniteville Manufacturing Company "for the purpose of Manufacturing, dying, printing and finishing all goods of which Cotton or other fibrous articles may form a part." An initial capital of $300,000 was authorized for the company, divided into shares of $500 each. Named with Gregg as incorporators were Hiram Hutchison, president of the Bank of Hamburg; Otis Mills, a Charleston grain merchant and future proprietor of the prestigious Mills House Hotel; and Joel Smith, a wealthy and influential planter and member of the house of representatives from Abbeville District. Passage of the bill met a brief challenge in the house—by what Hutchison described as "a few 'Bluffton Boys'"—including former Vaucluse proprietor John Bauskett. But Gregg had friends in the legislature as well, including Joel Smith and Charleston senator Ker Boyce, both of whom were soon to be among the company's largest stockholders. When debate finally abated, both chambers approved Graniteville's charter by sizable margins.[28]

Despite Gregg's assertions regarding the democratic nature of incorporated manufacturing companies, Graniteville backers had no intention of diffusing ownership of their company among the general public. "We intend to have No partners but those that Can pay," stated Ker Boyce. Likewise, Hiram Hutchison bluntly asserted that the four Graniteville incorporators planned to "*select*

27. [Gregg], *Enquiry into Granting Charters of Incorporation*, 5, 8, 11, 13. Pauline Maier has argued that similar arguments regarding the democratic potential of corporations gradually overcame entrenched prejudice against them as aristocratic vessels of special privilege. See Maier, "The Revolutionary Origins of the American Corporation," *William and Mary Quarterly*, 3rd series, 50 (January 1993): 51–84.

28. *Statutes at Large*, XI: 357–58; Lander, *Textile Industry*, 55–56; Hiram Hutchison to John Springs, December 19, 1845, Springs Family Papers, SHC.

our copartners" and did not wish "more than twenty Stockholders *in all.*" By 1849, when the entire capital was subscribed and paid in, approximately thirty stockholders held shares in the company, with a majority of these divided among some of the wealthiest and most prominent capitalists in South Carolina, and perhaps the entire South. Gregg invested $30,000 of his own money in sixty shares of Graniteville stock. Joining him with eighty shares was Charlestonian Ker Boyce, a semiretired merchant, factor, politician, and former president of the state's largest private bank, the influential Bank of Charleston. Boyce was arguably the South's premier venture capitalist, whose net worth upon his death in 1854 amounted to almost $1 million in stocks and bonds. Bank of Hamburg president Hutchison purchased eighty shares as well, and convinced his friend John Springs of York District to make a $15,000 investment. Springs had retired from his life as a planter and slave trader, but spent much of his later years investing in an impressive array of bank and railroad stocks. By the time of his death in 1853 he was worth almost $500,000, two-thirds of which consisted of stocks and bonds in bank, railroad, insurance, and manufacturing enterprises. Springs and Hutchison also brought in William Wright, another York District resident, who took thirty shares of Graniteville stock. Like Springs, Wright was a retired planter with an impressive portfolio of investments, which eventually grew to include 2,540 shares of stock in no fewer than nine different bank corporations in the Carolinas. The only active planter among the largest investors (at eighty shares) was Joel Smith of Abbeville District, who owned one hundred slaves and $25,000 in real estate in 1850. However, at the time of his death five years later, Smith's slave holdings had decreased to seventy-nine, while the bulk of his $400,000 estate consisted of stockholdings in ten banks, three railroads, three insurance companies, and two manufacturing firms. Together, these six men owned 360 shares of Graniteville stock and provided more than half of the company's initial capital.[29]

Even lesser investors in the Graniteville factory boasted considerable wealth,

29. Ker Boyce to James Henry Hammond, December 12, 1845, James Henry Hammond Papers, Library of Congress; Hiram Hutchison to John Springs, December 19, 1845, Springs Family Papers, SHC; "List of Stockholders and Numbers of Shares in the Graniteville Manufacturing Company [1846]," Gregg/Graniteville Papers, USC-Aiken; Stockholder Account Book, Graniteville Manufacturing Company Papers, SCL. For biographical information on Ker Boyce, see *Biographical Directory of the S.C. Senate,* 1:169–71; for Hiram Hutchison and John Springs, see Lacy K. Ford Jr., "The Tale of Two Entrepreneurs in the Old South: John Springs III and Hiram Hutchi-

with the Charleston merchant community looming especially large on the list of stockholders. Incorporator Otis Mills (ten shares) owned a personal fortune estimated by an R. G. Dun agent at $200,000, while census takers placed the figure at $380,000. Other Charleston investors included commission merchants Howland and Taft (ten shares), a pair of Massachusetts natives whose partnership earned enviable profits from selling South Carolina cotton to New England mills. Merchant and financier James Lamb took twenty shares in the Graniteville factory, as did retired merchant Robert Martin. Conspicuously absent among Graniteville stockholders were investors from the factory's immediate vicinity, namely, Edgefield and Barnwell. Aside from Bank of Hamburg president Hutchison and cashier John J. Blackwood (ten shares), the only other Edgefield stockholders were Vaucluse veterans James Jones and James G. O. Wilkinson. Their assets, however, lay in manufacturing experience, not significant capital wealth. Each man only took two shares of Graniteville stock. Ker Boyce solicited James Henry Hammond "to be a Corporator with us" (an invitation that garnered William Gregg's hardy approbation), but Barnwell District's largest planter and slaveholder declined the offer.[30]

The spectacular result of the arrival of Gregg and his fellow men of capital to the Horse Creek Valley was the creation of one of the premier examples of industrial capitalism in the entire South. Stockholders met at Hamburg in March 1846 to organize their company, electing Gregg as president and choosing four additional directors. In the same month, the Graniteville company purchased 9,000 acres of land on Horse Creek just below Vaucluse—land mostly owned by Gregg, James Jones, and Ker Boyce and for which they re-

---

son of the South Carolina Upcountry," *SCHM* 95 (July 1994): 198–224; Michael Tadman, "The Hidden History of Slave Trading in Antebellum South Carolina: John Springs III and Other 'Gentlemen Dealing in Slaves,'" *SCHM* 97 (January 1996): 6–29; for William Wright, see "Will of William Wright," June 13, 1857, Will Transcripts, York County, vol. 3, 419–30, SCDAH; for Joel Smith, see 1850 population census and slave schedules for Abbeville District, and Package 3950, Box 140, Estate Papers, Abbeville District (SCDAH).

30. "List of Stockholders [1846]," Gregg/Graniteville Papers, USC-Aiken; Credit Reports, South Carolina, vol. 6 (Charleston), 33, 194, R. G. Dun & Co. Collection, Baker Library, Harvard Business School; 1850 Manuscript Census Returns, Population, Charleston District, SCDAH; *Biographical Directory of the S.C. House*, 5:151–52 (James Lamb); "Report of the President of the Graniteville Manufacturing Company, April, 1849," 2, Gregg/Graniteville Papers, USC-Aiken; Ker Boyce to James Henry Hammond, December 12, 1845, James Henry Hammond Papers, Library of Congress.

ceived a handsome compensation. Construction contracts went out shortly thereafter and Gregg traveled north to secure the necessary machinery. Divesting himself of Vaucluse, and eventually quitting his Charleston business, Gregg made Graniteville his all-consuming focus. The great work proceeded slowly over the next three years, but stockholders remained sanguine about their prospects, buoyed in large part by Gregg's infectious optimism. "Mr. G. thinks our factory will not be *surpassed*, if equalled in any respect, by any in the Union," reported John J. Blackwood to John Springs, "he having visited the best." By July 1848, with the installation of looms and spindles proceeding in earnest, Blackwood gleefully purchased the first two bales of cotton for Graniteville as "a sort of a *breakfast* for the machinery." Within another year, the Graniteville factory was spinning ten bales of cotton daily and turning off cloth that already enjoyed an enviable demand in markets as far away as Philadelphia.[31]

Visitors to Graniteville were dazzled by what they observed. "I have visited Graniteville [and] was highly gratified," wrote John W. Brodie to a friend and advised his family "not to let you rest until you carry them there." Dominating the manufacturing village was the massive granite factory building, two stories in height, with an attic, and 350 feet in length. Equally impressive was its power system. Granite dams diverted water from Horse Creek and a tributary down a mile-long canal to the factory, where it turned a set of turbines that produced 116 horsepower apiece. When full operations commenced in the fall of 1849, Graniteville's 9,245 spindles and 300 looms turned out 12,000 yards of cotton shirting, sheeting, and drills per day, plus a sizable quantity of No. 14 yarn, all of which found a ready market in Charleston, Philadelphia, and New York. With a $300,000 capitalization and a yearly output valued at an estimated $275,000, Graniteville dwarfed all other manufacturing establishments in Edgefield and Barnwell, as well as the rest of South Carolina. Gregg's closest rival in scale was its Horse Creek neighbor, Vaucluse, by then employing one hundred operatives and turning out $70,000 worth of cotton goods annually. In comparison, no saw or grist mill in Edgefield and Barnwell districts em-

31. *Edgefield Advertiser,* March 18, 1846; March 25, 1846; Ledger-Stockholder Accounts, 1846–50, Graniteville Manufacturing Company Papers, SCL; Edgefield Deeds, Book DDD, 557–59, SCDAH; *Report of the President, 1867,* 5–6; John Springs to Andrew Baxter Springs, March 6, 1846; Hiram Hutchison to John Springs, May 16, 1846; John J. Blackwood to John Springs, August 25, 1847, July 13, 1848, June 4, 1849; all in Springs Family Papers, SHC.

ployed more than a dozen hands or had a capital investment of more than $12,000, with most mills worth considerably less.[32]

Gregg also kept his pledge to uplift the physical and moral condition of the surrounding poor white population. More than three hundred operatives, mainly young women and teen-aged children, found employment at Graniteville, where they were quickly exposed to Gregg's habits of industry and the clockwork routine of the cotton factory. Daily operations at Graniteville commenced at daylight and continued through a twelve-hour workday that ceased at 7:30 P.M. Bells signaled the beginning and end to the daily labors, as well as the rigid breaks for breakfast and lunch. In this manner, the cotton mill carried out a seventy-two-hour work week, Monday through Saturday, throughout the year. Not everyone took to the regimen. While Gregg claimed no difficulty in procuring hands for Graniteville, keeping them was another story. Even before the factory was complete, Hiram Hutchison sagely predicted that "there will be some difficulty in *disciplining* 300 Carolinians at once." Experience bore out Hutchison's premonition. By 1851, Graniteville treasurer James Montgomery noted many factory operatives "do not succeed—do not like the work nor the regulation," and after much time and expense to themselves "return to their former residence."[33]

The inculcation of moral behavior was not confined within the factory walls. Surrounding Gregg's mill was a village of some nine hundred white inhabitants, giving Graniteville the largest white population of any town in

32. John W. Brodie to Jacob Stroman, November 7, 1849, Stroman Family Papers, SCL; *Edgefield Advertiser,* September 13, 1848; *De Bow's Review* 7 (1849): 456; *Hunt's Merchants' Magazine* 21 (December 1849): 671–72; 1850 U.S. Census, Edgefield District, S.C., Industry, SCDAH, 589–99.

33. Lander, *Textile Industry,* 61–62; Mitchell, *William Gregg,* 60–61; *De Bow's Review* 8 (January 1850): 27–28; *Hunt's Merchants' Magazine* 21 (December 1849): 672; Hiram Hutchison to John Springs, April 22, 1846, Springs Family Papers, SHC; James Montgomery to Benjamin C. Yancey, October 14, 1851, Benjamin Cudworth Yancey Papers, SHC. Several articles have subjected the Graniteville workforce to scrutiny. See Tom E. Terrill, "Eager Hands: Labor for Southern Textiles, 1850–1860," *Journal of Economic History* 36 (March 1976): 84–99; idem, "Murder in Graniteville," in *Toward a New South? Studies in Post-Civil War Southern Communities,* ed. Orville Vernon Burton and Robert C. McMath Jr. (Westport, Conn., 1982), 193–222; David C. Ward, "Industrial Workers in the Mid-Nineteenth Century South: Family and Labor in the Graniteville (SC) Textile Mill, 1845–1880," *Labor History* 28 (summer 1987): 328–48. The classic work on the persistence of preindustrial culture among nineteenth-century industrial workers remains Herbert G. Gutman, "Work, Culture, and Society in Industrializing America, 1815–1920," *American Historical Review* 78 (June 1973): 531–88.

Edgefield or Barnwell. Employees and their families were sheltered in rows of Gothic-style cottages and boarding houses, all built and maintained by the company and all subject to Gregg's lengthy list of behavioral restrictions. "The maintenance of a moral character" was required of all who wished to work and dwell at Graniteville and Gregg did not hesitate to dismiss and evict those who failed to maintain such a standard. Two churches were also built by the company, as well as a school that required the attendance of all Graniteville residents between the ages of six and twelve. Most important, at least to Gregg, temperance in his village was rigidly enforced. The sale or use of alcohol was forbidden in Graniteville, not only by employees, but by all who dwelled in the village. Leases to town lots had temperance clauses inserted, with leaseholders also bound to forbid "any riotous proceedings that may tend to demoralize the village." Those found guilty of infractions were subject to fines and even forfeiture of their lease. As early as 1848, even before the factory commenced full operations, Graniteville possessed its own temperance society. The cause of abstinence was even advanced by the village landscaping, as a spring-fed fountain gushing in the courtyard before the mill provided Graniteville inhabitants with "a perpetual lecture in favor of cold water." According to Gregg, the strict moral accountability demanded by the Graniteville company elicited little, if any, protest. "The restraints above named are willingly acquiesced in by the people," he told New York journalist Freeman Hunt, "and we have one of the most moral, quiet, orderly, and busy places to be found any where."[34]

Not everyone, however, was convinced that Gregg's largesse produced such laudable results. A contributor to the *Edgefield Advertiser* professed deep dismay at the long hours that Graniteville operatives were "doomed to toil." The Edgefield factory seemed too willing to ape the labor grinding practiced in northern factories. The critic lamented the sight of "so many poor, puny looking children . . . there confined and breathing a polluted atmosphere for thirteen hours per day." How would such poor, ignorant creatures ever be able to "take an honorable position in society?" Better for Graniteville to follow the northern example of recently enacted ten-hour laws than to sacrifice the sons

34. *Hunt's Merchants' Magazine* 21 (December 1849): 672; *De Bow's Review* 8 (January 1850): 27–28; *Edgefield Advertiser*, July 19, 1848; September 6, 1848; September 13, 1848; February 27, 1850; John Springs to Andrew Baxter Springs, March 3, 1848, Springs Family Papers, SHC. Examples of temperance clauses in Graniteville leases can be found in Edgefield Deeds, Book FFF, 259–61, 335–36, 362–63, 391–92, 411–12, 432–34; Book GGG, 233–34, 264–66, 276–78, 433–34, 473–74.

and daughters of South Carolina "at the shrine of wealth and ambition." A former employee of the Graniteville weaving department likewise saw benefits in a ten-hour law. "There is no class of people as much oppressed by labor as the operatives in Cotton Factories," he declared. A ten-hour law in South Carolina would save "the poor female and orphan children" of Graniteville from being sentenced to toil "thirteen hours per day, from year to year." Others leery of Gregg's industrial revolution cast a wider net. In a letter to James Henry Hammond frequently cited by historians as de facto evidence of widespread anti-industrial sentiment in the Old South, Charleston banker Christopher Memminger expressed broader misgivings over Gregg's model of white wage labor in the South:

> I find an opinion gaining ground that slaves ought to be excluded from mechanical pursuits, and everything but agriculture, so as to have their places filled with whites; and ere long we will have a formidable party on this subject. The planters do not perceive how it affects their interest, and very frequently chime in with this cry. I think of our friend Gregg of Graniteville, with those who are agog about manufactures, without knowing it, are lending aid to this party, which is in truth, the only party from which danger to our Institutions is to be apprehended among us. Drive out negro mechanics and all sorts of operatives from our Cities, and who must take their place. The same men who make the cry in Northern Cities against the tyranny of Capital—and there as here would drive all before them all who interfere with them—and would soon raise hue and cry against the Negro, and be hot Abolitionists—and every one of those men would have a vote. In our Cities, we see the operation of these elements—and if the eyes of the planting community are opened, the danger may be averted. Fill Barnwell District with some hundred Lowellers, and how do you think they will vote at elections?[35]

But those voicing concern over the possibly adverse impact of Gregg and Graniteville were remarkably few and generally overwhelmed by those who saw a positive lesson for the South in the granite factory on Horse Creek. Three weeks after printing the story of "puny" children "breathing a polluted atmosphere" inside the mill, the *Edgefield Advertiser* reprinted observations made by

---

35. *Edgefield Advertiser,* November 21, 1850; August 31, 1854; September 28, 1854; Martin, "Advent of Gregg and Graniteville," 414.

the *Charleston Courier*, which emphasized Graniteville's handsome housing, free schooling, two churches, and the "bright eyes" of the factory operatives. "No one visiting Graniteville, and learning the excellent regulation by which it is governed, but must wish," the *Courier* believed, "that there were many more such Manufacturing communities in our State." Local politicians also rose to defend Graniteville by censuring those calling for ten-hour laws to regulate labor conditions. Edgefield senator James P. Carroll told a public meeting at Graniteville that such an act might suffice "for the pauper population of England," but not for the "Freeman or Republicans" that occupied Carolina cotton mills. Senate candidate William C. Moragne concurred. If Graniteville employees had a grievance, they should undertake "a friendly conference with the Directors of the Company, instead of applying to the Legislature to interfere."[36]

By a wide margin, observers approved of what they saw at Graniteville and the factory quickly became a source of immense pride for Edgefield District and the state. A writer for *De Bow's Review* went so far as to assert that both Old and New England could take a common lesson from Graniteville in cotton manufacturing, "especially if they have any regard for the physical, mental, moral, and social welfare of their operatives." Far from being seen as a threat to the Old South's way of life and "peculiar institutions," Graniteville was hailed as a welcome addition, both economically and socially. The factory became the shining example of the type of economic diversity demanded for years by reformers, who sought to reduce, and perhaps even eliminate, South Carolina's galling dependence on northern factories. Even more important was Graniteville's presumed benefit to South Carolina's landless white population, whose poverty and poor prospects for economic advancement created a haunting specter of home-grown class conflict among slaveholders, who saw in this nascent proletariat the possibility of social discontent and political mobocracy. "*It is this great upbearing of our masses that we are to fear,*" Charleston manufacturer James H. Taylor warned his fellow South Carolinians ominously, "*so far as our institutions are concerned.*" Taylor saw no better way to remedy the problem than by providing poor whites with remunerative, steady, and disciplined industrial employment. James Henry Hammond echoed similar sentiments. Ignoring the warning of his friend Christopher Memminger, Hammond told the South Carolina Institute in 1849 that by directly tying poor whites to cot-

36. *Edgefield Advertiser*, December 12, 1850 (reprinted from the *Charleston Courier*, December 2, 1850); August 31, 1854; September 9, 1854.

ton production through employment in southern textile mills, they would gain a self-interest in sustaining "the social institutions of the South." "The fact cannot be denied," Hammond told the Institute, "that property is more secure in our slave States, than it is at present in any other part of the world; and the constant and profitable employment of all classes among us, will increase rather than diminish that security."[37]

Eyewitnesses credited Graniteville with transforming what had been a backward, immoral, poverty-stricken part of the state into a prosperous, moral, and, most important, contented population. The *Edgefield Advertiser* reprinted a litany of favorable reports from other state newspapers, extolling the industry and morality of Graniteville's operatives. Local writers added identical declarations. "For the good that has been done already by means of this large manufacturing establishment, the District, aye the State, owe a debt of thanks to its enterprising founders." Of Graniteville's success, the *Edgefield Advertiser* contended that "there are few of any profession in this State, who will not rejoice at it." Nor would the accolades heaped on Graniteville be consigned to industrial boosters. The diary of planter David Gavin overflowed with polemics against the northern society, yet included hosannas to Gregg as well. "Wm Gregg is a great man," confided Gavin, who felt assured that Graniteville's success had demonstrated "how correct [Gregg] was in his precept and how good his example has been."[38]

In this light, the introduction of large-scale, free labor manufacturing into South Carolina seemed hardly revolutionary at all. Indeed, prosouthern pundits argued just the opposite. By diluting the possibility of class conflict among whites and striking a blow at the sway held by northern industrial interests, Graniteville seemed to strengthen, not threaten, the conservative regime of cotton and slavery. Gregg had pulled off the impressive task of making large-scale manufacturing palatable to southern spokesmen in his state. Furthermore, the favorable reception of his arguments in favor of wage labor advanced the Edgefield and Barnwell political economy to the very brink of capitalist society. While denying that wage labor should replace slavery, Gregg's experiment at Graniteville nevertheless gained a qualified acceptance of wage labor

37. *De Bow's Review* 8 (January 1850): 25; 27 (November 1859): 606; James Henry Hammond, *An Address Delivered Before the South-Carolina Institute at its First Annual Fair, on the 20th November, 1849* (Charleston, 1849), 34.

38. *Edgefield Advertiser*, October 5, 1854; January 18, 1854; David Gavin Diary, December 15, 1862, SHC.

in the agrarian landscape. And if Gregg neglected to point out the irony inherent in turning to free labor as a means of strengthening slavery, it mattered not. It was apparently lost on most planters as well.

In September 1841, Hamburg speculators Howard & Garmany bought the season's first bale of cotton from Edgefield planter John Mosely, paying ten and one-half cents per pound in money from a South Carolina bank. But rather than forwarding the bale to Charleston for export to New England or Europe, it was sent to John Bauskett at his Vaucluse factory. The following day, Bauskett returned the cotton to Hamburg in the form of a fine article of cloth that was immediately placed for sale on store shelves. It was a telling series of transactions. At perhaps no other time did the ideal political economy envisioned by southern agrarians come closer to becoming a reality. The hegemony of agriculture over commerce and manufactures seemed absolute. Cotton traders like Howard & Garmany would presumably be out of business without the staple production of surrounding agriculturists. Similarly, the existence of Vaucluse would be pointless without a steady diet of Carolina cotton to feed its machinery. Furthermore, the string of exchanges was entirely contained within the borders of South Carolina, requiring neither Georgia banks and factors, nor New England factories, to transform the cotton bale into the necessities of civilized life in Edgefield and Barnwell. By 1850, it appeared that the agrarian landscape of Edgefield and Barnwell had digested its doses of industrial and commercial capitalism with remarkably few unwanted effects.[39]

Appearances soon proved deceiving. Even as district agriculturists congratulated themselves on maintaining their economic sovereignty and position over commerce and industry, their limits of their hegemony were gradually being revealed. By the latter decades of the antebellum period, the merchant enclaves, railroad corporations, and cotton factories dotting Edgefield and Barnwell began exerting themselves in ways that had little effect on the predominance of cotton and slavery, but which would strike at the assumptions that had guided entrepreneurship and economic development in the agrarian landscape for generations. Merchants, corporations, and "men of capital" may have strengthened Edgefield and Barnwell's most cherished institutions, but a day for reckoning was soon forthcoming.

39. *Edgefield Advertiser,* September 16, 1841.

CHAPTER SIX

THE ELEVATION OF COMMERCE

THE MERCHANT'S ASCENT AND THE DIVERGENCE

OF TOWN AND COUNTRY

The pursuits of commerce must be liberalized, the commercial class must be elevated in public opinion to the rank in society which properly belongs to it.

MERCHANTS CONVENTION, Augusta, Georgia, October 1837

IF ONE NEEDED EVIDENCE of an agrarian majority in the landscape of western South Carolina, the election of 1840 provided ample proof. In May of that year, "a large and respectable" gathering met at Hamburg to promote William Henry Harrison for the presidency, as well as the Whig Party in the state at large. Some three hundred men attended the rally, led by Bank of Hamburg president Wyatt W. Starke, with participants including some of the leading merchants and bank stockholders in Hamburg and the district: Henry L. Jeffers, Thomas Kernaghan, William Garrett, and Jeremiah W. Stokes. Their platform accused Van Burenites of hereditary pretensions and stifling the republican principle of rotation in office. In their stead, Hamburg Whigs called for political reform and an end to the corruption and cronyism they associated with the Democratic Party. Unanimously resolved, the Hamburg assembly vowed to "use our influence in promoting the election of Gen. W. H. Harrison to the presidency" and bring about an end to the "deleterious effects" of the

Epigraph from *Minutes of the Proceedings of a Convention of Merchants and Others, Held in Augusta, Georgia, October 16, 1837; with an Address to the People of the South and South-Western States, relative to the establishment of a Direct Export and Import Trade with Foreign Countries* (Augusta, 1838), 8–9.

Democratic Party "upon the agricultural and mercantile interests of the country." Two months later, Whigs reconvened at Hamburg in search of suitable candidates for the state legislature. William Garrett, a planter and Bank of Hamburg director, and Andrew J. Hammond, the aristocratic grandson of Indian trader LeRoy Hammond, were chosen as state house candidates, while in the temporary Whig euphoria of that summer, Starke was brought out to challenge the congressional seat held by Francis W. Pickens.[1]

Edgefield Democrats quickly dashed Whig hopes for success, working both privately and publicly to smother the infant opposition party in its cradle. "If it can be done with delicacy," Democratic candidate James P. Carroll quietly confided the need "to throw cold water upon the Harrison Movement in Hamburg." Even a single Whig candidate, Carroll believed, could pose a threat to the Democratic Party in the district. James Henry Hammond declined an offer to attend the Whig rally in Hamburg, citing his preference for Van Buren and belittling their cause by suggesting that the meeting might be more profitably employed in campaigning for a new road across Horse Creek into Hamburg. "I would cheerfully give a hundred or two for [that] purpose," Hammond told the invitation committee. The columns of the *Edgefield Advertiser,* one of the upstate's most ardent Democratic and states' rights newspapers, chimed in with blunt denunciations of both the strength and platform of the Whig movement in Hamburg. "Not having talent enough themselves," the *Advertiser* accused the Hamburg Whigs of inflating their numbers with members from neighboring Augusta. "There was a large crowd," admitted the *Edgefield Advertiser,* "but the far larger part was from Georgia." The newspaper warned South Carolina Democrats not to be duped by the tricks of the Hamburg Whigs. "The South will not be dictated to by a Hamburg Convention," declared the *Advertiser,* "nor will we suffer [Harrison] to be *forced* upon us by the manoevers of a few *Bank men* who have ruined the country and wish to saddle the mischief upon the present Administration."[2]

---

1. *Edgefield Advertiser,* April 21, 1836; March 28, 1839; May 21, June 11, July 23, and September 17, 1840; John A. Chapman, *History of Edgefield County From the Earliest Settlements to 1897* (Newberry, S.C., 1897), 140–42; Orville Vernon Burton, *In My Father's House are Many Mansions: Family & Community in Edgefield, South Carolina* (Chapel Hill, 1985), 135–36; W. Edwin Hemphill, Clyde N. Wilson, et al., eds., *The Papers of John C. Calhoun,* 28 vols. (Columbia, 1959–2003), 15:327, 337.

2. James P. Carroll to James Henry Hammond, June 5, 1840, and James Henry Hammond to M. R. Smith, May 20, 1840, James Henry Hammond Papers, Library of Congress; *Edgefield Advertiser,* June 4, 1840.

The result of the campaign, if not foreordained, was certainly predictable. Even Starke, the Whig movement's local leader, saw the handwriting on the wall and quickly withdrew his candidacy for Congress. When the ballots were counted in October, the Whig defeat in Edgefield was absolute. Garrett and Hammond finished dead last in a field of thirteen. Of the twenty-two election boxes in the district, the two men carried only the Whig stronghold of Hamburg, while failing to earn even a single vote in several rural precincts. Statewide, election returns strongly paralleled the results in Edgefield District, with Whigs winning just one congressional seat and a mere fifteen of the 169 seats in the General Assembly. Though Whigs claimed some of South Carolina's wealthiest and most influential merchants and planter-entrepreneurs among their ranks, the election of 1840 made painfully clear the popular weakness of the party in state politics. By 1842, the Whig Party was dead and buried in South Carolina.[3]

Hamburg Whigs lost in large part because of their party's national platform. From the outset of the campaign, Democratic leaders harped on Whig support for a national bank, an institution much despised by upcountry agrarians, who still feared a "Hamiltonian" coalition of government and commercial interests. While Hamburg Whigs deliberately kept their platform vague, state and national party leaders frequently went on record in favor of an expanded government role in economic development, especially through internal improvements and a reconstituted national bank. The economic nationalism of the Whig platform made South Carolina Democrats blanch, seeing in it too much opportunity for enhancing federal influence in state affairs. With the nullification and "gag rule" controversies providing explicit reminders of the potential dangers of active government, Carolina agrarians flocked to the Democrats to defend them against the aristocracy and sundry "isms" that Whig merchants and planter-entrepreneurs seemed bent on introducing.[4]

But while the Whig defeat of 1840 demonstrated their decidedly limited popular influence in state and local politics, merchants in Edgefield and Barnwell nevertheless continued to increase their commercial sway. By 1854, no fewer than 170 mercantile and trade establishments could be found in the two

3. *Edgefield Advertiser*, September 24 and October 24, 1840; Hemphill et al., *Calhoun Papers*, 15:355. On the failure of the Whig Party in South Carolina, see Lacy K. Ford Jr., *Origins of Southern Radicalism: The South Carolina Upcountry, 1800–1860* (Oxford and New York, 1988), 160–75.

4. Ford, *Origins of Southern Radicalism*, 173–75.

TABLE 5. Value of Goods, Wares, and Merchandise Sold

YEAR	BARNWELL	EDGEFIELD
1853	$331,680	$581,200
1854	$367,700	$579,000
1855	$448,000	$518,950
1856	$420,400	$562,980
1857	$410,700	$575,630
1858	$442,005	$590,970
1859	$399,105	$599,200
1860	$461,300	$627,050

SOURCE: *Reports and Resolutions, 1853–1860.*

districts. While Edgefield saw its mercantile activities plateau during the 1850s, the amount of trade in Barnwell—the late bloomer of the two districts and main beneficiary of the Charleston and Hamburg railroad—posted impressive gains, with the business of its mercantile community increasing by almost 40 percent in the last eight years of the decade. By the final year of the antebellum era, the annual sales of Edgefield and Barnwell merchants surpassed $1 million (table 5).[5]

Regardless of their popular weakness, the merchant class in Edgefield and Barnwell demonstrated a growing influence during the latter decades of the antebellum era, particularly in persuading the state legislature to make the districts more attractive to commercial interests. As trade increased in the years following the rise of Hamburg and the completion of the railroad, merchants in Edgefield and Barnwell worked to improve the transaction of business in the districts. The focus of this activity revolved primarily around the subject of liquid capital, seeking ways to expand its supply and to encourage its employment in commercial activities. In doing so, merchants not only pursued an obvious desire to enhance the quantity and quality of business in the districts, but

5. *The Southern Business Directory and General Commercial Advertiser* (Charleston, 1854), 308, 311–12.

they also worked to gain special consideration for commercial capital from state government.

Undoubtedly, much of the change sought by merchants was motivated by self-interest. They stood to be the primary beneficiaries of local banking facilities or limited liability partnerships. Likewise, the desire to rid neighborhoods of itinerant peddlers would also redound to the benefit of established tradesmen by reducing competition. But while such efforts demonstrated sound business instincts, much of the language invoked by merchant interests to achieve these changes also cast them as patriotic and valued defenders of southern interests. Many of the mercantile petitions that wound their way to the state house manipulated sectional fears over economic subservience and the security of their "peculiar institutions." Whether such actions were cynical manipulation or honest patriotism depended largely upon the eye of the beholder. In either case, merchants and their supporters gained significant concessions by cleverly combining the interests of their class with those of their region. In the process, Edgefield and Barnwell witnessed the elevation of commerce within its agrarian landscape and its increased consideration by state legislators.

While parts of this commercial transformation garnered support from both merchants and agriculturists—albeit for different reasons—such would not prove the case with another aspect of the merchant's ascent, namely, the growth of towns in the districts. Although both town and country shared a dependence on King Cotton, the transformation of crossroads villages into commercial towns also demonstrated a growing rift between rural and urban dwellers. As mercantile interests came to dominate the economic, political, and social affairs of district towns, the patina of harmony between town and country would give way to mutual suspicion and even outright hostility between the two realms. And, with the achievement of corporate status, towns gradually worked to isolate themselves from the control and influence of the agrarian landscape.[6]

Along with their stores, shops, and factorage houses, the burgeoning new merchant class in Edgefield and Barnwell also brought cries for banking facilities into the Carolina interior. For most of the antebellum era, a circulating medium

6. David Goldfield argues that mutual reliance on cotton created "greater distinctions . . . between cities than between town and country" in the Old South. Goldfield, *Cotton Fields and Skyscrapers: Southern City and Region, 1607–1980* (Baton Rouge, 1982), 36.

of commercial exchange was scarce in both districts, as well as in the rest of the middle and upcountry. Lines of credit, though generally available, traveled a tenuous route from the interior to the factors and commission houses of Charleston or Savannah and were usually employed only by the larger interior planters. As for specie or reliable paper money, even the wealthiest district residents had trouble securing adequate supplies of cash prior to the 1830s. Even during the pre-1819 cotton boom, Abbeville planter Andrew Norris lamented the shortage of cash money or its equivalent. "In the part of the Country I live there is no chance of getting Bills of exchange nor even Post Notes," Norris told James Edward Calhoun. The depression ushered in by the Panic of 1819 made matters even worse. "Money is very scarce here," wrote Norris in 1823, nor could any be borrowed, since "one half of our inhabitants are fruitlessly engaged in the attempt almost constantly." The situation was made worse by the fact that what little currency circulated in the western districts came largely from Georgia banks. Not only were Georgia bills subject to heavy discounts in South Carolina—and occasionally refused outright—but they were not receivable by state tax collectors. Aggravating matters further, the most convenient source of South Carolina bank notes was the city of Augusta, whose bankers exchanged their notes for those of its neighboring state at yet another discount, further depreciating Georgia paper in the Carolina interior.[7]

Though inconvenient at times, the shortage of a reliable circulating medium was at least bearable to agrarians in Edgefield and Barnwell. Credit was generally available to those who desired it, albeit at a distance, and a planter's accounts could be settled annually after his cotton crop was sold, usually through the services of an urban cotton factor. In such a system, a planter's financial transactions were largely confined to a reconfiguration of credits and debits on a few ledger sheets, not a series of cash exchanges. Once the cotton crop was sold, outstanding accounts were settled and new ones opened. The bulk of a planter's purchasing activities was confined to this brief period of the

7. Ford, *Origins of Southern Radicalism*, 62–63; William W. Freehling, *Prelude to Civil War: The Nullification Controversy in South Carolina, 1816–1836* (New York, 1965; New York, 1968), 44–45; Andrew Norris to James Edward Calhoun, September 28, 1818; Andrew Norris to James Edward Calhoun, May 1, 1823; both in James Edward Calhoun Papers, SCL; "Petition of Sundry Inhabitants praying the establishment of a branch of the bank of the State of South Carolina to be established at Hamburgh in Edgefield District," Petitions, ND-2170 [ca. 1821]; "Petition of Sundry Citizens of the Town of Hamburg praying the establishment of a Branch Bank of the State of South Carolina at Hamburg," Petitions, 1830–72; both in General Assembly Papers, SCDAH.

agrarian calendar. And if a planter was fortunate enough to hold a balance in his favor, it generally existed as a credit on the books of his factor, not as a purse full of specie winding its way back into the interior.[8]

However, with the commercial expansion that followed the founding of Hamburg, convenient access to banking facilities and currency became a growing concern, especially to district merchants. Hamburg had not yet completed its first year of existence before agitation arose in the town for a bank, either a branch of the state's financial arm—the Bank of the State of South Carolina (BSSC)—or a newly chartered private institution. The legislature obliged with a bank charter in 1822, but subscriptions were inadequate to fulfill the capital requirements of the charter and the proposed bank failed to materialize. Undeterred as usual by his own disheveled finances, Henry Shultz briefly operated his own "Bank of Hamburg" during the 1820s, whose notes were backed largely by Shultz's Hamburg property. Within months of opening, however, Shultz suspended specie payment and within two years his bank faded into oblivion.[9]

Despite the growing demand to expand the money supply in the interior, South Carolina legislators were slow to authorize new banks or to expand existing institutions. Many state solons had little desire to charter competition to the BSSC, whose profits went into the state treasury. Nor was the BSSC keen to see the creation of inland rivals. Although begged repeatedly throughout the 1820s and 1830s for a branch bank, BSSC directors balked at the invitation and remained skeptical over "the capacity of [Hamburg] to sustain a Bank." Finally deciding to test the commercial waters, BSSC directors obliged Hamburg with an agency in 1831. Unfortunately for Hamburg merchants, it failed in the Panic of 1837 after its agent fell in arrears to the parent bank in Charleston, leaving BSSC officials to pursue a judgment on his bond in order to recoup their losses.[10]

8. Harold D. Woodman, *King Cotton and his Retainers: Financing and Marketing the Cotton Crop of the South, 1800–1925* (Lexington, Ky., 1968; Columbia, S.C., 1990), 30–48.

9. "Memorial of Henry Shultz to the Legislature at the Session of 1821," Petitions, 1821–29, General Assembly Papers, SCDAH; Charles G. Cordle, "The Bank of Hamburg, South Carolina," *Georgia Historical Quarterly* 23 (June 1939): 150–51.

10. Freehling, *Prelude to Civil War*, 46; Alfred Glaze Smith Jr., *Economic Readjustment of an Old Cotton State: South Carolina, 1820–1860* (Columbia, 1958), 195–98; "Report to the Senate. Bank of the State. November 1830," Miscellaneous Communications, 1830–10; "Report of the Prest. of the Bank of the State of SoCa on Loans made to corporations," Miscellaneous Communications, 1841–

However, commercial interests in the districts, and Hamburg in particular, continued in their persistent demands for a bank. In a market requiring tens of thousands of dollars a week to conduct its normal business, and considerably more during the fall cotton harvest, merchants repeatedly noted that a banking facility was "necessary to the successful prosecution of their commerce." In addition, they decried the worrisome influence of Georgia capital in Carolina commerce. Lacking a bank of their own, Hamburg merchants were forced to borrow funds from Augusta banks, which permitted "the monied capital of another State . . . to find active and profitable employment—and even regulate and controul all operations in [the] great staple of our country." Invoking the language of economic sovereignty, petitioners asserted that until a bank was established at Hamburg, "instead of becoming a Rival, she must dwindle into a mere appendage of Augusta, and become a warehouse for cotton & for groceries belonging to its merchants." Other memorials resorted to similar claims. If left dependent upon Augusta banks, "the Merchants of Hamburg are necessarily tributary to the Brokers and private Capitalists of the former place." Nor were merchants the only ones suffering from the situation, since Hamburg cotton buyers inevitably issued discounted Georgia currency to planters in payment for their crop. Thus, with no bank of their own, "the profits of business in Hamburg, are in a good degree divided with the Capitalists of another State, and the ultimate direction of its trade, made to depend chiefly on their will." It was a situation bound to continue, bank supporters argued, until "unsafe Bills of Foreign Banks" were replaced with "a currency regulated by our own laws and guarded and preserved by our own Citizens."[11]

Relief finally came in 1835, when the South Carolina General Assembly chartered the Bank of Hamburg, with a capital stock of $300,000. Unlike its predecessor of the previous decade, this Bank of Hamburg had no difficulty in meeting the capital requirements of its charter. The entire capital stock was

---

15; both in General Assembly Papers, SCDAH; J. Mauldin Lesesne, *The Bank of the State of South Carolina: A General and Political History* (Columbia, 1970), 133–34. For memorials seeking a Hamburg branch of the BSSC, see Petitions, ND-2154 through 2170, 1830–72; Presentments, 1822–12; all in General Assembly Papers, SCDAH.

11. Freehling, *Prelude to Civil War,* 45; Edgefield, *Carolinian,* January 30, 1830; "Petition of the Inhabitants of Hamburg praying the Establishment of a Bank at that place," Petitions, ND-2169; Petition of Citizens of Edgefield for the establishment of a branch of BSSC at Hamburg, Petitions, ND-2162 [1826]; "Memorial of H. Schultz and others for a Bank at Hamburg South Carolina," Petitions, ND-2625 [ca. 1835]; all in General Assembly Papers, SCDAH.

oversubscribed within days of opening its books, and by April 1836, wagons loaded with specie began arriving to guarantee the bank's paper emissions. For the remainder of the antebellum era, aside from brief suspensions following the Panics of 1837 and 1857, the Bank of Hamburg proved itself an exemplary institution, providing a sound circulating medium that sustained and considerably expanded the region's commerce. It proved lucrative to stockholders as well, paying dividends of between 6 and 12 percent annually. When the bank sought a renewal of its charter in 1852, its stockholders could justifiably claim that the Bank of Hamburg had been "of great service and utility, not only in furnishing commercial facilities to the merchants of the Town of Hamburg, but in promoting the agricultural and manufacturing interest and prosperity of that section of the State in which the said Bank is located."[12]

Observing the profitability of the Bank of Hamburg, Charleston banks finally took notice and moved into the area as well. The powerful Bank of Charleston set up an agency at Hamburg, while the Southwestern Railroad Bank located an agency of its own at Aiken. For Aikenites, the agency was somewhat of a disappointment, since, like Hamburg, they had also pushed hard for a branch of the BSSC for their town. Bank of Hamburg managers, however, frowned upon Charleston competition as much as they did that from Augusta. "I dislike to see any of the Ch[arle]st[o]n Banks striking their Agents about us," declared Bank of Hamburg cashier John J. Blackwood, who took unabashed pride after his institution "broke down the Agency sent here by the B[an]k of Ch[arle]st[o]n. I would like to keep all others away."[13]

Despite the services rendered to both merchant and planter interests by the Bank of Hamburg, agrarians in Edgefield and Barnwell remained decidedly ambivalent toward banks and banking. And in times of economic upheaval and

12. Cordle, "Bank of Hamburg," 151–53; *Edgefield Advertiser,* April 14, 1836; "Petition of the Stockholders of the Bank of Hamburg S. Ca. Praying a Renewal of their Charter," Petition, 1852–17, General Assembly Papers, SCDAH. For Bank of Hamburg dividends, see the *Edgefield Advertiser,* 1836–60, *passim,* and "Statement of Dividends received from the Bank of Hamburg So. Ca. [1837–1850]," Robert Latta Papers, SCL.

13. John J. Blackwood to John Springs, July 21, 1849, Springs Family Papers, SHC; "Memorial of Sundry Citizens of Barnwell and Edgefield, praying for the establishment of a Branch of the Bank of the State of South Carolina in the Town of Aiken," Petitions, 1838–19, General Assembly Papers, SCDAH; *Aiken Telegraph and Commercial Advertiser,* July 8, 1835; *Edgefield Advertiser,* November 4, 1841; James Gadsden to James Edward Calhoun, August 20, 184[?], James Gadsden Papers, SCL.

specie suspension, their ambivalence quickly evolved into outright hatred. Even before the Panic of 1837, Francis W. Pickens declared bitterly that "the whole Banking System is a fraud upon the world and *we must never* sustain it," adding the observation that "the capitalists of the non-slave holding states live by it." The Fourth of July celebration at the rural Edgefield District neighborhood of Meeting Street used even less uncertain terms to denounce the banks. "They have become swindling machines, managed by speculating gamblers," discounting notes at 7 percent and redeeming them with shin-plasters, while lending their specie out of state at twice the rate. A toast demanded that the legislature "annul their charters or inflict a sufficient penalty, to prevent such licentious fraud."[14]

Antibank sentiment bubbled over into the ensuing decades. James Henry Hammond spent much of the 1840s denouncing banks in general, and the BSSC in particular, seeing too many parallels between that institution's influence in state government and that formerly wielded by Nicholas Biddle's despised Bank of the United States in national affairs. Likewise, with its paper emissions encouraging a host of speculative schemes, the BSSC embodied to Hammond the "dangerously misguided notions of progress" running rampant in modern society. Nor was the threat less tangible because the bank customer was a planter. "When he becomes a borrower, even if it be to hold his produce, or to purchase lands and laborers," Hammond declared, "he becomes as much a speculator as the merchant or broker, and is entitled to no more indulgence." The Panic of 1857 brought forth yet another stream of antibank polemics, surpassing even those inspired by the economic disruptions of the late 1830s.[15]

But banks were in Edgefield and Barnwell to stay, as was the paper currency they circulated. After a customer of the *Edgefield Advertiser* paid for his subscription in despised "shin-plasters," the newspaper accepted the payment with a shrug. "Shin-plasters are the order of the day," admitted the editors, "all Bank notes now can lay claim to no more honorable title." But even discounted paper money was better than no money at all, and if "the exigencies of the times should constitute Cockle shells the circulating medium . . . we would receive

14. Francis W. Pickens to Richard Crallé, January 28, 1837, F. W. Pickens Papers, SCL; *Edgefield Advertiser*, July 20, 1837.

15. Drew Gilpin Faust, *James Henry Hammond and the Old South: A Design for Mastery* (Baton Rouge, 1982), 276–78; Clyde N. Wilson, ed., *Selections from the Letters and Speeches of the Hon. James H. Hammond, of South Carolina* (Spartanburg, S.C., 1978), 62; Ford, *Origins of Southern Radicalism*, 324–37; Lesesne, *Bank of the State*, 52–116.

Cockle shells as money." William Gregg made an even more succinct statement of the agrarian landscape's newfound dependence on banks. "Who is it that can say he is not a debtor to the banks?" Gregg asked in 1858. "Every man, who owes a village or country store account, is indirectly a debtor to the banks," he sagely observed. Being indebted to a local, rather than "foreign" institution may have been slightly more palatable, but the outcome was largely the same. Banks had become a fixture in the lives of planter and merchant alike in the districts, although the former remained far less resigned to the fact than the latter.[16]

Besides seeking the expansion of commercial capital, district mercantile interests also worked to gain special privilege for it through the authorization of limited liability partnerships. From 1837 to 1839, delegations from Edgefield and Barnwell joined those from across the South at a series of commercial conventions held at Augusta and Charleston. Spurred by the economic malaise of the late 1830s, attendees combated southern commercial dependence with a series of simplistic panaceas to cure their region's economic ills: diversified agriculture, increased investments in manufacturing and commerce, boycotts of northern goods, and, in particular, direct trade with Europe. The results were predictably disappointing. As one historian observed, the solutions put forward at the conventions amounted to "a combination of wishful thinking, Southern nationalism, and muddled economic reasoning." Lacking the capital requisite to undertake a region-wide diversification, as well as the willpower to shun foreign goods and credit, delegates achieved little in the way of reducing southern subservience to cotton and northern commerce.[17]

But in the aftermath of their convention at Augusta in October 1837, merchants scored a noteworthy success in gaining legislative acceptance for limited partnerships. It was an effort geared toward the needs of commerce, and more specifically, the needs of southern merchants. As chair of the convention's

16. *Edgefield Advertiser*, January 25, 1838; William Gregg, *Letter of William Gregg to Thornton Coleman, Esq., June 8th, 1858* (Charleston, 1858), 8.

17. Woodman, *King Cotton and His Retainers*, 139–53, quotation 149. For the specific activities of the commercial conventions, see *Minutes of the Proceedings of a Convention of Merchants and Others, Held in Augusta, Georgia, October 16, 1837* (Augusta, 1838); *Minutes of the Proceedings of the Second Convention of Merchants and Others, Held in Augusta, Georgia, April 2d, 1838* (Augusta, 1838); *Minutes of the Proceedings of the Third Commercial Convention, Held in Augusta, Georgia, in October, 1838* (Augusta, 1838); and *Proceedings of the Fourth Convention of Merchants and Others, Held in Charleston, S.C., April 15, 1839, For the Promotion of The Direct Trade* (Charleston, 1839).

reporting committee, George McDuffie expressed his optimistic belief that the southern states contained "a sufficiency of capital" to meet its needs, "if motives could be presented to give it proper direction." To meet this end, McDuffie argued that no measure would be as effective as "a law limiting the responsibility of copartners to the sums which they shall put into the partnership." Thus, planters and "men of fortune who have retired from business" could invest a portion of their surplus capital in new commercial concerns—"under the management of men of character and capacity"—without risking their entire fortunes. Not only would such a measure assure the public that the partnership's credit rested on "the substantial foundation of the capital paid in," but limiting liability would "effectually direct the capital and enterprize of our citizens into channels where it is so much wanted," that is, out of agriculture and into commerce. Convinced by their own argument, convention delegates returned home to memorialize their respective legislatures on the subject of limited partnerships.[18]

Led by SCC&RR superintendent Alexander Black, a delegation of Charlestonians presented a petition on the subject to the South Carolina legislature in December 1837. "With the intention therefore of emancipating ourselves, from our dependence upon the North," the petitioners asserted that the legalization of limited partnerships would be highly beneficial "for the encouragement of the Trade and Commerce of the State." Similar laws had been employed in Europe and many northern states for years, by which their commerce had benefited greatly. "If these States have experienced the advantage of this Law," the petitioners asked the General Assembly, "can any good reason be assigned why South Carolina and all the Southern & South Western States should not do likewise?" Apparently, however, some members of the legislature found "good reason" and objected to the bill and its provisions. Observing this opposition, the *Edgefield Advertiser*, which supported the measure, grew pessimistic over the bill's chance for success. "It contemplates the establishment of a new principle in our system," observed the newspaper, "and *may* lead to extremes of speculation and fraud." However, the bill found strong support from many influential house members, including Ker Boyce, the champion of commercial interests in South Carolina. After further debate, the legislature finally agreed to the request of the petitioners.[19]

18. *Convention Minutes, October 16, 1837*, 11–14, quotation 11.

19. "Memorial of the Committee appointed . . . by the late Convention of Merchants at Augusta . . . suggesting the expediency and necessity of a Law authorizing limited copartnerships,"

The new act authorized the use of limited partnerships "for the transaction of any mercantile, mechanical or manufacturing business," or for the transportation of passengers and cargo. Only banking and insurance concerns were excluded from employing this new arrangement. Under the provisions of the new law, limited partnerships consisted of a general partner or partners, who ran the business and were liable for all debts of the partnership, and one or more "special partners," who contributed "in actual cash payments" a sum of capital to the common stock of the partnership and who was liable only to the extent of this investment. To discourage abuses, additional clauses forbade special partners from withdrawing their capital under the guise of dividends or profits, and also to prevent either general or special partners from claiming a preference for themselves over outside creditors in cases of insolvency.[20]

Finding the new arrangement advantageous, a handful of Edgefield and Barnwell merchants soon after formed limited partnerships with local capitalists. Shortly after passage of the act, Augusta merchant George M. Newton invested $5,000 as a "special partner" in the Hamburg store of general merchant John O. B. Ford. Newton's infusion of capital helped to place Ford's business among the dominant general merchandise houses in Hamburg for most of the 1840s, until Ford sold out and relocated to New York City at the end of the decade. James M. C. Freeland and James A. Talbert likewise made use of the law, forming a limited partnership to operate a dry goods business in Edgefield. As general partner, Freeland ran the business, while Talbert, the special partner, contributed $3,666.66 to the joint venture.[21]

Although used to advantage by some, limited partnerships never became commonplace in the districts or the state. Few mercantile businesses operated on a scale that made limited partnerships particularly beneficial, while larger entrepreneurial endeavors preferred the corporate form of enterprise. On a regional note, limited partnerships failed to attract idle wealth into commerce and manufacturing because the act did nothing to rid the South of its chronic shortage of capital. Those touting the benefits of limited partnerships greatly overestimated the investment capital held by most planters. In practical terms,

Petitions, 1837–73, General Assembly Papers, SCDAH; *Edgefield Advertiser,* December 7 and 21, 1837.

20. *Statutes at Large,* VI: 578–81.

21. Edgefield Deeds, Book 48, 498; Book GGG, 297–98, 403, SCDAH; Credit Reports, South Carolina, vol. 9a (Edgefield), 61, R. G. Dun & Co. Collection, Baker Library, Harvard Business School; *Edgefield Advertiser,* March 11, 1852.

the limited liability granted to "special" partners meant little as long as the capital for investment did not exist.

But the legislature's authorization of limited partnerships still had symbolic, if not practical, significance. While doing nothing to create new capital, the acceptance of limited partnerships demonstrated growing statutory consideration for commercial capital in South Carolina. As the *Edgefield Advertiser* aptly noted, limited partnerships were indeed a "new principle" in the state's political economy, one that placed the state among many in the Union that authorized similar arrangements during the middle decades of the antebellum era. But while legal and business historians have argued that northern legislators employed limited partnerships in an attempt to curb the spread of big business by replacing corporations with a watered-down substitute, the impetus behind partnerships in South Carolina was just the opposite. William Gregg correctly deduced that the act authorizing limited partnerships "amounts to the same thing in substance, as a general act authorizing the issuing of charters of incorporation." Unlike its northern counterparts, limited partnerships in Edgefield and Barnwell were intended to expand, not constrict, the influence of associated capital in the agrarian landscape.[22]

While banks and limited partnerships improved the transaction of business in the districts, mercantile interests in Edgefield and Barnwell also labored to raise the reputation of their calling by taking aim at the ancient practice of hawking and peddling. Predating the arrival of settled merchants, hawkers and peddlers were among the earliest commercial agents to enter the Carolina backcountry. While never as prevalent in the South as in other parts of the nation, these itinerants nevertheless spread a plethora of urban-produced goods across remote regions of the state. In doing so, they simultaneously introduced portions of the rural population to the nascent market economy evolving in antebellum America. It was not an entirely welcome event. Besides the shiny trinkets filling their packs and wagons, peddlers also carried a tarnished reputation for devious and unscrupulous trading. As a catalyst in the commercial osmosis percolating through the agrarian landscape, the peddler frequently embodied the conflicting emotions felt toward a market economy. He introduced por-

22. Ronald E. Seavoy, *The Origins of the American Business Corporation, 1784–1855: Broadening the Concept of Public Service During Industrialization* (Westport, Conn., and London, 1982), 97–98; [William Gregg], *An Enquiry into the Propriety of Granting Charters of Incorporation for Manufacturing and Other Purposes, in South-Carolina* (Charleston, 1845), 3–4.

tions of the countryside to a world of affordable commodities and the delights of consumer culture. But his reputation for deceit and duplicity often externalized agrarian misgivings over the integrity of the commercial culture intruding into their landscape. It was this latter representation that created particular anxiety among merchants in Edgefield and Barnwell. Although transportation improvements and growing competition initiated the decline of the antebellum peddler, settled merchants undertook a concerted effort to hasten his demise. In taking aim at the itinerants in their midst, district merchants not only sought to discredit a source of economic competition, but also to enhance the reputation of their profession, as well as the place of commerce, within the agrarian landscape.[23]

Despite persistent—and largely successful—efforts to curtail the activities of hawkers and peddlers, Edgefield and Barnwell never completely purged themselves of this roving class of traders. Even into the 1850s, sundry types of itinerant merchants and tradesmen could still be found in the districts. A handful of Hamburg businesses, such as Elias & Co. and the dry goods and clothing concern of Abraham Levy, employed peddlers to expand their local customer base or to drum up business during dull periods of the trading year. In a few instances, established businessmen began their mercantile careers as peddlers before putting down roots and opening up their own stores. Hamburg hardware dealer Alfred B. Church started out as a tin peddler, while John Leigh came to South Carolina as a traveling daguerreotypist before marrying and settling in Edgefield as a respectable, if unsuccessful, carriage maker.[24]

---

23. The standard work on peddling and itinerancy in antebellum America remains Richardson Wright, *Hawkers & Walkers in Early America* (Philadelphia, 1927). On the peddler as a purveyor of market culture, see David Jaffee, "One of the Primitive Sort: Portrait Makers of the Rural North, 1760–1860," in *The Countryside in the Age of Capitalist Transformation,* ed. Steven Hahn and Jonathan Prude (Chapel Hill, 1985), 103–38; idem, "Peddlers of Progress and the Transformation of the Rural North, 1760–1860," *Journal of American History* 78 (September 1991): 511–35; and Jackson Lears, *Fables of Abundance: A Cultural History of Advertising in America* (New York, 1994), 63–74. For the South, see Lewis E. Atherton, "Itinerant Merchandising in the Ante-Bellum South," *Bulletin of the Business Historical Society* 19 (April 1945): 35–59, and Harold D. Woodman, "Itinerant Cotton Merchants of the Antebellum South," *Agricultural History* 40 (April 1966): 79–90. On the persistence of peddlers in the postbellum era, see Lu Ann Jones, "Gender, Race, and Itinerant Commerce in the Rural New South," *Journal of Southern History* 66 (May 2000): 297–320.

24. Credit Reports, South Carolina, vol. 9a (Edgefield), 37, 39, 41, 63; R. G. Dun & Co. Collection, Baker Library, Harvard Business School.

Far more prevalent, however, was the persistent image of hawkers and peddlers as foreign and unscrupulous characters, purveying wares of dubious quality through sharp trading and dishonest business ethics. Since colonial times, South Carolinians complained about "divers persons . . . who pay no tax towards the support of this government," yet traveled throughout the region trading rum, sugar, and other wares with slaves "to the great prejudice of the planters and their masters" as well as "the store-keepers and shop-keepers in this Province." More than a century later, the pages of the *Edgefield Advertiser* warned "our country friends" to be "on their guard against a set of itinerant lawbreakers, pack-pedlers" that frequented rural neighborhoods. Not only did these roving peddlers trade with slaves, but the *Advertiser* further reported that the goods they offered "have . . . in some instances, been found to be the cast off and infected furniture of a hospital, the wearer of which renders himself liable to many loathsome disorders." R. G. Dun agents, too, held no great regard for the peddlers they came across in Edgefield and Barnwell. "No use talking or writing ab[ou]t such men," one agent advised, "g[oo]d today, gone tomorrow."[25]

Indeed, antipathy toward hawkers and peddlers in antebellum South Carolina seemed particularly virulent in Edgefield and Barnwell. As early as 1797, the Edgefield Grand Jury presented "a Great Greivance that hawkers & Peddlers are suffered to Vend their Goods in this state to the Great Injury thereof." Protests covered a variety of accusations, but the majority related to the peddlers' detrimental impact on the business and reputation of settled merchants in the districts. Inhabitants in and around the village of Cambridge, along Edgefield District's boundary with Abbeville, complained that the mobility of peddlers allowed them to evade taxes on their merchandise, giving them "a great and improper advantage over the mercantile part of the community." A petition from Barnwell District likewise pointed out the ease with which peddlers avoided the tax on stock in trade. A peddler could easily carry $10,000 in goods into their district, paying only $50 for a license and then quickly dodge the tax collector by leaving before the January first collection date. Settled merchants in Barnwell, on the other hand, would have to pay a state tax of $75 on the same amount of goods. Even worse, peddlers tended to siphon off specie

25. *Statutes at Large*, III: 487; *Edgefield Advertiser*, March 15, 1854; Credit Reports, South Carolina, vol. 9a (Edgefield), 47, R. G. Dun & Co. Collection, Baker Library, Harvard Business School.

from the districts, delaying the payment of debts to local merchants and carrying "ready money . . . entirely out of the State, without scarcely a probability of its ever finding its way back again."[26]

To distance themselves from the unsavory reputation given to trade by itinerant vendors, as well as to tar the image of the peddler even further, settled merchants in Edgefield and Barnwell presented themselves as respected members of the community, chief among the peddlers' victims and who wished mainly to protect others from such artifice. Peddlers injured "those merchants who have established themselves in the community," noted a Barnwell petition to the General Assembly, "whose interests, whose feelings, and whose Capital, will remain with Carolina." Similarly, Edgefield merchants asserted that the interests of peddlers were "not at all identified with the interest of the community; they have no abiding place amongst us—they are floating members of Society, who drain the country of its Capital." Furthermore, settled merchants presented themselves as the defenders of district consumers, seeking to rid Edgefield and Barnwell of a class of businessmen that made its living by persuading naïve country folk to swap their honest cash for shoddy and superfluous wares. "From the nature of the occupation," warned an Edgefield petition, peddlers "are eminently calculated to impose on the Weak and unsuspecting part of the community." Opponents of hawking and peddling in Barnwell made similar claims. Peddlers "introduce and vend to our Citizens such Articles or Commodities, as are of the most inferior quality, and by cunning and artifice induce the inexperienced and unwary to purchase from them at prices even higher, than the same articles of much superior quality could be purchased from the Shopkeepers and established Merchants of the Country." The dichotomy presented by local merchants and their supporters was clear: peddlers

26. "Presentments of the Grand Jurors in Edgefield County," Presentments, 1797–98; "Petition of Sundry Inhabitants of the village of Cambridge and it vicinity, praying for further restrictions on Hawking and peddling," Petitions, 1820–40; "Petition of Sundry citizens of Barnwell district praying that the licenses on hawkers and pedlers may be increased," Petitions, 1831–156; "Petition of Sundry citizens of Barnwell District praying that the price of license for hawking and pedling may be increased," Petitions, ND-647; all in General Assembly Papers, SCDAH. Christopher Morris found similar complaints made by merchants in Vicksburg, Mississippi, against flatboat retailers who temporarily set up business on the city's waterfront. Morris, *Becoming Southern: The Evolution of a Way of Life, Warren County and Vicksburg, Mississippi, 1770–1860* (Oxford and New York, 1995), 122–23.

were equated with refuse and deception; established town and country merchants with quality and integrity.[27]

Early efforts to curtail hawking and peddling met with mixed results. Doubting the constitutionality of an outright ban on hawkers and peddlers, the General Assembly instead responded to the 1797 presentment of the Edgefield Grand Jury by increasing the state license on peddlers to $250. However, in 1820, a senate committee rejected an effort by several upcountry districts to force peddlers to purchase a license from each district in which they conducted business, rather than a single state license. The committee believed that the amendment "would have led to the total prohibition of Hawkers & Pedling within the state." Such an act could not be justified, "unless [the committee] should have adopted the opinion that such trading was injurious to the Community & should be forbidden: but they have seen no sufficient reason for such an opinion." In 1825 the legislature approved district peddling licenses, but the fee was dropped to $50.[28]

It was not until the 1830s, when Edgefield and Barnwell merchants and their supporters began casting peddlers as a threat to slavery, that the legislature took active measures toward the practical prohibition of hawking and peddling. "The persons generally employed in this sort of traffick are men from the North," explained an 1831 Barnwell petition to the General Assembly, "whose principles and whose feelings are adverse to us and our institutions." The Barnwellers asserted that "*our peculiar institutions* instead of being treated with respect, are dangerously and insidiously attacked by many persons engaged in the business of pedling." The citizens of Edgefield painted an even more disturbing picture of the "demoralizing influence" of peddlers on the local slave population. "By facilitating the means of concealment," peddlers were "often the transporters of inflammatory materials calculated to incite this portion of the population to deeds of Violence & attrocity at which the heart Sickens." Following close upon the heels of Denmark Vesey's thwarted Charleston

27. "Petition of Sundry citizens of Barnwell," Petitions, 1831–156; "Petition of Sundry Citizens of Abbeville & Edgefield districts, praying that the sum paid for licenses of Hawkers & Pedlars shall be increased," Petitions, ND-259; Petition of Sundry citizens of Barnwell District," Petitions, ND-647; all in General Assembly Papers, SCDAH.

28. *Statutes at Large*, V: 307–8; VI: 265–66; "Report of the Comtlee of Grievances on the Present. of the Grand Juries of Edgefield & Greenville Counties," Reports, 1797–19; "Report of the Judiciary Committee on petitions from sundry inhabitants . . . on the Subject of Hawking & Peddling," Reports, 1820–67; both in General Assembly Papers, SCDAH.

slave insurrection in 1822, as well as the bloodletting of Nat Turner's full-fledged slave rebellion in Virginia in 1831, such pleas met with a prompt and favorable response from state legislators. In 1831 the fee for a license to peddle was doubled to $100, with a peddler required to provide a $1,000 recognizance for himself and $500 each for two local free holders acting as sureties. Furthermore, during the time for which a license was granted, hawkers and peddlers were required to be on "good behaviour, and especially refrain from all violations of the laws of this State against trading with negroes—against seditious or inflammatory publications or conduct—against gaming—and against the retailing of spirituous liquors without license." Four years later, not satisfied with the prohibitions of the previous act, the citizens of Aiken demanded that the existing laws regarding hawking and peddling "will be so far amended as to *exclude* that class of persons from trading within our limits." Again, the legislature reacted with vigor and increased license fees on itinerants to $1,000 and raised the penalty for peddling without a license to $5,000.[29]

The General Assembly retreated somewhat from these extremes, however, which essentially prohibited all hawking and peddling in South Carolina, by both natives and outsiders. In 1843 license fees for peddlers were returned to $50. But the sole granting power was vested with district road commissioners, who could grant or reject an application as they saw fit. In addition, to protect the state's "institutions" from foreign influence, the legislature required that a license to peddle be granted only to applicants who had been citizens of the respective district for the preceding ten years and legally entitled to vote at the time of application. Thus, the act met the demands of both constituencies wishing to restrict itinerant traders. Slaveholders saw their chattel shielded from a potentially subversive and demoralizing influence, while merchants received protection against outside competition. Once given control over the granting of peddling licenses, district road commissioners exercised the authority but rarely. In Edgefield, for example, commissioners seldom issued more than one or two licenses in a given year.[30]

29. "Petition of Sundry citizens of Barnwell," Petitions, 1831–156; "Petition of Sundry Citizens of Abbeville & Edgefield districts," Petitions, ND-259; "A Petition of Sundry Citizens of Aiken with regard to Hawkers & Peddlers," Petitions, 1835–62; all in General Assembly Papers, SCDAH; *Statutes at Large*, VI: 433–34, 529.

30. *Statutes at Large*, XI: 283–84. From 1847 to 1860, the annual reports of the Commissioners of Roads and Bridges for Edgefield District were printed in the *Edgefield Advertiser* in October and November, which listed licenses issued by the board during the previous year.

But the campaign against hawking and peddling was more than just an effort by merchants in Edgefield and Barnwell to rid themselves of an economic rival. It was also a campaign for respectability. With their victory, district merchants saw their status as the legitimate intermediaries between producers and consumers in the districts enhanced, placing local stores and shops at the center of commerce in both districts. In doing so, the merchant class in Edgefield and Barnwell acquired a growing air of social respectability for themselves and their profession. Furthermore, by manipulating the growing anxiety over outside threats to slavery, merchants found themselves accepted as trusted lieutenants in the districts' defense of the institution from both internal and external threats. In 1856 the *Edgefield Advertiser* reminded its readers that peddlers were "destitute of character, as a general thing, and are bad persons to be tampering and trading with our slaves." The most effective method of countering them, the newspaper advised, was for district inhabitants to patronize the merchants residing among them. "Our merchants are men of responsibility and character, who are tax-payers and supporters of the State and her institutions." Was it proper for "skulking" peddlers to be brought into competition with the respectable merchant class of Edgefield? The *Edgefield Advertiser* thought not and felt confident "that every orderly well disposed person will concur with us."[31]

Banking enlarged commerce in the districts, limited partnerships made it less risky, and the forced decline of peddling gave it greater respectability. But the most visible impact of the merchant class in Edgefield and Barnwell was their role in town creation. Hamburg remained the most conspicuous urban presence in the districts, but town growth was by no means restricted to Henry Shultz's offspring on the Savannah. Signs of the trend were visible elsewhere. While remaining the centers of local justice, the villages of Barnwell and Edgefield gained concomitant influence as commercial centers, as a growing array of stores and trade establishments sprouted around their court house squares.

31. Atherton, "Itinerant Merchandising," 57–59; Jaffee, "Peddlers of Progress," 532–33; *Edgefield Advertiser*, July 9, 1856. In December 1859, in response to public pressure following John Brown's raid at Harpers Ferry, the General Assembly passed an even stricter act regulating the conduct of itinerant salesmen, which required peddlers to obtain licenses from state treasurers and swear not to "infringe or interfere with the laws and regulations . . . made for the government of slaves and free persons of color." *Statutes at Large*, XII: 656–57; Steven A. Channing, *Crisis of Fear: Secession in South Carolina* (New York, 1970), 52–53.

At the time of Hamburg's founding, the village of Barnwell was home to a wooden court house, a jail, and little else. Its somnambulant population of slightly more than one hundred persons stirred only during court weeks and sheriff's auctions. But by the 1840s, spurred in large part by the completion of the SCC&RR ten miles to the east, Barnwell Court House saw its population jump to 750 inhabitants, including a thriving mercantile community. By the 1850s, business directories counted no fewer than sixteen general merchants in Barnwell Court House, besides a tailor, druggist, and coach maker. Many of these businesses flourished. Fifteen years after first opening a merchant-tailor establishment in the town, J. C. Buckingham saw his annual volume of trade rise to $10,000. Merchant J. J. Ryan operated two successful stores in Barnwell District, one at the court house and the other at Blackville on the line of the railroad, both of which he stocked with goods purchased in Charleston, New York, and Boston. By the 1850s, Ryan's enterprises were valued at $20,000.[32]

Edgefield Court House likewise emerged during the second quarter of the nineteenth century as a commercial center of growing importance to its district. Like its court house sibling to the south, the village of Edgefield expanded to include a significant merchant population who were, in the words of one historian, "urban-oriented even when they were not urban dwellers." By the 1850s, the "neat little village" visited by Robert Mills in the 1820s had grown to include dry goods dealers, grocers, merchant tailors, carriage makers, shoe manufacturers, clothiers, jewelers, druggists, and a number of men involved in sundry professional practices. The prosperity of some made them among the most prominent merchants in the district. Marshall Frazier set up a store in 1850 and in just six years became the leading dry goods and grocery supplier in town. Edgefield native Budd C. Bryan apprenticed as a clerk before opening his own general store in the village in the 1840s. Within five years, Bryan increased his worth to more than $10,000 and enjoyed a reputation for being "as s[a]f[e] a Merc[han]t as in the Dist[rict]." George Penn was a leading general merchant for decades in Edgefield Court House before selling out to his son, Edmund. Although his business failed in the late 1840s, the younger Penn re-

32. Robert Mills, *Statistics of South Carolina, Including a View of its Natural, Civil, and Military History, General and Particular* (Charleston, 1826), 360; William Gilmore Simms, *The Geography of South Carolina* (Charleston, 1843), 36; *Southern Business Directory, 1854*, 308; Credit Reports, South Carolina, vol. 3 (Barnwell), 77 and 93, R. G. Dun & Co. Collection, Baker Library, Harvard Business School.

covered quickly and by the end of the antebellum period was selling more than $30,000 worth of goods annually.[33]

Town growth in the districts became especially visible along the line of the SCC&RR, revealing the particular synergy between the railroad and district merchants. Even before construction began, SCC&RR superintendent Alexander Black promised that "populous villages will spring up in healthy parts of the country, adjacent to the route," which would in turn attract the trade of surrounding neighborhoods. Black proved a worthy prophet. While Aiken was the most prominent example of the railroad's visible hand in town development, other, more spontaneous, commercial enclaves sprouted along the line as well, particularly in the vicinity of the railroad's frequent turnouts. Built as sidings to pass trains and collect freight and passengers, these turnouts numbered no less than thirty by 1837, with several developing into notable centers of local trade. Within a decade or two, railroad stops such as Williston found themselves "doing a flourishing Business in a mercantile way." In 1842 more than one hundred Barnwell residents petitioned for a public road to Graham's Turn-Out, a railroad depot that also contained two stores, a post office, an election box, and a muster ground. Graham's had become "a place of some considerable importance" in their neighborhood, explained the petitioners, "from whence there is a great deal of Cotton and other produce shipped, and goods and merchandise received." In the mid-1840s, William Seaborn Bamberg and two brothers set up business near the South Edisto River at Lowry's Turn-Out and soon after "took hold of its affairs." Like Graham's, Lowry's also became the focus of neighborhood commerce, largely at the expense of the older trading crossroads of Buford's Bridge, which the railroad had bypassed. Within several years, the Bamberg brothers subsequently applied their name to the town—and later, the county—that they helped spawn.[34]

33. Woodman, *King Cotton*, 326. I agree with Orville Vernon Burton's opinion that the urban orientation of village merchants was present in both the antebellum and postbellum South. See Burton, *In My Father's House Are Many Mansions: Family & Community in Edgefield, South Carolina* (Chapel Hill, 1985), 28, 344n. For descriptions of Edgefield Court House's merchant and professional population, see ibid., 28–29, and *Southern Business Directory, 1854*, 311; *Edgefield Advertiser*, April 26, 1856. On individual merchants, see Credit Reports, South Carolina, vol. 9a (Edgefield), 31, 67, and 70, R. G. Dun & Co. Collection, Baker Library, Harvard Business School.

34. *Report of a Special Committee Appointed by the Chamber of Commerce, To Inquire into the Cost, Revenue and Advantages of a Rail Road Communication Between the City of Charleston and the Towns of Hamburg and Augusta* (Charleston, 1828), 19–20; *Semi-Annual Report of the Direction of the South-*

The village of Blackville became an especially vivid example of the railroad's transforming influence on Barnwell District. Little more than a cluster of log houses and a dismal tavern when the railroad arrived, Blackville blossomed over the next two decades into one of the SCC&RR's busiest cotton receiving points between Charleston and Hamburg. While the town's antebellum population peaked at only 150, it seemed almost every Blackville resident was involved in the town's flourishing traffic in cotton and mercantile goods. By 1849, residents claimed at least a dozen stores and trade establishments, with combined sales reaching as much as $100,000 annually. Blackville citizens boasted that "there is no place in the Southern Country, of the same size, that can equal it in the amount of its annual business." Convinced of their town's potential, residents even changed its name, deciding that "Black-ville is exceedingly inappropriate for a town, which . . . will soon divest itself of all the characteristics of a village." They rechristened the town "Clinton," after General James Clinton of Revolutionary War fame, but recanted two years later and restored the original designation. In a burst of sectional patriotism, residents decided that their town was a more fitting monument to Alexander Black, a founding-father of the SCC&RR, rather than General Clinton, "a *Northerner,* and one to whom we are in no immediate and direct manner indebted, however useful his services may have been to the United States."[35]

As district commerce concentrated in these merchant enclaves, towns increasingly became "a place apart" from the plantations and farms in the agrarian landscape. Though both revolved around the production and marketing of agricultural staples, town and country nevertheless underwent a separation that

Carolina Canal and Rail Road Company, July 10, 1837 (Charleston, 1837), 4; *Southern Business Directory, 1854,* 308; Credit Reports, South Carolina, vol. 3 (Barnwell), *passim,* R. G. Dun & Co. Collection, Baker Library, Harvard Business School; "Petition of Sundry Citizens of Barnwell District praying that the Village of Williston be incorporated," Petitions, 1854–0102; "Petition for a Road in Barnwell District," Petitions, 1842–35; both in General Assembly Papers, SCDAH; M. M. Brabham, *A Family Sketch, and Else, or Buford's Bridge and its People* (Columbia, 1923), 107–9; Barnwell County Deeds, Book DDD, 27, SCDAH; N. Louise Bailey, Mary L. Morgan, and Carolyn R. Taylor, eds., *Biographical Directory of the South Carolina Senate, 1776–1985,* 3 vols. (Columbia, 1986), 1:91.

35. Samuel M. Derrick, *Centennial History of South Carolina Railroad* (Columbia, 1930), 96–97; *Southern Business Directory, 1854,* 308; Simms, *Geography of South Carolina,* 36; "Petition of the Citizens of 'Blackville,'" Petitions, 1849–63; "Petition of Sundry Citizens of the Town of Clinton and its Vicinity," Petitions, 1851–39; both in General Assembly Papers, SCDAH.

went beyond mere metaphor. As the historian David Carlton observed in the postbellum South Carolina piedmont, the greatest significance of this plethora of towns came in making their "businessmen *into* a class," with attitudes and goals distinct from the surrounding countryside. This separation became official with acts of incorporation granted by the General Assembly, which legally marked the transition from country village to municipality. The court house villages of Barnwell and Edgefield were the first in the districts to gain municipal status, receiving charters in 1829 and 1830, respectively. Hamburg and Aiken followed suit five years later. By 1860, no fewer than eight incorporated towns could be found in the districts, where none had existed a generation before.[36]

The primary consequence of these incorporations was the creation of town councils, consisting of an intendant and wardens invested with powers to enact by-laws and ordinances for the security and welfare of their respective towns. Resident merchants quickly became fixtures on town councils in the districts. From the time of Hamburg's incorporation on, merchants dominated the ranks of intendant and warden in their town. By the 1840s and 1850s, merchants such as Budd C. Bryan, E. B. Presley, Edmund Penn, and Abner Bushnell served at varying intervals on the Edgefield town council, while hotel proprietor Frank Schwartz, grocer Jacob Cook, and dry goods dealers Henry Wessels and John Mosely all served as wardens in Aiken during the same period.[37]

At first glance, advancement from country village to incorporated town

---

36. Morris, *Becoming Southern*, 114; David L. Carlton, *Mill and Town in South Carolina, 1880–1920* (Baton Rouge, 1982), 26. On town development and the urban process in the antebellum South, see Goldfield, *Cotton Fields and Skyscrapers*, 28–79; Morris, *Becoming Southern*, 103–31. The eight towns achieving incorporation were Barnwell Court House (1829), Edgefield Court House (1830), Hamburg (1835), Aiken (1835), Blackville/Clinton (1849), Bamberg (1855), Williston (1858), and Buford's Bridge (1859). *Statutes at Large*, VI: 398–400, 416–18, 530–32, 537–40; XI: 558; XII: 401, 612, 680. The village of Ninety Six, located just across the Edgefield District border in Abbeville District, became incorporated in 1861. *Statutes at Large*, XII: 779–82. Hamburg received an earlier corporate charter in 1827, but its provisions were apparently never put into effect. *Statutes at Large*, VI: 326–28.

37. Town council members were gleaned from the *Edgefield Advertiser*; petitions in the General Assembly Papers, SCDAH; Credit Reports, South Carolina, vols. 3 and 9a, *passim*, R. G. Dun & Co., Collection, Baker Library, Harvard Business School; Barnwell *Palmetto Sentinel*; and the *Charleston Courier*.

seemed a logical, almost natural, progression. However, in Edgefield and Barn-well districts, this was seldom the case. Corporate status for district towns was never an automatic occurrence, nor was such standing achieved without frequently overcoming vocal opposition. In essence, incorporation meant creating a new government, with authority over residents and visitors alike. Unlike business corporations, whose by-laws extended only to their shareholders, municipal corporations wielded their authority over all persons within their limits, whether resident or not, and who could not decline the obligations a municipality imposed upon its citizens. In addition, these new towns steadily worked to extend the powers granted in their initial charters, especially those relating to taxation of town residents and their property. When Henry Shultz attempted to preserve his control over Hamburg by blocking efforts to incorporate his town, he echoed the sentiments of all those leery of municipal authority. "The true policy should be to have as few restrictions on the inhabitants as possible," Shultz believed, "and by all means to avoid the burthens, taxes, &c. which these petty corporations are so fond of imposing." In an agrarian landscape long suspicious of government in general, and active government in particular, the creation of a municipal authority was seldom welcomed by rural segments of the population, particularly those who found themselves residing within or adjacent to these newly created town boundaries. A more unabashed example of a Hamiltonian combination of government and commercial interests could scarcely have been imagined.[38]

The movement for incorporation initiated with a desire to implant order on unruly elements—black and white—which growing villages seemed to attract all too frequently. Residents seeking a town charter for Barnwell Court House described the "many evils to the morals and good order of society," particularly intemperance, which thrived in their village for want of incorporation. Likewise, Aikenites found themselves "frequently disturbed by disorderly persons," who acted with impunity because village residents lacked the authority to enact municipal regulations. Inhabitants of Edgefield Court House provided

---

38. "Memorial of Henry Shultz, respecting the town of Hamburg, & his assignment to the State," Petitions, 1828–25, General Assembly Papers, SCDAH. On municipal corporations, see Joseph Stancliffe Davis, "Corporations in the American Colonies," in *Essays in the Earlier History of American Corporations*, 2 vols. (Cambridge, Mass., 1917), 1:49–74; William E. Nelson, *Americanization of the Common Law: The Impact of Legal Change on Massachusetts Society, 1760–1830* (Cambridge, Mass., 1975), 133–34; Seavoy, *Origins of the American Business Corporation*, 21–23.

a particularly detailed list of daily affronts contributing to "the great moral contamination of the young & unreflecting" in their village: gambling, trading with slaves, public intoxication, neglected streets, inattention to the cleanliness of backyard privies, "Riots & affrays" during public assemblies, and "profane swearing." In addition, an overly democratic spirit of enterprise had overrun the public square in Edgefield "with the stalls of cake sellers & other petty chopmen."[39]

Initial charters reflected these limited demands by confining town councils to largely regulatory powers. Entrusting oversight to elected town councils, the General Assembly vested them with the power to appoint constables, levy fines, and enact ordinances judged necessary "for preserving health, peace, order, and good government" within town boundaries. Municipal officials seldom hesitated to exercise their newfound authority and passed a steady stream of laws aimed at civilizing their new municipalities in both appearance and manner. Ordinances enacted in Edgefield Court House permitted the town council to incarcerate intoxicated slaves, as well as to fine persons that discharged firearms in public places or blocked sidewalks with their horses. The Edgefield council even considered hiring a public cowherd to prevent cattle from defecating in village streets. The Aiken town council levied $20 fines on persons engaging in horse racing or cock fighting within the corporate limits and forbade merchants and tradesmen from conducting business on the Sabbath. The council also appointed themselves as a health commission, with authority to inspect all town property and correct nuisances to the public health as they saw fit.[40]

These municipal powers quickly became a source of conflict between town councils seeking to expand their authority and those who wished it curtailed. As older towns grew and new ones came into existence, town councils and their supporters repeatedly sought to add new powers to their charters as well as to usurp those previously wielded by officials at the district level. In so doing, councils not only worked to soften the rough edges of their towns, but also to

39. "Petition of Sundry citizens of the Village of Barnwell praying for incorporation," Petitions, 1827–137; "Petition of the citizens of Aiken praying an act of Incorporation," Petitions, ND-3905 [ca. 1835]; "Petition of the inhabitants of the Village of Edgefield for a charter of incorporation," Petitions, ND-558 [ca. 1830]; all in General Assembly Papers, SCDAH.

40. *Statutes at Large*, VI: 398–400, 416–18; *Edgefield Advertiser*, May 25, 1837; June 15, 1837; June 17, 1841; October 9, 1850; *The Charter of the Town of Aiken, with the By-Laws and Ordinances, passed by the Town Council, June, 1860* (Charleston, 1860), 16, 19–21.

distance themselves from the cultural and political influence of the surrounding countryside.

Revenue for town treasuries became a particularly contentious issue. Town officials repeatedly made the observation that without adequate finances, their authority was essentially rendered null and void. Constables had to be paid. Streets needed to be kept in repair. The town council of Aiken echoed the sentiments of its sister towns in the districts by declaring that its "present financial resources . . . are totally incompetent to defray the expenses incidental to the maintenance of a proper municipal authority." Unable to meet their income requirements only by collecting fines, town councils pressed for alternatives to augment town coffers. The authority to tax within town boundaries became the most obvious method of raising revenue. In 1839 the legislature empowered the town council of Aiken to tax real estate within their corporate limits, as well as carriages kept for hire. Two years later, Aiken was authorized to extend its taxing powers to include slaves, free blacks, and the sale of merchandise. By 1851, Barnwell received the right to collect up to $300 per year in taxes on town property. Hamburg received especially generous tax privileges in its 1835 charter, granting authority to levy taxes on land, slaves, free blacks, stock in trade, drays, carts, horses, mules, hogs, "and in general on all and every kind of property, both real and personal, within the corporate limit." By the early 1850s, largely to cover municipal investments in two railroad companies, Hamburg taxes had expanded to include dogs, insurance agencies, sales at auction, and an additional impost on real and personal property to pay the interest on railroad bonds. By this time, even the relatively minuscule towns of Blackville and Williston had acquired extensive rights of taxation from the General Assembly.[41]

While the burdens of municipal taxes were largely confined to town residents, rural residents grew perturbed when towns sought to usurp revenue sources previously earmarked for the districts at large. In 1835, to help in "guarding more effectively against the abuses" of liquor dealers in the town of Edgefield, the state legislature granted the Edgefield town council the power to grant or refuse retail licenses in the town, a power previously held by district road commissioners. During the next few years, Edgefield also received sole

41. "Petition of the Town Council of Aiken in behalf of themselves and the Citizens, Praying for an amendment of the charter of the Town of Aiken," Petitions, 1841–36, General Assembly Papers; *Statutes at Large*, VI: 539; XI: 74, 180; XII: 104, 258, 323–24, 369–70, 549, 612–13.

power to grant licenses for taverns and billiard tables as well as permission to tax nine-pin allies. However, all fees still went to the road commissioners of Edgefield District. Believing themselves to be "a fitter depository of these powers than the Board of Commissioners of Roads," the town council not only petitioned to retain licensing authority within town limits, but also for the privilege of keeping the fees and taxes emanating therefrom. District road commissioners adamantly opposed the demand, claiming that a "large portion" of district road funds accrued from the town. If deprived of that revenue, commissioners warned that "it will be indispensable to resort to taxes upon the people" to construct and repair roads and bridges in the district. Those residing beyond town boundaries were even less enamored with the actions of the Edgefield council. Some 125 citizens of Edgefield District declared that giving road revenues to the town of Edgefield "is gross injustice, for it is nothing more nor less, than taxing the people of the District generally . . . to give to the Village to be used as they may wish."[42]

The rift between town and country that began over control of road funds became an outright chasm when councils succeeded in exempting town residents from district road levies. For generations, road upkeep had been the responsibility of all who resided within ten miles of a public highway, underscoring the reciprocal obligations of residents to the economic welfare of their neighbors. But town councils increasingly balked at this legal and cultural precedent, preferring that town hands focus their attention on the streets and alleys within corporate boundaries, not the roads of their rural neighbors. As early as 1834, the Barnwell town council asked to exempt town inhabitants from the authority of district road commissioners, believing that rural public roads were benefiting at the expense of street upkeep within their town. When Edgefield Court House made a similar request the following decade, road commissioners and rural inhabitants protested that "if the Village hands be taken from

---

42. "Memorial of the Town Council of Edgefield, praying an alteration of their charter," Petitions, ND-4058 [1835], General Assembly Papers, SCDAH; *Statutes at Large*, VI: 537; XI: 71, 181, 415. "Counter Petition of Certain citizens of Edgefield Village and of the district against a proposed amendment of the Charter in regard to keeping in repair of the Public Roads," Petitions, 1841–39; and "Petition of Sundry Citizens of Edgefield praying *repeal* of Sixth Section of 1847 Act granting village of Edgefield right to keep money arising from granting of licenses to retail liquors, keep Taverns, Billiard Tables, & 9-Pin alleys within the corporate limits," Petitions, 1848–57; both in General Assembly Papers, SCDAH. For other protests against the Edgefield town council, see Petitions, 1847–56, 57, and 58, General Assembly Papers, SCDAH.

these [public] roads . . . past experience has demonstrated, that these roads cannot be kept in adequate repair." But Edgefield town inhabitants countered that responsibility for both town streets and rural highways made the road duty required of them "considerably greater . . . than that required of other hands in the neighbor hood . . . and much more than their fair proportion." By the 1850s, the state legislature regularly granted town dwellers in Edgefield and Barnwell exemptions from road levies beyond their corporate limits, leaving rural residents to blame towns for the deterioration of their already sorrowful public roads. "Towns & Cities dont do their duty in keeping up the roads," groused members of the Beech Island Agricultural Club. "Every man living in Ease & Luxury in the citys gets his living out of the planter," the agriculturists asserted, "and they should build the roads & keep them up & not take our negros off the plantation to do it." An article in the *Edgefield Advertiser* complained that village merchants profited the most from good roads, yet contributed the least toward their upkeep. "The road worker—he is the merchant's customer," the newspaper added, too often found his proceeds eaten away by the added expense of hauling his crop over deteriorated highways. However, when the same road hand settles accounts with his merchant, "he finds the profit of the merchant includes this extra cost, and he is therefore indirectly taxed with this additional sum, which the merchant and season co-operating produced."[43]

District towns made other, even bolder, attempts to expand their influence, much to the alarm of agrarian residents in Edgefield and Barnwell. When Hamburg tried to expand its town limits by one-half mile in all directions in the early 1840s, farmers in the vicinity quickly spoke out against the endeavor, seeing "no propriety in subjecting farms, country settlements, & mill seats, to a heavy taxation for Town purposes." Also working to thwart the effort was the SCC&RR, which owned much of the land abutting Hamburg's southern boundary. Extending the town's limits, asserted the SCC&RR, would not only subject the railroad "to a most onerous corporation Tax," but also inflict "great inconvenience from corporate regulations." Defeated in the attempt to expand its borders, the Hamburg council was again thwarted several years later when

43. "The Petition of the Intendant and Wardens of the Village of Barnwell praying for an exemption from working on certain Roads," Petitions, 1834–9; "Counter Petition of Certain citizens of Edgefield district," Petitions, 1841–39; "Petition for Recharter of the Town of Edgefield," Petitions, 1853–101; all in General Assembly Papers, SCDAH; *Statutes at Large*, XII: 341, 548, 612, 613, 696; Proceedings of the Beach Island Agricultural Club, November 5, 1859, Records, Beech Island Farmers Club, 1846–1934, SCL; *Edgefield Advertiser*, November 5, 1845.

they sought to tax the capital stock of the Bank of Hamburg. Noting its service "in affording every facility to the Merchants of purchasing the produce of the Planters," Bank of Hamburg stockholders quickly convinced the legislature that a municipal tax upon bank stock would be an "unequal and unjust" burden. Farmers residing within the extensive town limits of Blackville scored another success by confining municipal property taxes to town lots and banning any tax upon slaves employed exclusively in agriculture.[44]

But victories against the steadily expanding power of town councils were few, and generally confined only to the most bald efforts to secure new sources of town revenue. More often than not, the state legislature continued to expand the authority and autonomy of district towns. In 1860 Barnwell succeeded in extending its corporate limits by one-quarter mile in all directions, despite strenuous opposition from those who viewed the annexation as "mercenary or at least purely financial in conception & purpose." Planter Laurence P. Hext sought unsuccessfully to halt the action by arguing that "it is not customary . . . to Extend the municipal regulations and authorities of a Town Council, over plantations and their appurtenances."[45]

With municipal power a growing presence in antebellum Edgefield and Barnwell, opponents of the trend not only worked to rein in town councils, but frequently tried to revoke existing town charters or block the enactment of new ones. The tiny villages of Williston and Ninety Six made repeated applications

44. "The Counter Petition of sundry Citizens of Hamburg against the amendment of its charter for incorporating said Town," Petitions, ND-5723 [ca. 1841]; Petition of SCC&RR "Praying they may not be embraced within the boundary Limits of Hamburg," Petitions, ND-3497 [ca. 1844]; "Petition from the Town Council and sundry Citizens of Hamburg—praying than an Act be passed authorizing said Town Council to impose a Tax on the Capital Stock of the Bank of Hamburg," Petitions, ND-5728 [1859]; "Counter Petition of Sundry Citizens of Hamburg So Ca Praying that the charter of said town be not amended," Petitions, ND-5717 [1859]; "Report of the Committee on Finance & Banks on the Memorial of the Town Council of Hamburg asking permission to tax the stock of the Bank of Hamburg and the counter memorial of the stockholders in said Bank," Reports, 1859–89; "Petition to the Legislature of So. Ca. for Amendment to the Charter of Blackville," Petitions, 1860–77; all in General Assembly Papers, SCDAH; *Statutes at Large*, XII: 783.

45. "Petition of Sundry Citizens of Barnwell, C.H. praying an amendment of their Charter and an extension of the limits of the same," Petitions, ND-5781 [ca. 1860]; "Petition of L. P. Hext praying that no change in the charter of the town of Barnwell be granted," Petitions, 1860–78; both in General Assembly Papers, SCDAH.

for a town charter before overcoming local opposition, which maintained "that to impose the onerous duties of an Incorporated Town upon so few residents . . . is oppressive." In 1849 some twenty-six Barnwell District residents opposed the renewal of Aiken's charter, complaining that its council enacted "frivolous, unnecessary and unequal ordinances," and burdened residents with taxes, "partial administration of justice and the inefficient operation of our Town & ordinances." Opponents of the recharter of Edgefield in 1853 declared themselves disgusted with the "arbitrary regulation" of town managers—particularly a recently enacted ban on liquor sales within town limits—and preferred instead to be again placed under "the general law of the country." Such a return to district authority would save town opponents from being subjected to "a petty power which is as unlawful and unjust in its operations as it is undignified and contemptible in its being."[46]

But like the merchant class that provided much of their population, towns had arrived to stay in Edgefield and Barnwell. Coupled with the creation of banks and limited partnerships, as well as the hastened demise of hawking and peddling, town development demonstrated the increasing influence of merchants in the districts. While none of the changes were inherently hostile to the interests of district agrarians, neither were they the offspring of a commercial class dragooned into submission by the numerical superiority of planters and yeomen. Through the efforts of the local mercantile community, commerce began to emerge from the subordinate position envisioned by agrarian theorists and practitioners in Edgefield and Barnwell. Admittedly, such efforts succeeded in part because mercantile practitioners could meld their economic aspirations with the political and social concerns of district agrarians. But they also prevailed in no small measure because of the persistence and cohesion demonstrated by merchants and their supporters. Far from assuming "a servile attitude towards the planters," merchants in Edgefield and Barnwell actively—and successfully—elevated the place of commerce in the agrarian landscape, seldom with the blessing of district planters and frequently over their vocal opposition. And, with the establishment of incorporated towns,

46. "Petition of Sundry Citizens of Barnwell praying that the Town of Williston be *Not* Incorporated," Petitions, 1854–101; "Petition of Sundry Citizens of the town of Aiken in Barnwell Dist., Praying that the charter of incorporation of said Town be not renewed," Petitions, ND-3902 [1849]; "Petition of Sundry citizens of Edgefield District, praying that the Town of Edgefield be not rechartered," Petitions, ND-3976 [1853]; all in General Assembly Papers, SCDAH.

merchants created their own particular realm in which the needs of commerce predominated.[47]

Nor would challengers to agrarian hegemony in Edgefield and Barnwell be confined to district merchants. Simultaneous to the contests between town and country, additional conflict arose between district residents and the SCC&RR. As the railroad corporation matured as a business entity in Edgefield and Barnwell, tensions developed between the company and the surrounding community, straining the shaky harmony between the two that existed following the railroad's completion in the 1830s. But unlike district merchants who transformed the practice and perception of commerce by tying their economic interests to the political concerns of area slaveholders, the SCC&RR would challenge the interests of both town and country residents in Edgefield and Barnwell.

47. Eugene D. Genovese, *The Political Economy of Slavery: Studies in the Economy and Society of the Slave South,* 2nd ed. (Middletown, Conn., 1989), 20. The growing position of the merchant and town in antebellum Edgefield and Barnwell predated a similar rise that would occur in the postbellum South Carolina interior. See Carlton, *Mill and Town,* 13–39; Lacy K. Ford Jr., "Rednecks and Merchants: Economic Development and Social Tensions in the South Carolina Upcountry, 1865–1900," *Journal of American History* 71 (September 1984): 294–318. For another example of the growing divisions between town and country in antebellum South Carolina, see Bruce William Eelman, "Progress and Community from Old South to New South: Spartanburg County, South Carolina, 1845–1880" (Ph.D. diss., University of Maryland, College Park, 2000), 58–69.

CHAPTER SEVEN

FROM INTRASTATE TO INTERSTATE

THE RAILROAD AND THE DEMISE OF *Publici Juris*

No corporation can be considered as well managed, where the public or individual interests are made paramount to that of the corporation.

TRISTRAM TUPPER, President, SCC&RR Company, 1841

IVESON L. BROOKES HATED the SCC&RR. The Baptist minister traced
the source of his animosity to the time of his marriage to Mrs. James J. Myers.
The wealthy Edgefield widow owned a sizable plantation near Hamburg,
through which the SCC&RR wished to pass its railroad. Company officials
dispatched superintendent Alexander Black to negotiate a free right-of-way
through the land. Mrs. Myers initially demurred, but she finally capitulated before Black's "artful persuasion" and "the interposition of some neighbors."
Shortly after the exchange, however, Mrs. Myers married the Reverend Brookes,
who, as the new owner of the property, decided to "interpose my veto" upon
the agreement until new arrangements for the right-of-way could be made
with the railroad. Upon meeting Brookes, Black condescendingly informed
him that all his neighbors had granted the SCC&RR a right-of-way without
charge, and implied that Brookes should follow their magnanimous example.
But Brookes cared little about the actions of his neighbors, retorting that "I did
not look upon the R.R. Company as entitled to deeds of charity, being already

Epigraph from *Semi-Annual Report to the Stockholders of the South-Carolina Canal and Rail-Road
Company. Made on the Third Monday of July, 19th, 1841* (Charleston, 1841), 4.

a Wealthy class of enterprising individuals well able to pay for a privilege thro the benefit of which their wealth was to be greatly enhanced." Brookes not only insisted that the SCC&RR pay for the privilege of passing through his land, but that the company also indemnify him against any damages the railroad might inflict. This time, it was Black who demurred. But after further discussion, Black apparently consented to Brookes's demands. All he asked in return from the good Reverend was that they postpone fixing the terms of settlement until after the railroad had been built, so that an assessment of damages could be more accurately ascertained. Once the road was completed, Black assured Brookes that he would call again and adjust everything to his satisfaction.[1]

Years passed, however, and Black never paid the promised call upon the Reverend Brookes. In the interim, Brookes found that "my apprehension of disadvantage from the passing of the R Road thro' my premises were correctly founded." Within a decade of its completion, the railroad, which Brookes neither wanted nor needed (he lived almost within sight of Hamburg), had become an exasperating nuisance. At the onset of construction, motley work gangs pillaged his timber, then compensated Brookes with "a torrent of abuses" after he attempted to interpose "measures of restraint" upon them. Once complete, the railroad subjected Brookes to further "inconveniences & dangers" by obstructing his wagon path and frightening his horses and livestock with its passing trains. In addition, his fields and woodlands along the line were exposed to "falling fires" spewed from steam engines. Most galling of all, however, the railroad came to constitute "a great thoroughfare for every rouguish negro that chooses to plunder my property to convey to market his ample booty!" Brookes accused neighborhood slaves, as well as those in the company's employ, of stealing his firewood and carrying it by cars to the railroad's depository at Hamburg ("doubtless within the knowledge & sanction of some . . . R.R. agents," Brookes believed). As long as the railroad existed, Brookes lamented that these evils "will be I suppose perpetual."[2]

The final straw came early in 1837, when construction gangs returned to Brookes's plantation to embank the railway. When Brookes confronted the contractor with a demand to halt "any further trespass until I should have things adjusted according to original intention," the "Irishman" snapped that he was backed by the SCC&RR and that "when he was ready should proceed

---

1. Iveson L. Brookes to Tristram Tupper, March 21, 1837, Iveson L. Brookes Papers, SCL.
2. Ibid.

regardless of my opposition." Exasperated, Brookes set forth his case to SCC&RR president Tristram Tupper and warned him that further attempts to appropriate his property for the "private use of a wealthy company of speculators will be considered as adding insult to Injury & treated accordingly." Writing Tupper in March, and again in August, Brookes reiterated the reasons why the railroad had become "a perpetual nuisance" to his plantation, and fixed the sum of $2,500 "as the least amount for which I feel willing to put up with the disadvantages of the R.R." When Tupper refused to make adequate restitution, Brookes engaged an attorney and ordered a lawsuit to be "immediately commenced against the Company." Unless the railroad agreed to his terms, Brookes warned Tupper that "the whole operations of the R R company on my premises must be considered a wanton trespass & be treated accordingly by me." The threatened suit was merely the opening broadside in Brookes's personal war with the SCC&RR. During the next two decades, Brookes would take the company to court again, this time for blocking the road between his farm and Hamburg. Between lawsuits, Brookes made continual protests against the railroad's detrimental influence on the discipline of his slaves and the safety of his horses and livestock.[3]

The Reverend Brookes may have been the most vocal critic of the railroad in Edgefield and Barnwell, but he was by no means alone in his misgivings. During the latter stages of the antebellum era, district residents joined Brookes in questioning whether the railroad remained a faithful servant of the public interest. In its first years of existence, the SCC&RR had been touted as a quasi-public enterprise whose aims and ambitions coincided with those of the community it served. The belief that the railroad was *publici juris* led to its securing eminent domain powers from the state, as well as acquiring a free right-of-way through most of Barnwell and Edgefield—the Reverend Brookes notwithstanding. However, in spite of the fascination railroading held in the two districts, an inchoate feeling also began to emerge among the local popu-

3. Brookes to Tupper, March 21, 1837; Iveson L. Brookes to Tristram Tupper, August, 1837; Tristram Tupper to Iveson L. Brookes, September 25, 1837; Iveson L. Brookes to Tristram Tupper, October 10, 1837; all in Iveson L. Brookes Papers, SCL. On Brookes's later confrontations with the railroad, see "Edgefield District, In Equity, June Term, 1854. Iveson L. Brookes, vs. The South Carolina Railroad"; John Bauskett to Iveson L. Brookes, May 28 and 30, 1853; Josias Keadle to Iveson L. Brookes, June 28, 1852; George B. Lythgoe to Iveson L. Brookes, March 20, 1848; "1858, R.R. act for stock killed"; H. T. Peake to Iveson L. Brookes, September 13, 1860; all in Iveson L. Brookes Papers, SCL.

lace that the railroad may not be an unquestioned blessing. To be sure, popular opinion, when backed by the state legislature and the courts, could still influence railroad policies. In cases of livestock killed by passing trains and the curtailment of Sunday operations, the company conceded to legal and social pressures and altered operations to conform with public demands. But as the antebellum era progressed, the railroad grew less responsive to public opinion. Whereas the first decade of railroad operations in Edgefield and Barnwell was marked by declarations of common interests between the SCC&RR and the community it served, by the 1850s the relationship was devolving into mutual mistrust and antagonism.

Changes within the SCC&RR heightened the discord. By the 1840s, the railroad had overcome most of its technical and managerial teething pains and undertook a concerted effort to realize the sanguine expectations of profits held by company stockholders. Besides securing rate increases and aggressively cutting costs, the company also entered into a merger with the Louisville, Cincinnati & Charleston Rail Road Company (LC&CRR). The latter corporation had been formed in the mid-1830s as an ambitious, but ill-conceived, attempt to construct a transmontane railroad from Charleston to the Ohio River. Despite enjoying enormous financial backing from the South Carolina legislature, the LC&CRR managed to build only a short, albeit lucrative, spur connecting Columbia with the SCC&RR at Branchville. With the blessing of the state legislature, the two railroads combined in 1844 to form the South Carolina Rail Road Company (SCRR).[4]

Besides greatly increasing the scope and income of the railroad, the formation of the SCRR also transformed the relationship between the corporation and the people of Edgefield and Barnwell. While company officers and stockholders justified their conduct as a legitimate effort "to realize for themselves a portion of the benefits resulting from this enterprize," many inhabitants of Edgefield and Barnwell saw such actions as "a breach of faith with the people." At the same time, confrontations between the SCRR and the public transformed the state's traditional role as disinterested arbiter between public and private interests. By sanctioning rate increases and route alterations by the

---

4. *Statutes at Large*, XI: 254–55, 295–96. On the history of the LC&CRR and formation of the SCRR, see Samuel Melanchthon Derrick, *Centennial History of South Carolina Railroad* (Columbia, 1930), 128–91; Ulrich Bonnell Phillips, *A History of Transportation in the Eastern Cotton Belt, To 1860* (New York, 1908; reprint, New York, 1968), 168–202; and Alfred Glaze Smith, *Economic Readjustment of an Old Cotton State, South Carolina, 1820–1860* (Columbia, 1958), 160–71.

SCRR, state legislators revealed a growing willingness to gratify the demands of corporate capital in antebellum South Carolina. And when the General Assembly permitted the SCRR to bypass Hamburg with a railroad bridge over the Savannah River into Augusta, legislators essentially abandoned their role as protector of intrastate interests in favor of the expanding interstate outlook of the railroad.[5]

Besides the Reverend Brookes, livestock owners in general residing near the railroad experienced the mixed blessings of having a railroad pass through one's neighborhood. Engines and cars exacted an alarming toll on cattle, horses, hogs, and other stock roving along the railroad's path. Brookes lost a horse to a SCRR locomotive after the unfortunate animal fell into a railroad cut near Aiken. Passing trains proved even more lethal to his cattle. In a single year, Brookes lost an ox, two milk cows, and a cow and calf to run-ins with locomotives and company hands. A. R. Danner lost four milk cows, a steer, and two heifers to SCRR engines and cars, which sped through his land at rates up to twenty-five miles per hour. Nor was the destruction of livestock the only adverse effect of steam trains on neighboring property. The whistle of a railroad engine cost Beech Island resident James M. Miller the sale of a friend's horse. After hearing the whistle, the horse "showed a great disposition to run," which revealed its lack of stamina to the customer. "If he blowed so in Feby.," the prospect asked, "what would he do in July?"[6]

These were not isolated events. As the SCRR expanded operations in the 1840s, it spent an ever increasing amount of time and money in settling claims for livestock lost to company trains. By 1850, collisions had become so frequent that SCRR officials sought to exculpate themselves by asserting that such accidents were an unavoidable consequence of railroad operations. As such, they argued that the company could not be held responsible "for the damage which ensues from the ordinary use of said engines and cars." State jurists, however,

---

5. *Semi-Annual Report of the Direction of the South-Carolina Canal and Rail-Road Company, To July, 1838* (Charleston, 1838), 3; "Petition of the Sundry Citizens of Barnwell, Lexington, & Orangeburgh Districts, protesting an increase in rates by the S.C.R.R.," Petitions, ND-3602 [1839], General Assembly Papers, SCDAH.

6. "1858, R.R. act for stock killed"; H. T. Peake to Iveson L. Brookes, September 13, 1860; both in Iveson L. Brookes Papers, SCL; *A. R. Danner v. The South Carolina Rail Road Company,* 38 S.C.L. (4 Richardson), at 329 (1850); James M. Miller to Benjamin C. Yancey, February 3, 1857, Benjamin Cudworth Yancey Papers, SHC. See also Derrick, *Centennial History,* 124–25.

dismissed the argument. "It would give dangerous license and indemnity to the destruction of cattle," observed Judge Edward Frost, "if the Company and its engineers were protected by a presumption of law, that the destruction is inevitable." In addition, Frost noted that the SCRR's own rule, which charged engineers for the value of livestock destroyed, was an admission by the company that "the destruction may be avoided with care." It was a decided victory for district agriculturists. Although accidents between trains and cattle would continue, it was restitution from the SCRR that became unavoidable. Between 1850 and 1855, the SCRR paid no less than $15,967.58 in compensation for stock mutilated and killed by company trains. In 1857 alone, the company disbursed $4,388.08 among state farmers for livestock lost to the railroad.[7]

If livestock suffered from normal railroad operations, so too, argued some, did the morals of the community. While planters and yeomen achieved a victory over the SCRR in defense of property values, other local residents struck a blow in defense of Christian morals by forcing the SCRR to curtail its Sunday operations. In its first years of service, the company ran trains on the Sabbath but rarely, albeit for fiscal rather than spiritual reasons. In 1838 Tristram Tupper expressed misgivings as to whether the income from Sunday trains would exceed the additional expenses and wages such policies would entail. However, his doubts became moot after the company accepted a mail contract from the federal government, which required the running of at least two trains on Sunday. To offset the cost of this arrangement, SCC&RR officials added passenger cars to mail trains, then later began running separate freight trains on the Sabbath as well. By 1849, a dismayed visitor to Aiken found the SCRR running its passenger and freight cars on Sunday the same as any other day. "How dreadful to see the command of God, 'to keep holy the sabbath' thus trampled upon," she lamented.[8]

7. *Danner v. SCRR*, at 338. Livestock losses were compiled from *Proceedings of the Stockholders of the South Carolina Railroad Company*, 1851 through 1856 (Charleston, 1851–56), and *Annual Reports of the President and Directors and the General Superintendent of the South Carolina Railroad Company, For the Year Ending December 31st, 1857* (Charleston, 1858). The precedent set forth in *Danner* for cattle losses was extended to the killing of horses by company trains in *Joseph Murray v. The South Carolina Railroad Company*, 44 S.C.L. (10 Richardson), at 227 (1857).

8. *Semi-Annual Report*, July 1838, 5–6; *Semi-Annual Report*, January 1939, 7–8; "Trip to Aiken S.C. with sister Wilder in the Spring of 1849," anonymous travel journal, SCL. See also Derrick, *Centennial History*, 126–27.

Nor was this traveler alone in her sentiments. As the business of the SCRR expanded in the 1840s and 1850s, a growing number of Edgefield and Barnwell residents took umbrage at the continual violation of the Sabbath by company trains. Both the law and religious custom required that "men of all occupations, desist from their weekly labors on the Sabbath," yet the company habitually carried on Sunday operations. Indeed, Sabbath violations by the SCRR were deemed particularly grievous, since the "the immense number of persons in its employ, enable it to exert a most injurious influence" upon the moral foundations of local communities. Not only did Sunday operations deny SCRR employees the traditional day of rest to restore body and spirit, but the "noise and bustle and business" of company trains disrupted Sabbath observances in every town and hamlet along their path. The state's Episcopal Church put forth a question to the SCRR that was undoubtedly shared by others: "Men in other pursuits, and under other institutions, under equal pressure of business, yield their pressing demands to the obligations of the moral law, and the corresponding influence of the public sentiment. Are Rail Roads to constitute the almost solitary exception?"[9]

Disappointed in their hopes that the SCRR would correct the evil by its own volition, Edgefield and Barnwell inhabitants lent their voices to a chorus of protests demanding the cessation of all Sunday railroad activity. In 1849 residents joined citizens from seven other districts in petitioning the legislature to instruct state proxies to obtain a suspension of all SCRR operations on the Sabbath. Although admittedly loath to interfere in the religious and business habits of its constituents, legislators nevertheless deemed it "in their proper sphere to promote the cause of social morals, and to encourage the due observance of the Sabbath." As a result, the assembly instructed state proxies "to use their best efforts" to obtain the petitioners' objective at the next annual meeting of the SCRR.[10]

9. "Memorial of Sundry Citizens . . . against Rail Road Operations on the Sabbath," Petitions, ND-4011, 4018, and 4025 [1849]; "Memorial of certain Citizens of Barnwell, praying the State to instruct her proxies in the Rail Road Company to procure a suspension of Rail Road operations on the Sabbath day," Petitions, ND-4019 and 1849–68; all in General Assembly Papers, SCDAH; *Proceedings of the Stockholders of the South-Carolina Railroad Company, 1854* (Charleston, 1854), 9, 11.

10. "Report of the Committee on the College, Education, & Religion on Sundry Memorials relating to Rail Road Operations on the Sabbath-day," Reports, 1849–140, General Assembly Papers, SCDAH.

Support also existed among SCRR stockholders for ending Sunday trains, but action on the matter progressed slowly. In February 1851, SCRR president Henry W. Conner told stockholders that conducting business on the Sabbath "was done in order to accommodate the public wants and requirements, as a matter of imperative necessity, and not of voluntary choice." Even if the company agreed to terminate Sunday service, Conner believed so many exceptions would have to be made that there would be "continual violations of the rule." But as protests against Sunday operations continued, SCRR directors gave greater consideration to proposals put forth to satisfy such demands. By 1853, stockholders agreed to suspend all Sunday labor on the SCRR, "except as regards the carrying of the public mail and other cases of emergency." The action seemed to strike a happy medium between the SCRR and the public. In 1856 stockholders passed a resolution in support of a decision to discontinue all Sunday freight traffic. The following year, the SCRR superintendent reported that except for two Sunday passenger and mail trains, "there is an entire cessation of business along the whole line on that day."[11]

In spite of recurrent complaints over the unwanted consequences of SCRR operations, Edgefield and Barnwell nevertheless evinced a fascination for railroads that bordered on a mania. A contemporary stranger to the districts might have supposed that the Reverend Brookes was the lone railroad critic in the area. The completion of the SCC&RR to Hamburg in 1833 touched off a frenzy for railroads in the districts that lasted throughout the antebellum period. By 1861, the state legislature had chartered no fewer than twelve companies to run railroads within or through the two districts. Most of the impetus behind this myriad of railroad schemes came from district towns. As early as the mid-1830s, the towns of Edgefield and Barnwell had each secured charters from the state legislature to construct railroad links with the SCC&RR. Merchants and planters in and around Edgefield Court House twice obtained railroad charters for their town, while their counterparts at Barnwell Court House secured no less than three railroad charters. Hamburg obtained four railroad charters in

11. *Proceedings of the Stockholders of the South-Carolina Rail Road Company, 1851* (Charleston, 1851), 22–23; *Proceedings of the Stockholders of the South-Carolina Rail Road Company, 1853* (Charleston, 1853), 14–17; *Proceedings of the Stockholders of the South-Carolina Rail Road Company, 1856* (Charleston, 1856), 7; *Annual Reports of the President and Directors and the General Superintendent of the South Carolina Railroad Company, For the Year Ending December 31, 1857* (Charleston, 1858), 8; Derrick, *Centennial History,* 217–19.

the 1850s alone, thanks to the efforts of bankers Hiram Hutchison, Jeremiah W. Stokes, and John J. Blackwood, as well as leading Hamburg merchants such as Charles Hammond, Andrew Burnside, Josiah Sibley, and Edward J. Buckmaster. Even smaller towns and villages in the districts displayed grandiose railroad ambitions. In the late 1850s, Barnwell District merchants George J. Priester, Leroy Wilson, and cousins Hampton and Josiah J. Brabham worked diligently to raise subscriptions for a railroad to connect Buford's Bridge with either the SCRR or the recently completed Charleston and Savannah Railroad.[12]

Edgefield District displayed a particular eagerness to add to its paltry railroad mileage, which amounted to only a short section of the SCC&RR near Hamburg. Besides efforts to build a road of their own, Edgefield residents also tried to persuade other South Carolina railroads to pass lines through their district. In 1836 merchants and planters in Edgefield Court House beseeched the LC&CRR to locate their route through the district, and appointed commissioners to gather stock subscriptions in order to sway company officials. In 1853, the state legislature authorized the Greenville and Columbia Railroad to construct a branch road through Edgefield to Aiken, which the *Edgefield Advertiser* promoted with vigor and the Edgefield town council encouraged with a $30,000 subscription. The following year, public meetings in Edgefield and Lexington districts promised large stock subscriptions to the Columbia and Hamburg Railroad, if the company would run its line through southern Edgefield.[13]

However, despite the undeniable enthusiasm manifested for each scheme, none of these efforts came to fruition. Except for a tiny section of the Greenville and Columbia Railroad that passed across the northern tip of Edgefield District, neither Edgefield nor Barnwell acquired any additional railroad mileage in the antebellum era. Bickering over route selection was a standard dilemma in most railroad development schemes, but lack of capital was the common denominator in every failure. While popular demand and public levies had been the primary requirements for traditional internal improve-

12. Railroads chartered in Edgefield and Barnwell included two Edgefield Rail Road Companies (1834, 1855), three Barnwell Rail Road Companies (1835, 1847, 1861), the Savannah River Valley Railroad Company (1852), the Branchville and Savannah Railroad Company (1853), the Wateree and Hamburg Railroad Company (1853), two Columbia and Hamburg Railroad Companies (1853, 1858), the People's Railroad Company (1859), and the Buford's Bridge Railroad Company (1861). *Statutes at Large*, VII: 396–404, 422–28; XI: 364–65, 475–81; XII: 171–72, 238–39, 248–52, 393–400, 593–95, 660–62, 761–62, 807–8.

13. *Edgefield Advertiser*, October 6, 1836; March 22, 1854; and *passim; Statutes at Large*, XII: 253.

ments like public highways, railroads needed breathtaking amounts of money. Organizers of the Hamburg-backed Savannah River Valley Railroad, for example, estimated a need for between $1.5 and $2 million to complete their proposed ninety-mile route from Hamburg to Anderson Court House. Even the shortest branch railroads sought capitalizations in excess of $100,000, and local railroad boosters repeatedly found themselves embarrassed by their inability to raise even relatively modest amounts of capital. In July 1847, Hamburg banker John J. Blackwood observed the excitement among the inhabitants of Edgefield Court House for a renewed railroad scheme to connect their town with Aiken. But when calls for subscriptions went out the following month, Blackwood found that the enthusiasm had "cooled down, since the $150,000 *promised,* added up to only $71,000 when the books were opened." Similar stories could be applied to almost every failed railroad venture in Edgefield, Barnwell, and beyond, as local residents came to realize that enthusiasm alone might build a public highway, but not a railroad. SCRR director Ker Boyce found that "if you will go to a Rail Road Meeting you will always hear the Loudest and Longest speech made by ones that have not a dollar to put in." After another Edgefield railroad project fell well short of its capital needs, an exasperated booster exclaimed, "Shall it always be said of us that we do things thus in Edgefield? . . . Shall it always be said of us, that we *plan* everything and *execute* nothing?" Nor did Edgefield's leading capitalists escape the dilemma. In a desperate bid to finance his capital-starved Savannah River railroad project, company president Hiram Hutchison authorized stockholders to pay installments with interest-bearing notes instead of specie, but to no avail. Although Edgefield and Barnwell were among the wealthiest districts in the state agriculturally, their inhabitants could not—or would not—convert their wealth into the investment capital necessary to construct a railroad of their own. Lacking access to urban venture capital and unable to secure fiscal succor from the General Assembly, corporate entrepreneurship in the districts succeeded only on a modest scale, if it succeeded at all.[14]

The desire to connect with the SCRR and participate in the transportation revolution of the era inspired a brief, but frantic, plank road mania in Edge-

14. "Memorial of the Sav. River Valley Railroad Co.," Petitions, 1853–57, General Assembly Papers, SCDAH; John J. Blackwood to John Springs, July 6, 1847 and August 25, 1847; both in Springs Family Papers, SHC; Ker Boyce to James Henry Hammond, October 25, 1847, James Henry Hammond Papers, Library of Congress; *Edgefield Advertiser,* July 20, 1853; December 7, 1853.

field and Barnwell during the early 1850s. Plank roads had become popular the previous decade in several northern states, especially New York, where inhabitants were attracted by the low cost and simple construction technique. Heavy wood planks were laid across stringers set in a roadbed. The result was a smooth surface over which heavy loads could be carried with relative ease and speed. Seen as inexpensive alternatives to railroads, plank roads were touted as an affordable, efficient means by which Edgefield and Barnwell could be integrated into larger markets and join the economic modernity ushered in by the railroad. Initially, the boom showed great promise. At least five plank road companies were chartered in the districts, backed by the boundless enthusiasm but limited capital of district merchants and their surrounding communities. Besides the advantage of cost, plank road boosters also presented "moral" considerations that underscored the growing ambivalence among district residents toward railroads in general and the SCRR in particular. Plank roads would not kill livestock or risk setting fires with sparks from passing locomotives. Furthermore, the capital invested in plank roads would remain within Edgefield and Barnwell. "The money expended for iron, Locomotives, Cars &c., for a Rail Road is sent out of the State," claimed a plank road enthusiast from Edgefield, "while the amount expended for a Plank Road, is retained in the State, and even in the District." Finally, it was argued that plank roads held certain democratic advantages, which would release the public from the economic and social restrictions dictated by railroad corporations:

> When completed, the [Plank] Road will be here, accessible to every one, benefitting every one, injuring no one, and can be at all times, and at all hours, by the poor and rich, old and young. It is somewhat different with Rail Roads. Having certain hours of departure, the traveller is obliged to leave, when the regulation of the Company requires, or he cannot travel at all . . . A Rail Road may pass through a man's plantation, and within twenty yards of his Gin House, and unless there is a station or turn out at the place, he may be compelled to wagon his Cotton, and other produce, five or six miles to a station . . . Turn-outs are expensive, and are only constructed where the wants of the Company require.[15]

15. *Edgefield Advertiser,* September 12 and 26, 1849. Charters were granted by the General Assembly to the Hamburg & Edgefield Plank Road Company (1849), the Graniteville Plank Road Company (1849), the Savannah Plank Road Company (1850), and the Central Plank Road Company (1850). *Statutes at Large,* XI: 583–87, 598–603; XII: 24, 322. A fifth company, the Edgefield &

Two roads were actually completed in Edgefield District. The Hamburg & Edgefield Plank Road Company connected the respective towns with a twenty-six-mile plank road by the mid-1850s, while a second company built a nine-mile stretch of plank road extending north from Edgefield to the rural crossroads of Cheatham. Unfortunately, the boom soon went bust. Wooden planks decayed rapidly, which subjected customers to jolting that exceeded that caused by the districts' notoriously poor public highways. Furthermore, the optimistic expectations of stockholders for profits soon proved illusory. Agriculturists patronized plank roads only when hauling loaded wagons to market, preferring dirt roads for their return and thus denying plank road companies a return toll. Investors soon found the value of their stock deteriorating as rapidly as the roads themselves. The constant need for replanking devoured income and reduced plank road stock to a fraction of its par value. Nor did plank road companies prove better than the SCRR in filling the obligations of public servant. Residents considered the failure of plank road companies as not only economic, but moral as well. "The spirit of their charter, if not the letter, places them in the attitude of a corporation bound to keep their work of public utility in complete condition, or else give it up entirely," wrote one irate patron of the Hamburg and Edgefield plank road. The dismal condition of the route left the company "morally and legally culpable; and if the evil progresses we do not see why their charter should not be held forfeited." By the end of the decade, the Hamburg & Edgefield Plank Road Company was insolvent, its president bankrupt, and its road a decayed ruin "too censurable to merit either patience of forbearance . . . It is the subject of every traveller's abuse."[16]

In contrast to the struggling railroad schemes of Edgefield and Barnwell, the SCC&RR seemed to be positively thriving. With the issue of an additional

Cheatham Plank Road Company, was authorized by Governor John L. Manning in 1853. *Edgefield Advertiser,* September 7, 1853; *Statutes at Large,* XII: 322. Evidence of the plank road mania in Edgefield and Barnwell is amply recorded in the pages of the *Edgefield Advertiser,* 1847–53, *passim.* On the national plank road boom of the 1840s and 1850s, see George Rogers Taylor, *The Transportation Revolution, 1815–1860* (New York, 1951, 1968), 29–31; John Majewski, Christopher Baer, and Daniel B. Klein, "Responding to Relative Decline: The Plank Road Boom of Antebellum New York," *Journal of Economic History* 53 (March 1993): 106–22.

16. *Edgefield Advertiser,* August 13, 1856; April 7, 1858; Credit Reports, South Carolina, vol. 9a (Edgefield), 37, 45, R. G. Dun & Co. Collection, Baker Library, Harvard Business School; *Statutes at Large,* XII: 804.

13,000 shares of stock during the 1830s, the SCC&RR expanded its capitalization from $700,000 to $2 million by the end of 1842. In that same year, the
Charleston and Hamburg route conveyed almost 34,000 passengers and more
than 92,000 bales of cotton, netting the company receipts totaling $349,834—
more than twice the amount earned just eight years earlier. On the eve of its
merger with the LC&CRR, the condition of the SCC&RR never seemed better. Income was up, expenses were down, and the railroad's only remaining debt
was its $100,000 loan from the state, for which the legislature had granted an
additional ten years to repay. Aside from its enviable financial position, the
SCC&RR also drew satisfaction from the public benefits its road provided.
Not only did the railroad provide a convenient means of conveying passengers
and freight, but land values advanced along the entire Charleston and Hamburg route. Even those who owned no land near the railroad frequently gained
employment or otherwise profited from the business of the road. By 1839, Tristram Tupper could tell his stockholders with gratification that "the opportunity for improvement has not been lost to the good citizens who have been re-
alising from our large expenditures."[17]

Indeed, it seemed that everyone was profiting from the "large expenditures"
of the SCC&RR—everyone, that is, except for company stockholders. Apart
from the knowledge that their enterprise proved a great advantage to the
public, SCC&RR stockholders found little remuneration from their sizable
investment. Dividends were minimal throughout the 1830s, with almost all income from receipts and stock installments used to offset unexpectedly high construction costs. Stockholder meetings became an annual forum for SCC&RR
officials to offer explanations for the lack of profits, followed by sanguine pre-
dictions that a steady stream of dividends would soon be in the offing. But the
situation showed little improvement in the following decade. From 1840 to
1842, the SCC&RR paid no dividends. Its successor, the SCRR, fared slightly
better. Between 1844 and 1849, the SCRR declared dividends as high as five and
two-thirds percent, but profits generally fell well short of this level. In 1847 and
1848, the SCRR paid its dividends in scrip instead of cash, and for the second
half of 1848 the company declared no dividend at all.[18]

17. Derrick, *Centennial History*, 120–21; *Semi-Annual Report*, July–December, 1838, 10; *Semi-
Annual Report*, July–December, 1842, Table D.

18. Derrick, *Centennial History*, 121; *Semi-Annual Reports*, 1835–42, *passim; Annual Report*, 1851,
Statement No. 4.

While much of this profit dilution could be blamed on managerial inexperience and the unexpectedly high cost of building and maintaining their railroad, some company officials felt the SCC&RR's dividend woes were inherent in its role as public servant. Most prominent in expressing this point of view was president Tristram Tupper, who held that his stockholders lacked remuneration in large part because their railroad served the public *too* well. In Tupper's opinion, his company had made "large outlays to accommodate the public, without looking for an adequate return." Company directors, first and foremost, needed to represent the interests of SCC&RR stockholders and not allow corporate policy "to be opened for debate, as a public measure." "This accounts for the ruin of so many Joint-stock Companies," explained Tupper. "Those who manage them, either attend too much to public opinion, or to their own interests opposed to that of the Company." Tupper's growing exasperation over his company's role as public servant began manifesting itself in corporate policy, which not only sought to reduce operating costs, but also demonstrated his growing distaste for the tenet of *publici juris.* Shortly after his election to office in 1837, Tupper placed notices in local newspapers soliciting aid in "preventing and detecting depredations on [SCC&RR] property," particularly the theft of timber, iron, nails, and other materials stored along the line of the road. In that same year, Tupper urged an increase in the acquisition of landed property by the SCC&RR, particularly woodlands, in order to provide a source of cheap fuel and render the railroad independent of local suppliers "who would otherwise take advantage of the continual demand for these articles." For a time, the railroad marketed surplus wood at bargain prices to area residents, but quit the practice after local woodcutters complained that they had been "compelled to almost abandon the business" by the SCC&RR's cut-rate prices. In his final piece of advice to stockholders upon his departure in 1843, Tupper again betrayed his mistrust of the public his railroad served by recommending that all deeds conveyed by the SCC&RR should include the stipulation "that in no instance the occupant should complain, that the ordinary business of the Company was a nuisance."[19]

19. *Edgefield Advertiser,* February 23, 1837; *Semi-Annual Report,* January–June, 1837, 5–6; *Semi-Annual Report,* July–December, 1842, 25; *Proceedings of a Meeting of the Stockholders of the South-Carolina Rail-Road Company, Held at the Hall of the S.W. Rail-Road Bank, Tuesday, November 17, 1846* (Charleston, 1846), 5–6; *Semi-Annual Report,* July–December, 1842, iii–iv, 12–16, quotations iv, 14, 15.

Tupper reserved his most strident entreaties for demanding an increase in passenger and freight rates. By the terms of the company's 1828 charter, SCC&RR rates were set at five cents per mile for passengers and thirty-five cents per hundred miles for each one hundred pounds of freight. But by the middle of 1836, dismayed SCC&RR officials noted that receipts continued to lag behind expenses due in large part to the inadequate fares "fixed by our Charter." Two years later, Tupper complained that "the rate of toll on this road is quite too low," particularly after taking into consideration the fact that the SCC&RR carried passengers and freight at up to half the cost of other overland conveyances with as much as a fourfold saving in time. Expressing his belief that the public was "sensible of all these advantages" provided by the railroad, Tupper averred that it would "readily yield to the circumstances which demands an increase of fare . . . by which means only its very heavy expenses can be sustained." As a result, in 1838 the railroad secured a fare increase from the General Assembly, which permitted an almost 50 percent advance in passenger and freight rates.[20]

Implementing the new rates in 1839 and 1840, the SCC&RR made considerable reductions in its corporate debts. But before the benefits of increased income could reach stockholders in the form of dividends, nervous directors ignored Tupper's warnings and reduced rates in an ill-conceived attempt to increase freight receipts diminished by the depression that followed the Panic of 1837. The action proved popular among planters, factors, and merchants (whom Tupper observed were "always represented in the meetings and the boards"), but did nothing to improve the fiscal state of the company. The rate cut was a violation of Tupper's guiding policy: stockholder interests should not be sacrificed for the benefit of public demand. Or, as Tupper explained, "we should not increase the outlay to transport 100,000 packages at 75 cents, each, making $75,000, when without a greater outlay, 75,000 packages, could be had at one dollar, making an equal sum of $75,000." Until greater dividends were realized, or company stock could be disposed by holders at par, Tupper urged that the SCC&RR "do nothing for the public, not required by the charter, to the cost of the Shareholder."[21]

However, while sound business practice, higher freight and passenger rates

20. *Statutes at Large*, VIII: 360, 484; *Semi-Annual Report*, January–June, 1836, 3–4; *Semi-Annual Report*, January–June 1838, 3; *Semi-Annual Report*, July–December, 1838, 10–11.

21. *Semi-Annual Report*, July–December, 1842, 13.

merited a hostile reaction from the riding public. Soon after the increase went into effect, a public gathering at Barnwell Court House declared that the measure was "a hardship, and should be repealed." The act infringed upon the compact between the company and the state, which granted the former certain privileges in return for specified duties performed on behalf of the latter. "Any departure from the terms of said compact," declared the Barnwell meeting, "is a violation of good faith, and should be resisted." Shortly after the above public meeting, more than two hundred Barnwell residents took their complaints to the state legislature and denounced the measure as "entirely gratuitous and unnecessary," which constituted "a breach of faith with the people":

> When the South Carolina Canal & Rail Road Company was incorporated, many privileges were granted to them by your Honorable Body, and the inhabitants of the Country through which the road was to pass, made relinquishments of their lands and prepared to submit to all the inconveniences which a great thorough fare like the Rail Road in their vicinity would occasion, with the expectation which was held out to them, that the convenience of the Road, Cheapness of travelling &c. would fully counterbalance any—nay exceed any injury they would receive from its passage.[22]

Not only was this "reasonable hope" in danger of going unfulfilled, but the memorialists asserted that higher rates threatened to "put it out of the power of a great many of them to use the Road as a general means of travelling." Unless the legislature repealed the increase, Barnwell residents feared the SCC&RR's success would "embolden them to further exactions, untill a passage on the road will amount to many as an entire prohibition."

But the legislature stood by the SCC&RR. Simply put, legislators explained, "the Company had been entirely mistaken" in estimating the cost of building and operating its railroad. Although the SCC&RR faithfully administered its road upon the terms contained in its charter, "it was found by experience that, at the same rates, the Road could not be made to yield any sufficient interest to warrant its continuance." With profits negated by unforeseen expenses, the result would have been either "a sacrifice ruinous to those inter-

---

22. *Edgefield Advertiser,* September 19, 1839; "Petition of citizens residing in Barnwell District, Praying *a Repeal of so much of the A.A. 1838* as authorized an Increase of the rates of Transportation on the Charleston & Hamburg Rail Road," Petitions, 1839–69, General Assembly Papers, SCDAH.

ested or a waste of the whole Capital invested." But more than SCC&RR stockholders stood to lose by a failure of the company. "It will be borne in mind too that the State had now become more closely linked with the matter," noted legislators, by its $100,000 loan to the SCC&RR. If the line continued to be unprofitable, it would not only spell the ruin of the SCC&RR, but result in a substantial loss to South Carolina taxpayers as well. "Under these circumstances," legislators explained, "it became necessary to choose between evils, and in preference to a Sacrifice of the interests involved in the Road, the State determined to allow an increase of the Tolls." Surely the petitioners could not wish "that the Road should be kept up by their Fellow Citizens without a commensurate benefit to all?"[23]

While all agreed that stockholders in the SCC&RR—and later the SCRR—should receive "a commensurate benefit" from their railroad, Edgefield and Barnwell residents never completely rid themselves of the notion that freight and passenger tolls were frequently less than equitable. "It is a subject of universal complaint," observed William Gregg, "that small matters receive so little attention by the agents of the Road that persons are deterred from shipping." Such sentiments were muted during the early 1840s, as competition from Savannah River steamboats and a general economic malaise prevented the railroad from charging the maximum rates permitted by its amended charter. However, complaints over railroad tolls reemerged later in the decade, after the SCRR initiated a sliding rate scale that favored passengers and freight traveling up the railroad from Charleston, particularly interstate cargo passing the entire line to Hamburg and into neighboring Georgia. To many in Edgefield and Barnwell, the SCRR's encouragement of interstate freight demonstrated a decided bias in favor of out-of-state customers over those at home, an action decidedly at odds with the tenets of economic sovereignty. "We cannot see the propriety or the *justice* of reducing the fare in favor of travel to the upper regions of Georgia," exclaimed the *Edgefield Advertiser*, "and not likewise reduce it to encourage travel to the upper parts of our own State." Upcountry hay growers likewise languished under the SCRR's rate system, with director William Gregg noting in 1847 that "the Columbia & Hamburg stables were

23. "Report of the Com. of Ways & Means on the Petition of the Citizens of Barnwell & Orangeburg, praying a Repeal of the act authorizing the South Carolina Canal & Rail Road Company to increase their rates and on the Bill to Repeal the said Act," Reports, 1839–76, General Assembly Papers, SCDAH.

supplied by the cheap rate of freight with Eastern Hay" imported through Charleston. A spokesman for Edgefield's stoneware makers, signing himself "One of the People," called SCRR rate schedules a "great obstacle to Southern industry and Southern independence." "So long as freight is cheaper from New York than from Aiken," Edgefield potters could not hope to compete with northern rivals. As a result, Charleston would remain a market for northern produce instead of home manufactures, and "One of the People" demanded that the state legislature stop the SCRR from stifling "the growing interests of the State by what is nearly akin to a restrictive Tariff."[24]

But the state had no interest in forcing a reduction in SCRR rate schedules. On the contrary, legislators had become a deeply interested partner in the SCRR's drive for profitability. Besides its $100,000 loan to the SCC&RR, the state legislature had also guaranteed $2 million in LC&CRR bonds to support the fledgling company. When the two railroads formed the SCRR in 1844, the successor company found itself indebted to the state of South Carolina to the tune of almost $2.5 million in principal and interest. While SCRR directors and stockholders seemed unconcerned about the debt and its repayment, the subject quickly became a source of understandable anxiety to the General Assembly, and both houses soon pressured the new company to repay its obligations to the state. In particular, legislators demanded that the SCRR expand its cost-cutting efforts in order to increase company profits. In a joint resolution passed in December 1844, the legislature declared that "as a large Stockholder, and as otherwise under liabilities for the South-Carolina Rail-Road to a large amount," the state of South Carolina possessed a deep interest in all measures that would "promote its prosperity." As such, both the state and the SCRR would benefit from any measure "that will reduce the expenses of traveling and freight on said Road."[25]

Bypassing the issue of freight rates, the legislature instead turned its attention to Hamburg and the "heavy charges on produce, goods and passengers" incurred in crossing the Savannah River from the SCRR terminus into Augusta. This costly and time-consuming bottleneck proved a particular barrier

24. Derrick, *Centennial History*, 216–17; William Gregg to James Henry Hammond, November 17, 1847, James Henry Hammond Papers, Library of Congress; *Edgefield Advertiser*, June 20, 1849; May 13, 1852.

25. Derrick, *Centennial History*, 164–65, 204–5; *Annual Report*, February 1845, 4–5; "Resolutions instructing Commrs. appointed to represent the State in the S.C. Rail Road Co." Resolutions, 1844–32, General Assembly Papers, SCDAH.

to the efficient operation of the railroad. As such, representatives deemed "the removal, or considerable reduction" of this obstacle to be "of great public importance" and should "engage the early decided action of the South-Carolina Rail-Road Company and its Directors." At the February 1845 annual meeting of SCRR stockholders, state commissioners advised the company that the passage of a track across the Savannah River at Augusta was absolutely necessary "to effect the reduction of expenses . . . on trading, produce, & goods."[26]

The SCRR directorate was well aware of the situation. Although the Hamburg railroad was originally conceived as a means of strengthening the economic sovereignty of South Carolina, company officials gradually realized that a narrowly intrastate outlook placed detrimental restrictions on the business of their railroad. Despite the sanguine faith among generations of Edgefield and Barnwell residents in the virtue of mitigating the presence of "foreign" commerce in local economies, the South Carolina interior simply could not supply the cotton and freight necessary for the profitable operation of the Charleston and Hamburg line. The remedy for this situation became apparent when SCRR officials looked across the Savannah River and observed the progress made by the Georgia Railroad and the Western & Atlantic Railroad in expanding the Augusta hinterlands westward across Georgia and into Tennessee and Alabama. By the mid-1840s, SCRR officials estimated that Georgia railroads carried more than 100,000 bales of cotton into Augusta, almost all of which found its way to the city of Savannah. Seeing the profits from carrying southwestern cotton pass tantalizingly before their eyes, SCRR president James Gadsden found himself "deeply impressed with the importance of removing all existing interruptions to a free intercourse between the Carolina and Georgia sides of the Savannah River." In short, in order to survive and thrive, the SCRR needed to adopt an interstate business philosophy and to convince the General Assembly to do the same.[27]

26. *Annual Report,* February 1845, 4–5; "Report of the Commissioners appointed to represent the State in the meetings of the So Carolina Rail Road Company & the So. Western Rail Road Bank," Misc. Communications, ND-169 [1845], General Assembly Papers, SCDAH.

27. *Reports by the President of the So. Ca. Rail Road Company, and of A Committee of Seven Appointed by the Stockholders, on the Change of Location of the Present Depot, and Work Shops on Mary and Line Streets, with the Advantages, Objections, and Probable Cost of Each New Location Suggested. Also, The Engineer's Report upon Inclined Plane, &c.* (Charleston, 1846), 20–21. On the growing interstate perspective of the SCC&RR and SCRR, see *Semi-Annual Reports,* July–December, 1836, 9–10; January–June, 1840, 10; July–December, 1840, 6–7; January–June, 1843, 9–13; *Annual Report,*

Since its inception, the SCRR had always maintained something of an interstate outlook. Charleston boosters who had promoted and backed the original scheme had their eyes fixed on the rich cotton hinterlands of Augusta. Indeed, capturing this trade for the city of Charleston had been the railroad's initial raison d'être, a goal that even overshadowed interest in the potential for profits that might be earned by the railroad. But Charleston's interstate vision had been grounded in the tenets of economic sovereignty. The economic benefits provided by the railroad were intended to build up Charleston and Hamburg at the expense of Savannah and Augusta. They were not intended to be reciprocal. Nervous residents of Augusta and Savannah had understood this while the Charleston-to-Hamburg railroad was still in its planning stages. But the interstate outlook put forth now by the SCRR made no such distinctions. Its focus was on the profit margin of the company, regardless of the effects, positive or negative, upon either South Carolina or Georgia.[28]

Before it could attain this goal, however, the SCRR needed to overcome the long-standing localism existing on both sides of the Savannah River. More specifically, the SCRR confronted the tradition of economic sovereignty head-on in the form of the Augusta Bridge. Spanning the Savannah River between Hamburg and Augusta, the bridge had remained the primary means of communication between the two towns since its construction by Henry Shultz in the mid-1810s. After Shultz lost the bridge in the Panic of 1819, it passed through the hands of several owners before winding up in the possession of the city of Augusta in 1840. As the new owner and franchise holder, the Augusta city council repeatedly exercised its chartered privilege to block the construction of any rival bridge in the vicinity, all the while collecting a lucrative annual income in bridge tolls. When the state legislature urged a connection with Augusta, a committee of the SCRR offered the Augusta city council $60,000 to purchase one-half of the bridge, with the stipulations that passage should be free and the bridge kept up at the joint expense of the city and railroad. The council promptly declined this and other offers and negotiations over the Augusta Bridge terminated soon after. Augusta leaders had no intention of aban-

1844, 21. On antebellum railroad development in Georgia, see Phillips, *History of Transportation*, 221–334, and Milton Sydney Heath, *Constructive Liberalism: The Role of the State in Economic Development in Georgia to 1860* (Cambridge, Mass., 1954), 254–92.

28. Derrick, *Centennial History*, 1–19; Phillips, *History of Transportation*, 136–40.

doning their lucrative bridge monopoly or making it easier for the SCRR to carry their cotton trade away to Charleston.[29]

Nor was the rival town of Hamburg particularly eager to alter this state of affairs. Although Henry Shultz had spent the remainder of his life challenging the legitimacy of Augusta's title to "his" bridge, the Augusta Bridge monopoly was not entirely detrimental to Hamburg interests. Bridge tolls may have made it difficult for Hamburg merchants and factors to secure Georgia customers, but the continuation of the bridge monopoly also maintained Hamburg's status as the SCRR's western terminus. Indeed, by the 1840s, the SCRR depository had become Hamburg's economic raison d'être. The town had been dealt a series of economic setbacks during the decade. In 1847 the city of Augusta completed an impressive canal that not only harnessed the waterpower of the Savannah River, but also siphoned off much of the upriver cotton traffic previously collected by its cross-river rival. By 1849, local sources estimated that the canal had diverted from 10,000 to 12,000 bales of South Carolina cotton to Augusta, leaving Hamburg residents in fear "that in a year or two, all Carolina Cotton which passes down the River to this Town, will find a market in Augusta, and which, when once fully diverted from this market, we believe it will be extremely difficult to regain." In addition, construction of the state-supported Greenville and Columbia Railroad was under way in the South Carolina piedmont and progressing rapidly by the late 1840s, which threatened to further rechannel the flow of upcountry cotton away from Hamburg. By the end of the decade, a Charleston correspondent predicted that the canal and railroad would combine to place Hamburg "among the enterprises that *were* but *are not.*" Only by retaining its SCRR terminus could Hamburg continue as a prime collection and distribution point for upcountry cotton and produce, which in turn provided the livelihood of its mercantile community and a small army of draymen who conveyed SCRR freight and passengers back and forth over the Augusta Bridge.[30]

29. *Reports by the President of the SCRR and a Committee of Seven,* 6; "Report of the Commissioners appointed to represent the State in the meetings of the So. Carolina Rail Road Company & the So. Western Rail Road Bank," Misc. Communications, ND-169 [ca. 1845], General Assembly Papers, SCDAH.

30. "A Memorial of the Intendent & Wardens of the Town of Hamburg. Also, of Sundry Citizens of the Same Town, praying that an appropriation be made for improving in part the navigation on the Savannah River," Petitions, 1848-38; "Petition of Citizens of Hamburg, in the District

But the constant need for horse-drawn portage across the Savannah River had become an embarrassing inefficiency to SCRR management. Drayage over the Augusta Bridge not only created frustrating delays for customers, but increased shipping costs significantly. "I am now more than ever persuaded that the Rail Road as a freight Road to accommodate the Planters & Merchants of the interior will fail," confided James Gadsden, "if the dray, waggon, omnibus, & Bridge taxes are continued to the extent now exacted." One company committee estimated that the charges incurred in receiving and forwarding freight at the railroad's termini of Charleston and Hamburg "amounted to *more* than *one-half* of the entire cost of transit, over the 136 miles of the Rail-road!" Civility among SCRR passengers and draymen also suffered at the Hamburg depot. "Passengers are grievously annoyed whenever the cars arrive, by scrambling for full seats in the Omnibusses," complained a Hamburg journalist, "so much so, that they are in some fear of being injured by over-kindness." Competition for coach and omnibus passengers incited frequent brawls between Augusta and Hamburg draymen, and turned the Hamburg depot into a recurring site of "knock down and drag out scrape[s]" between rival drivers. In a particularly ugly incident, one stage driver shunned the use of his fists and instead attacked a rival with a lead bar.[31]

Hamburg merchants and residents appeared willing to tolerate such occasional embarrassments as long as their town remained the terminus of the Charleston and Hamburg line. A continuation of the Augusta Bridge monopoly not only denied South Carolina cotton easy access to Georgia warehouses and markets, but also kept the SCRR from bypassing Hamburg and completing its sought after connection with the Georgia Railroad. For Hamburg interests, the tradition of economic sovereignty that inspired their town's founding and early growth continued just as necessary for its future prosper-

---

of Edgefield, for an appropriation to improve the navigation of the Savannah River from the Town of Hamburg to the Mouth of the Augusta Canal," Petitions, ND-3338 [1849]; both in General Assembly Papers, SCDAH; Rosser H. Taylor, "Hamburg: An Experiment in Town Promotion," *North Carolina Historical Review* 11 (January 1934): 32–34; Orville Vernon Burton, *In My Father's House are Many Mansions: Family & Community in Edgefield, South Carolina* (Chapel Hill, 1985), 30–31, 344–45; *Edgefield Advertiser,* August 22, 1849. For the history of the Greenville and Columbia Railroad, see Phillips, *History of Transportation,* 340–46; Ford, *Origins of Southern Radicalism,* 224–26.

31. James Gadsden to James Edward Calhoun, October 16, 1841, James Gadsden Papers, SCL; *Semi-Annual Report,* July–December 1836, 10; *Edgefield Advertiser,* July 27, 1842; June 28, 1843.

ity. At the same time that SCRR president James Gadsden was urging South Carolina and Georgia to abandon their rivalry and discover "their true policy in the harmony of a *free and unrestricted trade*," the majority of Hamburg was backing Henry Shultz in his ongoing efforts to regain ownership of the Augusta Bridge and block any construction that could expedite such a connection.[32]

For a brief time, it appeared that Hamburg's interests might prevail. The Augusta Bridge charter remained valid through 1848, along with its stipulation that no rival bridge could be built in the immediate vicinity. Furthermore, the Augusta City Council continued to rebuff all efforts by the SCRR to buy part or all of the Augusta Bridge and refused permission to cross the Savannah elsewhere into the city. Internal policies within the SCRR also acted in Hamburg's favor. In the mid-1840s, president James Gadsden turned his company's attention to the construction of a branch line to Camden, South Carolina, which required several years and $600,000 to complete and left stockholders weary of further capital expenditures. Most encouraging of all to Hamburg interests, however, was the success Henry Shultz appeared to be having in regaining his share in the Augusta Bridge. Appeals to state and federal district courts failed to bring about a decisive opinion in the matter. By 1848, Shultz had an appointment with the U.S. Supreme Court for a final confrontation with the city of Augusta over lawful ownership of the bridge as well as remuneration for three decades of tolls and damages. Local residents backed Shultz in the struggle and lauded the perseverance he had shown in "contending against a large monied corporation." The uncertainty over bridge ownership left the SCRR leery of continuing its attempts to acquire a share in the Augusta Bridge. With legal title to the bridge muddied by years of legal wrangling, SCRR directors abandoned their efforts to control the existing bridge and instead worked to secure the right to construct a new bridge of their own.[33]

Hamburg's hopes of surviving as the SCRR terminus soon unraveled, due primarily to actions taken by the town's original source of succor: the South Carolina General Assembly. In 1845 the SCRR asked the General Assembly for the right "to construct and keep up a bridge across the Savannah River from

32. *Annual Report*, February 1846, 38; *Edgefield Advertiser*, January 14, 1846.

33. Derrick, *Centennial History*, 194–96, 200–201; *Statutes at Large*, XI: 322–23; *Edgefield Advertiser*, February 27, 1850; *Kennedy et al. v. The Bank of the State of Georgia et al.*, 12 U.S. Reports (8 Howard) at 586 (1850).

Hamburg to Augusta," after the expiration of the current bridge charter in 1848. Legislators responded in December by vesting the Augusta Bridge charter with the SCRR. Company directors accepted the charter, but soon questioned the wisdom of their action after Shultz's challenge for title to the bridge entered the federal courts. Furthermore, the proviso that the SCRR provide compensation to the bridge proprietors for the South Carolina side, at a price fixed by five commissioners, was viewed by both Augusta and Hamburg interests as an egregious misapplication of the state's power of eminent domain. Shultz and his supporters decried the action as the equivalent of "compelling one man to sell his property to another, not for the public good, but for private benefit." With all parties expressing dissatisfaction with the arrangement, the General Assembly repealed the act in 1848. Instead, charter to the bridge was returned to Shultz, but with the proviso that the SCRR "may be, and are hereby, authorized to construct a bridge across the Savannah River, at any point on said river, at or near Hamburg, for the purpose of transportation of freight and passengers." In essence, the General Assembly gave the SCRR its blessing to abandon Hamburg.[34]

Opposition from Augusta to the crossing was overcome by the deep pockets of the SCRR. In July 1852, company officials finally concluded "a satisfactory arrangement" with the Augusta City Council and not only gained permission to run a railroad bridge into the city, but also to construct two depots within city limits, including one adjacent to the Georgia Railroad depot to be used exclusively for interstate business. In exchange for these privileges, the SCRR paid the impressive sum of $150,000, part of which was covered by the Georgia Railroad and two smaller lines, all of whom were equally as eager as the SCRR to be part of a vast, new interstate system of common carriers. It was an impressive show of concerted action by rival railroad corporations, and one that reiterated the view of James Gadsden that "our Southern Rail-Roads are to be considered not exclusively State works, but as a part of a common system; the veins and arteries of a great commercial body, animating in the recip-

34. "Petition of the South Carolina Rail Road Company . . . For the privilege of a Bridge across the Savannah River at Hamburg, at the expiration of the present Charter," Petitions, 1845–51, General Assembly Papers, SCDAH; *Statutes at Large,* XI: 345–46, 525–26; Derrick, *Centennial History,* 200–201; *Annual Report,* February 1846, 25, 34; "Memorial of Henry Shultz & John McKinne Praying a renewal of their Charter for the Bridge across the Savannah River at Hamburg & Augusta," Petitions, 1848–82, General Assembly Papers, SCDAH.

rocal circulations of its trade the whole, and paralyzing by impediments, or restrictions no portion."[35]

The positive effects of completing this interstate connection soon manifested themselves in the bottom line of the SCRR. Within a year after completing the railroad bridge across the Savannah in 1853, new SCRR president John Caldwell observed that "its beneficial influence upon our business had been already sensibly felt." SCRR receipts advanced by 50 percent in the 1850s, which finally allowed stockholders to realize the long-awaited "commensurate benefit" of their capital investment. While SCRR dividends seldom reached 5 percent in the 1840s (and were generally much lower), the dividend rate never fell below 8 percent after 1853, and reached a particularly impressive 10 percent in 1856.[36]

But Hamburg would not share in the bounty of interstate railroad commerce. In 1853, its final year as the SCRR's western terminus, the town of Hamburg collected more than 140,000 bales of cotton at its railroad depot. Four years later, after the SCRR had perfected its connections with the Georgia Railroad, cotton receipts at Hamburg plummeted to 18,533 bales, while the new Augusta depots collected no fewer than 108,358 bales. Hamburg's pending demise was unmistakable, leading a steady stream of factors and merchants to either fail or abandon the town for greener pastures. R. G. Dun credit agents watched as the "general falling off in the trade of Hamburg" ruined hardware merchants Edward Henkle and George Robinson, as well as hotel owner John L. Doby. Longtime Hamburg businessman Henry L. Jeffers relocated his cotton factorage and commission business to Charleston, while Josiah Sibley and John Usher moved their substantial cotton and grocery business across the Savannah River to Augusta. Smaller merchants, such as John Osborn and A. M. Benson, experienced similar fates and either failed or left Hamburg to reestablish their businesses elsewhere. By 1860, even the pages of the *Edgefield Advertiser,* an enthusiastic booster of Hamburg, admitted the unpleasant truth that Hamburg "is not what she once was."[37]

The desertion of Hamburg by the SCRR merely punctuated three decades

35. *Annual Report,* February 1853, 7; *Annual Report,* February, 1847, 12.

36. *Annual Report,* February 1853, 7; Derrick, *Centennial History,* 209.

37. *Annual Report,* February 1853, table 2; *Annual Report,* 1857, table 2; Credit Reports, South Carolina, vol. 9a (Edgefield), 41, 42, 45, 46, 64; vol. 6 (Charleston), 189, R. G. Dun & Co. Collection, Baker Library, Harvard Business School; *Edgefield Advertiser,* September 26, 1860.

of transformation in the relationship between the railroad and the people of Edgefield and Barnwell. By the latter years of the 1850s, decades of confrontation with the SCRR over livestock losses, Sunday operations, rate increases, and the desertion of intrastate interests had created a widespread feeling among district residents that they were no longer partners in a shared patriotic undertaking, as they had once believed. Thirty years of SCRR operation might have provided Edgefield and Barnwell with new towns, increased property values, and an expanded cotton market, but such blessings were partially offset by the realization that the SCRR had grown far less subservient to public opinion. The end of the antebellum era saw the agrarian model of the corporation as an agent of public service and *publici juris* replaced by the corporate self-interest prevalent elsewhere in the "age of capital." By the 1850s, the public toasts that had declared the Charleston and Hamburg railroad to be "the pride and ornament of South Carolina" had been replaced by private mutterings over the "miserable monopoly" wielded by the SCRR. Members of the Beech Island Agricultural Club remained skeptical toward the perceived benefits of railroads to local agriculturists. "Rail roads have been a disadvantage to our farmers," declared one member. Prior to the completion of the SCC&RR, "a man could sell a boat load of Corn in the Augusta market as easy as he could now a wagon load," the planter observed, "and besides we were not at the expense of sacking."[38]

Self-interest begot self-interest, however, and the inhabitants of Edgefield and Barnwell soon showed signs of reciprocating the narrow economic relationship that now prevailed between the SCRR and the public. In 1850 the SCRR began work on a new route through the sandhills as a means to avoid the inclined plane at Aiken. Although the new route ran less than six miles in length, construction costs for the bypass amounted to more than $125,000. Extensive grading accounted for most of the total, but this time expenses also included sizable outlays for acquiring the necessary right-of-way. Like Iveson Brookes, landowners along this new route no longer looked upon the SCRR "as entitled to deeds of charity." In their eyes, the pursuit of profit had become the company's modus vivendi and made the SCRR no longer worthy of patri-

38. Eric J. Hobsbawm, *The Age of Capital, 1848–1875* (London, 1975); Aiken, *Aiken Telegraph and Commercial Advertiser,* July 8, 1835; Credit Reports, South Carolina, vol. 6 (Charleston), 142, R. G. Dun & Co. Collection, Baker Library, Harvard Business School; "Record of the Proceedings of the Beech Island Agricultural Club, 1856–1862," May 1, 1858, Records, Beech Island Farmers Club, SCL.

otic gifts of a free right-of-way as it had in the past. As a result, local landowners exacted thousands of dollars in compensation from the SCRR for the privilege of passing its new road through their properties. Mr. and Mrs. Henry L. Brown received $200 from the company for the right-of-way through their property near Aiken, while Mary Stewart received $100 from the SCRR along with a promise that the company would maintain a fence along the line and relocate her kitchen if it proved necessary for building the new road. Other landowners secured more than money from the SCRR. Graniteville investor James G. O. Wilkinson secured a lifetime travel pass for himself and his wife from the SCRR, while hotel proprietor Mary Schwartz had the company erect a "Stopping Place . . . before my House in Aiken" at which she would operate "a neat and comfortable Passenger House for the reception of Passengers."[39]

In the span of one generation, the railroad had traveled from public servant to private business. The SCRR all but admitted it and the residents of Edgefield and Barnwell came to understand it as so. What rang even more hollow, however, were pronouncements from the General Assembly that legislation passed at the behest of the SCRR served the public as well. It was difficult for district citizens to see how rate increases and the removal of the SCRR depot from their principal market town benefited their interests. Allowing and even encouraging such actions seemed far removed from the legislature's ancestral role as disinterested arbiter in local economic disputes and protector of public rights against the self-interest of individual entrepreneurs. But additional conflicts between agrarians and corporate interest awaited the inhabitants of Edgefield and Barnwell on the banks of Horse Creek, as the cotton factories at Graniteville and Vaucluse also arose to challenge the traditional balance between entrepreneurship and public welfare in the agrarian landscape. And, as in the altercation between Hamburg and the SCRR, the members of the General Assembly would once again be called upon to determine the outcome.

39. *Annual Report,* February 1851, 9; Derrick, *Centennial History,* 202–3; Barnwell Deeds, Book EE, 94, 263; Edgefield Deeds, Book GGG, 179–80, SCDAH.

CHAPTER EIGHT

"A DOMINEERING INFLUENCE"

GRANITEVILLE AND THE TRIUMPH OF MEN OF CAPITAL

We now have a great issue made up, the war is between capitalists in stocks & corporations, and capitalists in labour & land. The struggle is for ascendancy and if the former are sustained in their swindling career they will control & own the latter. I go for land & negroes.

FRANCIS W. PICKENS, 1837

AT THE TIME GRANITEVILLE was under construction in the late 1840s, William Gregg also commenced work on a summer house in the hills between his factory and the town of Aiken. Built on a plot of property owned in partnership with Graniteville investors Ker Boyce and James G. O. Wilkinson, Gregg named his retreat "Kalmia" after the ubiquitous flower found on the surrounding hillsides. After he retired from his Charleston mercantile career in the early 1850s, Kalmia became Gregg's year-round residence. Boyce and Wilkinson joined him, and in late 1852, the three men hired a surveyor to lay out the village of Kalmia. The twenty-four lots were large, containing slightly more than thirteen acres apiece, with a single street laid through the center of the village. The neighborhood quickly became a favored country retreat for several local and lowcountry gentlemen. Lowcountry scions Henry F. Porcher and Rene Ravenel soon joined Gregg and his Graniteville cohorts at Kalmia, as did Edgefield jurist and state senator James P. Carroll.[1]

Epigraph from Francis W. Pickens to James Henry Hammond, July 13, 1837, James Henry Hammond Papers, Library of Congress.

1. Broadus Mitchell, *William Gregg: Factory Master of the Old South* (Chapel Hill, 1928; New York,

It was at Kalmia, in the limelight of his newfound celebrity, that Gregg assumed the role of gentleman farmer. He quickly adapted to the part. Preferring peach blossoms to cotton bolls, Gregg planted a sizable fruit orchard on his Kalmia estate. Each year, after packing his harvest on site, he sent his peaches by railroad to Charleston, whence they traveled by steamship for final sale in New York just three days removed from the tree. The profits from this enterprise earned the respect—and envy—of area planters and many moved to imitate his example. "Gregg made $6,000 this year on some 30 acres of rather poor peaches," observed James Henry Hammond, which inspired him to attempt his own—less successful—investment in an Aiken orchard. Gregg's horticultural laurels also merited his inclusion in the exclusive Beech Island Farmers Club, whose meetings he attended regularly and where he took an active part in club debates. After clearing an additional $4,000 from his peach harvest in 1858, the *Charleston Courier* wrote of William Gregg: "manufactures and horticulture have alike owned the impulse of his enterprising spirit."[2]

But unlike the planter-manufacturers of an earlier generation, Gregg was not an agriculturist dabbling in industrial pursuits. He was a manufacturer first and foremost, whose agrarian endeavors, however profitable, remained a permanent sidebar to his manufacturing investments. Yet the apparent ease with which he brought his cotton factory to fruition masked the roadblocks that Gregg overcame on the path to industrial success. A series of setbacks delayed commencement of full operations at Graniteville. The company drying house took fire in April 1847 and consumed twenty thousand feet of choice lumber. In June 1848, the factory flooring had to be completely taken up and relaid to correct the shoddy labor of "incompetent workmen." Likewise, considerable time was lost in installing and learning to operate the factory's water turbines— a fairly new innovation in power generation, and one with which few available mechanics had experience. Even after the factory was complete and in full operation, inexperience on the part of both labor and management, coupled with a depressed market for textiles, led to disappointing initial results. Graniteville's balance sheet barely broke even in 1850 and showed a loss of more than $12,000

1966), 86–90; Edgefield Deeds, Book HHH, 430–32, 440, 464, SCDAH; John W. Brodie to Jacob Stroman, November 7, 1849, Stroman Family Papers, SCL.

2. James Henry Hammond to Harry Hammond, October 10, 1856, James Henry Hammond Papers, SCL; Entries, April 5, 1856; April 3, 1858; September 3 and November 5, 1859, Records, Beech Island Farmers Club, SCL; *Edgefield Advertiser,* September 10, 1856; July 28, 1858.

the following year. Maturity and revived demand, however, soon reversed the situation. By 1854, Graniteville directors were declaring substantial annual dividends and a buoyant Gregg announced to his stockholders that "had our establishment been as well organized, and supplied with skilful hands as at present, we might have paid dividends even in 1850 and '51."[3]

But bad luck and inexperience were not the only obstacles to confront William Gregg and his fellow men of capital. Besides introducing manufacturing of unprecedented scale and sophistication to Edgefield and Barnwell, Gregg also challenged the traditional norms of entrepreneurial behavior in the agrarian landscape. Whereas custom and law previously kept entrepreneurship reined to popular influence, actions by Gregg in the name of the Graniteville factory disrupted this long-standing—if tenuous—relationship. Part of the challenge would be social. In his compulsion to maintain the moral standard he set for his operatives, Gregg attempted to extend his benevolent despotism beyond Graniteville and define standards of behavior for neighbors and employees alike. But while Gregg's effort to expand the scope of his temperance crusade met with understandable antipathy from Graniteville's agrarian neighbors, it found remarkably little opposition from state legislators, who demonstrated a reluctance to check the growing demands of industrial capital in Edgefield and Barnwell.

This reluctance became even more pronounced when Gregg demanded special prerogatives for the riparian interests of Graniteville and Vaucluse in the Horse Creek Valley, which not only threatened the livelihood of neighboring sawyers, but also presaged a complete subversion of the regulated balance between entrepreneurship and the public good that had existed in Edgefield and Barnwell for generations. Well into the nineteenth century, legislators had checked the disruptive ambitions of planter-entrepreneurs—particularly district sawyers. Overt attempts to advance private economic interests at the expense of the commonweal remained few and futile. Gregg and Graniteville, however, escalated the debate, as well as the stakes involved. More important, in challenging the riparian traditions of the Horse Creek Valley, Gregg forced

3. Hiram Hutchison to John Springs, March 5, 1847; June 10, 1848; John J. Blackwood to John Springs, November 8, 1847; all in Springs Family Papers, SHC; Mitchell, *William Gregg*, 91–102; Felix Canfield to Felicia H. Canfield, September 12, 1850, Felicia Canfield Papers, SCL; *Report of the President and Treasurer of the Graniteville Manufacturing Company, for the Year 1854* (Charleston, 1855), 13.

state legislators to stand aside from their role as disinterested mediator and assume a partisan stance as the ally of men of capital in South Carolina, even at the expense of entrepreneurial prerogatives claimed by local men of property for generations.[4]

Gregg long touted that the moral reformation of poor whites would be one of the primary benefits of his mill and village at Graniteville. Temperance served as the keystone of this binary system of uplift and discipline. Indeed, many supporters believed his prohibition of alcohol to be foremost among the blessings bestowed upon Graniteville residents. "Intemperance, the curse of the laboring classes," was rarely seen at Graniteville, observed the *Charleston Courier*. A writer for the Lexington *Temperance Standard* considered Graniteville's history to be "closely identified with the history of the temperance cause in South Carolina." Even textile scion Amos Lawrence of Massachusetts believed that Graniteville's ban on alcohol "will bring better settlers around them & will make the land sell for three times the price it would command, if it was a '*rum place*.'" Gregg himself went so far as to forbid the keeper of the Graniteville Hotel from stocking wine and brandy for the accommodation of his guests. "We don't want a set of loafing wine-drinkers about the place," Gregg informed his factory supervisor. Public accommodations in his village were intended to serve only "that class of persons called business men or at least those who can restrain themselves sufficiently to conform to the moral rules."[5]

But Gregg frequently found his program of moral reform undercut by Graniteville residents outside his employ, and thus removed from the immediate shadow of his "benevolence." The business of Thomas Marshall drew Gregg's particular disapprobation, as the village merchant seemed bent on providing Graniteville residents with every type of amusement that Gregg detested. Marshall initially provoked Gregg's ire by renting his hall for public dances, which forced Gregg to take "some decided steps on the part of the company to put a stop to them." A Graniteville supervisor advised Marshall that if he persisted in holding balls, then "all connexion between him and the com-

4. Mitchell, *William Gregg*, 76–90.

5. *Charleston Courier*, January 21, 1860; *Edgefield Advertiser*, October 5, 1854; Amos Lawrence to Amos A. Lawrence, September 25, 1850, Amos A. Lawrence Papers, Massachusetts Historical Society; William Gregg to James Montgomery, December 31, 1850, William Gregg Papers, SCL; Mitchell, *William Gregg*, 82–84.

pany in interest and reciprocity would be severed." To further dissuade attendance at such gatherings, Gregg let it be known that female operatives found partaking "would have no further employment from the company."[6]

The quarrel between Gregg and Marshall escalated further when the merchant was found to be retailing liquor from his Graniteville store. Although the action was a clear violation of the temperance clause in all Graniteville leases, Marshall nevertheless felt justified in making public declarations that he had been forced to close his business because of "the spirit of *Monopoly* and *Persecution* that has been recently manifested toward us by the *President* of the Graniteville Manufacturing Company." The sanctimonious tone of Gregg's response undoubtedly did little to assuage Marshall's resentment. "When the excitement subsides, you will come to the conclusion that you have been in the wrong," Gregg replied, "and that I have done nothing more than my obligations to the Graniteville Company require of me." As the self-proclaimed "enemy to all evil doers," as well as a benefactor to those in need, Gregg stated that he could not be expected "to encourage those who would lay a snare in the way of persons whose weakness would subject them to become a burden instead of a support to their families."[7]

Gregg's temperance crusade aroused additional opprobrium in the fall of 1854, when he petitioned the General Assembly for a law forbidding the sale of alcohol within three miles of Graniteville. Property owners in the affected area jumped to denounce the attempted measure as neither right nor just. Rather than encouraging the temperance societies already existing in Graniteville, they accused company officers of instead trying to place restrictions on neighborhood residents "in order to have a domineering influence over them." While wishing the company every success in "all their laudable and legitimate enterprises," the counterpetitioners virulently opposed the attempt to "place our estates under any restrictions, for their imaginary benefit or aggrandizement whatsoever." Such forms of paternalism may have been fine for the poor white operatives of Gregg's factory, but were not to be suffered by the republican agriculturists of Edgefield District. Gregg should not be permitted to exercise the same kind of control over his neighbors as he did his employees.[8]

6. William Gregg to James Montgomery, March 20, 1851, William Gregg Papers, SCL.

7. *Edgefield Advertiser,* October 5 and 12, 1854; Credit Reports, South Carolina, vol. 9a (Edgefield), 56, R. G. Dun & Co. Collection, Baker Library, Harvard Business School.

8. "Petition for the passage of a Law to Prohibit the sale of Alcoholic Liquors in or within Three

State legislators rejected the prohibition request, but not because they agreed that such an act would give Graniteville officials "a domineering influence" over their neighbors. Rather, they saw no need to enact a special law to obtain the sought-after result. South Carolina was already "well provided" with laws regarding the sale of alcoholic beverages, "which if only properly enforced will of its own effect carry out the very object proposed" by Gregg and his supporters. The senate Judiciary Committee reminded the petitioners that local road commissioners, who were entrusted with the power of granting licenses to sell liquor, "can by their own act in withholding license from such as reside within 3 miles, carry out the object if they so please to do." While neither trodding on the authority of district road commissioners, nor appearing to capitulate before the Horse Creek manufacturers, the General Assembly nevertheless refused to condemn Gregg's plan of moral economy. It rejected Gregg's means, but not his desired end.[9]

Keen observers of the legislative scene might have anticipated the General Assembly's ambivalent response to those opposing Gregg's prohibition campaign, for in the previous session Gregg scored a notable success in reconfiguring the relationship between men of capital, agrarian entrepreneurs, and the General Assembly. If temperance was desirable to maintain the moral standing of factory operatives, hegemony over the waterpower of Horse Creek became absolutely essential for the profitable operation of the Graniteville factory. By undertaking to reconstruct the riparian laws of Horse Creek, William Gregg sought nothing less than a repositioning of the place of industrial capital in the agrarian landscape.

Conflict over water rights had long been a staple among agrarian entrepreneurs in Edgefield and Barnwell districts. Riparian confrontations declined somewhat following the passage of the inland navigation act of 1825, which made it illegal for mill owners to obstruct navigable waterways and required the unhindered navigation of rafts of lumber and timber. However, challenges

---

Miles of the Village of Graniteville," Petition, ND-4118 [1854]; "Memorial of Sundry Citizens of Graniteville & the neighborhood against the application of the Graniteville Manufacturing Co, to prohibit the sale of spirituous liquors within three miles of that place," Petition, ND-4117 [1854]; both in General Assembly Papers, SCDAH.

9. "Report of the Committee on Judiciary on Petition of citizens & Land holders in vicinity of Graniteville for a law to prohibit the sale of alcoholic liquors within 3 miles of said village," Reports, 1854–141, General Assembly Papers, SCDAH.

to the act began to reappear about the time that Gregg commenced textile production at Graniteville. A series of petitions from sawmill owners in Edgefield and Barnwell pressured the General Assembly to reconsider the provisions of the 1825 act, as those seeking to broaden economic opportunity again clashed with those equally committed to the prerogatives of private property. In 1852 a petition from Barnwell District attempted to have Tinker Creek, a Savannah River tributary, declared a navigable stream. The prayer claimed the creek was large and navigable, "capable of transporting to market an immensely valuable body of timber and lumber." If opened and cleared of obstructions, Tinker Creek could "confer an immense advantage on a large densely populated and industrious community, bringing thereby to market an extensive body of finely timbered lands and enabling the productive industry of a populous region to advance the general interest of the State." A presentment from the Barnwell District Grand Jury added its own weight behind the effort. To encourage "the proper development of the resources of this District," the Grand Jury recommended that all streams capable of being made navigable by the removal of artificial obstructions, "*be declared navigable*," and thereby open the door of opportunity even wider to any aspiring sawyer-entrepreneur in the district.[10]

However, established mill owners on Tinker Creek vehemently opposed these requests, citing the expense and disruptions such actions would have on their operations. If approved, these mill owners would be forced to give free passage to all rafts through their dams and require the installation and maintenance of passages at their own expense for public use. Mill owners deemed such an application "unreasonable." "The Mill owners have . . . succeeded in their enterprizes & have made many sacrifices in order to establish themselves," they declared. "They have developed the resources of the country adjacent to them & it would in their opinion be manifestly unjust to appropriate the fruits of their labours & toil to the benefit of others." The constant use of slopes through their dams would mean "that those who have been pioneers in an enterprize which is now profitable will have swept from them the just rewards of their labours." They further resented the injustice of having to cover the cost of alterations from their own pockets. "The property of the community has been made navigable by the industry of some of its members," they

10. "Petition of Sundry Citizens of Barnwell District Praying that Tinkers Creek be Declared a Navigable Stream," Petition, ND-3325; "South Carolina, Barnwell District, Suggestions of the Grand Jury of Fall Term 1852," Presentment, 18525–4; both in General Assembly Papers, SCDAH.

complained, yet it was these same entrepreneurs who were being asked to bear the burdens a declaration of navigability would incur.[11]

One of the memorialists who opposed declaring Tinker Creek a navigable stream was also responsible for a narrower interpretation of the navigation provisions in the 1825 act. In its May 1852 term, the South Carolina Court of Appeals considered the case of Levi Hickson, a planter and mill owner on Shaw's Creek, a branch of the South Edisto River in Barnwell District, who was indicted under the 1825 act for obstructing the stream with his mill dam. Hickson appealed, however, claiming Shaw's Creek was not used for rafting at the time he constructed his dam, and that the dam was in place over twenty years before the indictment against him was pursued. Although a lower court jury found Hickson guilty, the Court of Appeals found in his favor. Speaking for the court, Judge Josiah J. Evans asserted that Hickson's dam was not in violation of the 1825 act, since the creek above it had been made navigable only recently and through private means, "and neither Hickson or the Legislature have dedicated it to the public use." The court declared the indictment against Hickson could not be sustained under the terms of the 1825 act, "unless the stream was used, at the time and place of obstruction, for the purposes of navigation by boats, flats, or rafts of lumber or timber." Without an official declaration of navigability, rafters wishing to pass through Hickson's dam would have to do so at his pleasure.[12]

By the time the General Assembly met in November 1852, both established and would-be sawmill owners were pressuring for alterations to the 1825 act. After considering the petitions and counterpetitions regarding Tinker Creek, as well as the recommendation of the Barnwell Grand Jury, the house Committee on Internal Improvements decided to enact "a general law upon that and other kindred subjects," and reported a bill to that effect. The senate Committee on Agriculture and Internal Improvements also presented a bill on the same subject. Although it quickly passed through the house, the bill soon stalled in the senate. After a first reading, the senate returned the bill to committee, where it was tabled and no further action took place on the matter for the remainder of the session. The stipulations of the 1825 act remained in place for the time being.[13]

11. "Petition of Sundry Citizens of Barnwell District Praying that Tinker's Creek be not Declared a Public Stream," Petition, ND-3324, General Assembly Papers, SCDAH.

12. *State v. Hickson,* 39 S.C.L. (5 Richardson, 1852) at 451.

13. "Report of the Committee on Internal Improvements Declaring all Streams which may be

William Gregg undoubtedly followed these proceedings with great interest, for the provisions of the 1825 act were beginning to interfere with operations at Graniteville. In 1853 suits were brought against Graniteville by two sawmill owners on Horse Creek operating above the cotton factory. One plaintiff claimed the Graniteville dam obstructed the free navigation of Horse Creek, a stream declared navigable by the General Assembly in 1820. Although the Grand Jury of Edgefield threw out the indictment, a separate civil case against Graniteville brought by the second litigant continued. Gregg feared that this would not be the last lawsuit brought against his factory. Other sawmills operated on Horse Creek above Graniteville, all of which would be adversely affected by his dam blocking the stream. If Graniteville was to continue its operations unharassed by upstream mill owners, Horse Creek's thirty-three-year charter as a navigable river would have to be altered, or perhaps overturned outright.[14]

The opening broadside came when the Graniteville Company introduced a petition in both houses of the General Assembly at the start of its 1853 term. James Jones, now the sole proprietor of the Vaucluse cotton mill, joined Gregg in the effort. Their prayer followed the line pursued by Levi Hickson in his successful suit before the Court of Appeals the previous year. Gregg and Jones described the presence of shoals on Horse Creek that commenced before Graniteville, which continued upstream for several miles, and argued that the shoals blocked navigation through that section of the stream. The idea of using Horse Creek at Graniteville for raft navigation was, they asserted, of recent origin. Only since the construction of the Graniteville dam had water levels upstream risen and calmed to the point that rafting the section was "at all practicable." Furthermore, Gregg and Jones argued that the 1820 act regarding

---

made Navigable by the Removal of Obstructions to be Navigable Streams," Report, 1852–225; "Report of the Committee on Agriculture and Internal Improvements on the Petition of Sundry Citizens of Barnwell District praying that Tinker Creek be Declared a Navigable Stream, also on the Presentment of the Grand Jury of Said District on the same Subject," Report, ND-4055 [1852]; both in General Assembly Papers, SCDAH; *Journal of the House of Representatives of the State of South Carolina, Being the Annual Session of 1852* (Columbia, 1852; hereinafter cited as *House Journal*), 12, 88, 186; *Journal of the Senate of South Carolina, Being the Extra and Annual Session of 1852* (Columbia, 1852; hereinafter cited as *Senate Journal*), 36, 117, 175.

14. "William Gregg, President of the Graniteville Manufacturing Co., and Others Familiar with Horse Creek, Report on the Plausibility of Making Horse Creek Navigable for Rafts," Miscellaneous Communication, 1854–5, General Assembly Papers, SCDAH.

the navigability of Horse Creek clarified little, and "as it now stands has led parties into litigation." To remedy the situation, they requested that the assembly pass a new law "which shall more explicitly explain the charter of 1820 and define the obligations of Parties owning Mills and also the rights of those who may claim the privilege of rafting down the Stream." Committees of both the house and senate concurred with the request and recommended the passage of a new law regulating navigation on Horse Creek. At the same time, Barnwell senator James J. Wilson and the house Committee on Internal Improvements resurrected the previous year's bill regarding navigable streams.[15]

Adding to the debate, the house received a counterpetition from Edgefield District, "praying that the laws in relation to the navigation of Horse Creek be not repealed." The counterpetitioners protested the efforts of Gregg and Jones, claiming that if the laws regarding Horse Creek were repealed, it would "be greatly to the prejudice of their interests and in derogation of their just rights," specifically the right to use Horse Creek to raft their timber to market. They noted that the lands upstream from Graniteville "abound in valuable timber adjacent to five mill seats and Mills now in operation." A ready market existed for Horse Creek lumber in Hamburg, Augusta, and Savannah. However, if the assembly repealed existing legislation and thereby allowed Graniteville and Vaucluse to obstruct Horse Creek permanently, the Edgefield petitioners warned, "it would have a chilling effect upon the spirit of industry and enterprise." They further asserted that the actions of Gregg and Jones were merely petty reprisals against mill owners, who sought nothing more than the established right of free passage on Horse Creek.[16]

Debate over altering the navigation laws provoked much discussion in the assembly. But after much wrangling, a new act emerged from the various proposals of the previous two sessions. Entitled "An Act to Declare a Certain De-

15. *House Journal, 1853*, 13, 78; *Senate Journal, 1853*, 13, 58; "Petition of the Graniteville Company for an Act to Regulate the Navigation of Horse Creek," Petition, ND-3341 [1853]; "Report of the Committee on Internal Improvements upon the Petition of Wm. Gregg and James Jones in regard to Horse Creek," Report, ND-2971 [1853]; and "Report of the Committee on Agriculture and Internal Improvements on the Petition of Wm. Gregg and James Jones praying the Passage of a Law further regulating the Navigation of Horse Creek in the District of Edgefield," Report, 1853–32; all in General Assembly Papers, SCDAH.

16. *House Journal, 1853*, 100; "Petition of Sundry Citizens of Edgefield District Praying that the Laws in Relation to the Navigation of Horse Creek be not Repealed," Petition, ND-3340 [1853], General Assembly Papers, SCDAH.

scription of Streams Navigable, and for Other Purposes," the new law protected most aspects of the 1825 act, but with some significant changes. Upon passage of the new act, all streams that had been rendered navigable, or which were capable of being rendered so by clearing obstructions, were "declared navigable streams." Any person obstructing the same "shall be deemed guilty of a public nuisance." Landowners adjacent to navigable streams could continue to erect mill dams and were still required to construct and keep in repair adequate passages to permit "free navigation for rafts of lumber or timber." No distinctions were made among mill owners or the type of mill operated by such dams. The act further stipulated that those who erected dams "on such streams antecedent to their use for the purposes aforesaid" were now permitted to collect compensation from those wishing to use the stream for the defined purposes of navigation. The amount of payment was to be determined by the parties involved. If an amount could not be agreed upon, a neighboring magistrate was to select four nearby freeholders to determine a sufficient compensation. This aspect of the new act still required mill owners to provide access, even if their dam occupied the site before the stream became navigable. But, for the first time, owners received compensation for the expense and trouble caused by the passage of rafts.[17]

However, the new law also detailed certain parties who would be exempt from the provisions of the act: "*Provided,* That nothing herein contained shall be construed to extend to the navigation of Horse Creek, above a point known as Richardson's Shoals, on said Creek." Richardson's Shoals was the location of William Gregg's Graniteville factory. Although Gregg and James Jones did not obtain legislation that specifically regulated navigation on Horse Creek, the 1853 law achieved the same purpose. Neither Vaucluse nor Graniteville would be required to provide passage through or around their dams, nor would their daily operations be affected by fluctuating water levels that passing rafts would necessitate. In essence, Graniteville and Vaucluse would have at their command all the water from Horse Creek that they needed, regardless of the economic consequences to mill owners upstream.[18]

17. "Report of the Minority of the Committee on Internal Improvements, to whom was referred a Bill from the Senate entitled 'A Bill to declare a certain description of Streams Navigable and for Other Purposes,'" Report, ND-2940 [1853], General Assembly Papers, SCDAH; *House Journal, 1853,* 142, 193; *Statutes at Large,* XII: 268.

18. *Statutes at Large,* XII: 268.

Although Gregg and Jones won the battle, a number of Edgefield residents were not about to concede the war. At the start of the 1854 session of the General Assembly, 125 citizens of Edgefield petitioned to have the third clause of the new act repealed, and have Horse Creek again declared a public highway. In thorough detail, the petitioners recited the half century of legislative pronouncements declaring Horse Creek "a public & navigable Water Course from its source to its mouth." Citing acts of 1796, 1807, and 1820, they claimed, "Perhaps no other stream in South Carolina of equal length, breadth, and depth has been declared navigable by so many statutes, and had such heavy penalties imposed by Law for obstructing the passage of lumber and rafts down its waters." The petitioners further noted the remarkably straight and deep channel of Horse Creek, which made the navigation of lumber rafts possible from within two and one half miles of its source. The surrounding valley abounded in valuable stands of pine, and water from the creek already powered several sawmills, with more mill seats available. They also noted that the immediate area was occupied by a largely poor population, so that the only significant market for Horse Creek lumber was Augusta or Savannah "by means of navigation down Said creek & thence up and down the Savannah River."[19]

But the primary focus of their argument was not the practicality of rafting on Horse Creek, but rather their right to do so. In stating their case, they laid claim to the long-standing legal framework and tradition that for decades fostered and protected sawyer-entrepreneurs in "their usual employment" and the pursuit of their "general business & habits." Closing Horse Creek not only threatened to cut sawyers off from market access, but would mark a fundamental shift in the established political economy regulating Horse Creek. Sawmill operators who purchased and improved, or intended to improve, Horse Creek lands did so "upon the *Good faith* of the State which has so often assured its citizens by solemn enactments that the said stream should '*forever*' be a navigable one." Why should their hard work and labor, and the profits emanating from them, be sacrificed while Graniteville was allowed to prosper at their expense?

19. "Petition of Sundry Citizens of Edgefield District Praying the Legislature Pass an Act for the Repeal of so much of the 3rd Clause of an Act entitled "An Act to Declare a Certain Description of Streams Navigable, and for Other Purposes," as relates to Horse Creek in Edgefield District, and to declare the same a Public Highway," Petition, 1854–59, General Assembly Papers, SCDAH.

Many of them have likewise labored to improve the navigation of said stream above the dam of the Graniteville Company, yet if they cannot get relief from your Honorable Body, their labor in that regard would be lost, in addition to suffering a ruinous depreciation of their property and a general destruction of their business. Your Memorialists would further suggest that the slight inconvenience and expense to the Graniteville Company of keeping open said Creek to the navigation of rafts through their dam is not at all comparable to the enourmous and irreparable injury done to the land and Mill owners above on said stream by closing it up.[20]

William Gregg did not let his opponents have the last word. To counter the claims of the Edgefield residents, he presented legislators with a printed version of his arguments in favor of retaining Graniteville's exemption in the new navigation law. He contended that the natural obstruction of Horse Creek created by Richardson's Shoals made it impassable to rafts, even if the Graniteville dam was removed. The only feasible way to pass over the disputed section was by letting off the water collected behind the dam and flooding the rafts over the shoals. However, if the proprietors of Vaucluse and Graniteville were forced to let off large portions of their water power supply in order to pass rafts, Gregg contended the result would be "ruinous" to both operations. "Past experience has proven that even one mill pond, suddenly emptied above, cannot, in ordinary times, be filled again without embarrassment to machinery below," explained Gregg. Both Vaucluse and Graniteville already made "considerable outlays" in order to retain sudden floods so that machinery could keep operating while the flow of the stream was temporarily halted to restore mill ponds upstream.[21]

Nor did Gregg allow this argument to rest on his assertions alone. He included testimony from several men "of very large experience in the lumber business." They not only concurred with Gregg's assertions regarding the impracticality of rafting over Richardson's Shoals, but also with his claim that flooding rafts over the shoals would be absolutely detrimental to the operations at Graniteville. "I don't think that rafting could be carried on over the shoals below the Graniteville Dam," one mill expert claimed, "without making such heavy drafts on the Graniteville pond as would be destructive of the water

20. Ibid.
21. "William Gregg . . . and Others . . . , Report on the Plausibility of Making Horse Creek Navigable for Rafts," Miscellaneous Communication, 1854–5, General Assembly Papers, SCDAH.

power used for driving the machinery of the Graniteville factory." Another concurred: water from the Graniteville pond could not be used to raft lumber over the shoals "without stopping the greater part, if not all the machinery."[22]

The petitions supporting and opposing the Horse Creek exemption presented the General Assembly with a clear choice. By permitting the exemption to stand, the assembly would overturn a half century of legal precedent protecting the use of Horse Creek as a public highway. In doing so, the exemption would directly benefit only the cotton factories at Graniteville and Vaucluse at the expense of upstream sawyers and land owners, who expected the assembly to maintain free navigation on Horse Creek. If the assembly overturned the exemption to the 1853 law, it would continue to maintain the stream's traditional status and require Graniteville and Vaucluse to allow the passage of rafts through their dams. However, by pursuing this option, the assembly might seriously hinder, and perhaps mortally wound, the economic future of the cotton mills on Horse Creek.

If antebellum South Carolinians generally opposed the development of large-scale manufacturing per se, the General Assembly had a golden opportunity in the fall of 1853 to check the activities of the South's foremost preacher of the industrial gospel. If Graniteville was not exempted from the navigation laws, there existed a very real possibility that Gregg's factory would join other failed attempts at manufacturing in the state. But the assembly could not sidestep the issue either. Ignoring Gregg's petition would allow Graniteville to remain vulnerable to indictments under the acts of 1820 and 1825. In order to ensure success, legislators took an active role in supporting Graniteville and Vaucluse by upholding their actions from the previous session. The exemption of Graniteville and Vaucluse from the 1853 act remained law.[23]

Gregg's legislative victory consummated the transformation of Horse Creek by men of capital. The petty entrepreneurial activities of sawmill owners found little opportunity in the valley during the twilight years of the antebellum era, as the local landscape came to be dominated by grander enterprises. Graniteville and Vaucluse went on to prosper through the Civil War years and decades beyond, but were not the only incorporated companies to occupy the valley before the war. In 1849 Ker Boyce made his second manufacturing foray into the Horse Creek Valley when he and his colleagues received a charter to

22. Ibid.

23. *House Journal, 1854,* 120, 143.

incorporate the South Carolina Paper Manufacturing Company. Organized two years later, with a capitalization of $60,000, the factory was in a location that provided easy access to both the waterpower of Horse Creek and the transportation facilities of the South Carolina Railroad. Like Graniteville, Charleston capital loomed large in the undertaking. Gregg joined Boyce in the venture, as did Gregg's Charleston business partner, Hezekiah S. Hayden, Charleston printer and publisher Joseph Walker, and Charleston attorney B. C. Pressley. On the heels of Graniteville's success in effectively closing Horse Creek to raft traffic, the paper factory expanded operations and increased its capital stock to $100,000. In 1858 the Charleston capitalists leased the mill to a consortium of Georgia investors under the overall supervision of John and George Winter, a father-and-son team of paper manufacturers from Columbus. Renamed and rechartered, the Bath Paper Mills Company mill operated one of the largest paper factories in the antebellum South, supplying daily newspapers in Charleston, Augusta, and Savannah, and thereby enabling southern polemicists to print their antinorthern tirades on a product of southern domestic industry. By 1860, the factory employed thirty-five white operatives and consumed 1,400,000 pounds of rags and cotton waste to produce 900,000 pounds of paper worth an estimated $81,000.[24]

Men of capital in the Horse Creek Valley even invaded Edgefield District's tradition of artisan-based pottery manufacturing. In 1856 a collection of "Augustans, Charlestonians and enterprising Northerners" organized the Southern Porcelain Manufacturing Company, selecting a location near Graniteville situated on an unlimited supply of kaolin clay. Capitalized at $200,000, the

24. *Statutes at Large*, XI: 559–60; XII: 321, 599–600; "Petition of B. C. Pressley & others praying to be incorporated as a company for the manufacture of Paper," Petitions, ND-4451 [1849]; and "Memorial of the South Carolina Paper Manufacturing Company asking the privilege of increasing their Capital," Petitions, 1854–133; both in General Assembly Papers, SCDAH; *Edgefield Advertiser*, May 6, 1852; February 22, 1860; Jonathan H. Poston, *The Buildings of Charleston: A Guide to the City's Architecture* (Columbia, 1997), 305–6; Credit Reports, South Carolina, vol. 9a (Edgefield), 57, 71, R. G. Dun & Co. Collection, Baker Library, Harvard Business School; *Charleston Courier*, February 11, 1860; *Eighth Census of the United States, Industry, 1860*, Edgefield District, SCDAH. See also Ernest M. Lander Jr., "Paper Manufacturing in South Carolina Before the Civil War," *North Carolina Historical Review* 29 (April 1952): 220–27. On John G. Winter, see LeRoy P. Graf and Ralph W. Haskins, eds., "The Letters of a Georgia Unionist: John G. Winter and Secession," *Georgia Historical Quarterly* 45 (December 1961): 385–402, and Robert S. Davis Jr., "The Story and Records of the Winter Iron Works," *Alabama Review* 53 (July 2000): 199–205.

works were supervised by experienced Vermont porcelain makers and employed a cosmopolitan workforce of northern and southern operatives, as well as English, Scots, and Irish immigrants. Within two years of receiving its charter, visitors to the factory found "about 30 hands busily engaged" in making a wide assortment of ceramic wares, from China pitchers and fruit jars to fire brick and earthenware water pipes. Like its textile and paper manufacturing neighbors, the porcelain company sold the bulk of its production by means of urban agents in Charleston and Augusta, whence it diffused across a regional, and even national, market.[25]

Gregg's victory was not without some personal cost. His prestige among his neighbors suffered as the antebellum era wound to a close. Nor did all of his future attempts to rearrange the local landscape in his favor meet with the success of his campaign to rewrite the navigation laws of Horse Creek. An 1854 effort by Gregg and others to create a public highway between Graniteville and Aiken via Kalmia was blocked "in consequence of objections made by one or two individuals owning lands near Aiken." In 1856 Gregg won election to the General Assembly as one of six representatives from Edgefield, but with only the fourth largest vote total in the district. Two years later, Gregg found to his disbelief that his accomplishments as a manufacturer were a decided handicap in his 1858 bid for the Edgefield District senate seat. "I thought the Graniteville enterprise would have commended me to everybody," he declared in a public letter, "but not so; . . . Many persons are busy circulating reports of cruelty in overworking and underpaying the people of Graniteville." Gregg spent much of his dismal campaign refuting charges ranging from his being a northerner to accusations that he forcibly exacted twenty-five cents from each of his operatives to defray the cost of Graniteville's Fourth of July celebration. Although the accusations against him were unsubstantiated, opponents clearly believed Gregg's association with the Graniteville factory undermined his popular appeal. When the election finally took place, Gregg managed to claim only 44 percent of the vote tally.[26]

25. *Statutes at Large,* XII: 425; *De Bow's Review* 27 (November 1859): 607; *Edgefield Advertiser,* March 10 and May 5, 1858; *Charleston Courier,* February 25, 1860; J. Garrison Stradling, "The Southern Porcelain Company of Kaolin, South Carolina: A Reassessment," *Journal of Early Southern Decorative Arts* 22 (winter 1996): 1–39. See also Edwin Atlee Barber, *The Pottery and Porcelain of the United States,* 3rd ed. (New York and London, 1909), 186–90, 451. Barber asserts that Alexander H. Stephens was among the Georgia investors in the porcelain works at Kaolin.

26. "Petition of James G. O. Wilkinson & others, citizens of Edgefield District, praying that a

Outside the Horse Creek Valley, however, few looked upon Gregg and his nascent industrial corridor as anything but a blessing upon South Carolina and the South in general. The view became even more predominant as sectional tensions attained their apogee, with those giving practical application to domestic industry applauded as shining lights of southern patriotism and munificence. "At a time when non-intercourse and encouragement of home industry are the public watchwords," proclaimed the *Edgefield Advertiser* in 1860, "it is but right to 'keep it before the people,' that *Vaucluse, Graniteville, Bath*, and *Kaolin*, are four *home* factories now in active and successful operation." While each factory was lauded in turn, Graniteville remained the particular recipient of public accolades. "If *contentment* and *self-respect* contribute largely towards the sum of happiness," asserted another scribe, "then of a verity may it be said that Graniteville is a place to make the heart of the Philanthropist rejoice."[27]

But did the legislative favor bestowed on Graniteville, as well as the concomitant manufacturing boom along the banks of Horse Creek, signal the onset of a full-fledged industrialization in South Carolina? Hardly. Graniteville and its neighbors remained among the scant handful of large-scale factories in the state and the rest of the South. But if regional changes wrought by these few factories were negligible, transformations at the local level proved fundamental. While parallels can be drawn to other conflicts over water rights in the antebellum era, the struggle at Horse Creek nevertheless displayed peculiarities. The contestants were not locked in some battle between competing precapitalist and capitalist visions of the good society. Nor did the industrialization of Horse Creek signal the arrival of market relations to the valley. That transition occurred with the arrival of the sawmills, not Vaucluse or Graniteville. Rather, the contest was between market-oriented entrepreneurs, each claiming the right to profit from the exploitation of the resources around them, but locked in a struggle to define the terms upon which the contestants would compete. Graniteville and the sawmills surrounding it differed from each other

---

certain road leading from Aiken to Graniteville may be declared a public Road," Petition, ND-3081 [1854], General Assembly Papers, SCDAH; *House Journal, 1854*, 70; *House Journal, 1855*, 16, 213; *Edgefield Advertiser*, September 15, 1858; William Gregg, *Letter of William Gregg to Thornton Coleman, Esq., June 8th, 1858* (Charleston, 1858), 3; Tom Downey, "The Need for the Right Sort of Men: The Political Career of William Gregg, 1856–1858," unpublished paper presented at the *Seventh Annual UNC–Charlotte Graduate History Forum*, University of North Carolina–Charlotte, March, 1995.

27. *Edgefield Advertiser*, February 22, 1860; March 16, 1859.

in scale, but not in overall purpose: to participate in a market society and reap its rewards. In that respect, they differed little from the economic motivations of their planter brethren in the agrarian landscape of Edgefield and Barnwell, who had likewise charted and sailed the same course for generations.[28]

But while the legislature deemed Gregg and his factory posed no threat to the slaveholders' regime—indeed, most observers asserted the factory had just the opposite effect—the exemption bestowed on Graniteville nevertheless carried significant costs for Edgefield and Barnwell. After the passage of the 1853 act, Horse Creek became a power source exclusively. Those requiring a transportation route would have to look elsewhere. It was perhaps the boldest, and most successful in a string of attacks on the socioeconomic norms handed down for generations in Edgefield and Barnwell. Both sides in the contest shared a market orientation, but the men of capital in the valley needed a different political economy in which to thrive, one that bestowed privilege on incorporated capital by revising laws and traditions that previously limited the prerogatives of private property. Gregg's exemption from the navigation laws effectively gave him the ability to exclude upstream sawyers from Horse Creek. No sawmill owner along the stream, no matter how many slaves he owned or how long established, ever received such license. The legislature no longer regulated competition among Horse Creek entrepreneurs. Instead, it chose the winners and losers.

---

28. For other conflicts over riparian rights, see Gary Kulik, "Dams, Fish, and Farmers: Defense of Public Rights in Eighteenth-Century Rhode Island," in *The Countryside in the Age of Capitalist Transformation*, ed. Steven Hahn and Jonathan Prude (Chapel Hill, 1985), 25–50; Harry L. Watson, "'The Common Rights of Mankind': Subsistence, Shad, and Commerce in the Early Republican South," *Journal of American History* 83 (June 1996): 13–43; Theodore Steinberg, *Nature Incorporated: Industrialization and the Waters of New England* (Cambridge, 1991), 99–165; and Morton J. Horwitz, *Transformation of American Law, 1780–1860* (Cambridge, Mass., 1977), 34–42. Steven Hahn has written extensively on disputes between yeomen and planters over common rights to unimproved lands, with a particular emphasis on conflicts over fence and stock laws. See Hahn, "Hunting, Fishing, and Foraging: Common Rights and Class Relations in the Postbellum South," *Radical History Review* 26 (1982): 37–64, and *The Roots of Southern Populism: Yeoman Farmers and the Transformation of the Georgia Upcountry, 1850–1890* (New York, 1983), 58–63, 239–68. On competing visions of economic progress in the South, see Daniel Dupre, "Ambivalent Capitalists on the Cotton Frontier: Settlement and Development in the Tennessee Valley of Alabama," *Journal of Southern History* 56 (May 1990): 215–40. For a sophisticated recent analysis on the penetration of capitalism into Old South, see Mark M. Smith, *Mastered by the Clock: Time, Slavery, and Freedom in the American South* (Chapel Hill, 1997), esp. 94–127, 154–76.

CONCLUSION

BY THE END OF 1860, the inhabitants of Edgefield and Barnwell districts had been calculating the value of the Union for as long as most could remember. Nullifiers had blazed the way, using the Tariff of 1828 as their catalyst. Though initially cool toward nullifier warnings of the threat posed by a northern congressional majority, Edgefield and Barnwell eventually warmed to the movement. A crowd of three thousand attended a pronullification rally at Edgefield Court House, passing resolutions declaring the Tariff of 1828 to be "a gross and palpable violation of the spirit of the Constitution," and called on all southerners as freemen "to resist to the utmost limit of their constitutional power, this unrighteous scheme of tyranny in *disguise*." An overflow crowd at Barnwell Court House took a similar stand and listened intently when state senator Angus Patterson denounced the tariff as being passed "against our consent, and in violation of our rights as well as our interests." The efforts of the nullifiers bore fruit in the fall of 1832. The previously moderate electorate of Edgefield and Barnwell cast their votes in favor of nullification candidates by wide majorities.[1]

Nullification succeeded in part because its proponents convinced residents that more was at stake than simply overturning an unfair tariff. When antitariff men at Edgefield claimed they were forced to choose between "slavery" and a course "necessary to save them from ruin and degradation," the reference to slavery was more than metaphorical. If they yielded national power to a northern majority, South Carolinians would suffer much more than political en-

1. Edgefield, *Carolinian*, January 23, 1830; *Charleston Mercury*, August 4, 11, 1828; Chauncey Samuel Boucher, "Sectionalism, Representation, and the Electoral Question in Ante-Bellum South Carolina," *Washington University Studies* 4 (October 1916): 44.

slavement. It was a point Angus Patterson made clear early in the nullification campaign. "One of the avowed objects of the Tariff, is to favor free labor, as it is called, at the expense of slave labor," he told a Barnwell gathering, "to render the latter species of labor unprofitable and indeed valueless, and thereby incline and force us to assent to a system of emancipation, through the agency of the General Government." If the tariff were allowed to stand, Patterson foresaw slavery as the next logical target of northern tyranny. "This question will be pressed upon as sure as we exist, and on the same grounds, and by the same arguments by which the Tariff was imposed."[2]

In the postnullification era, pointing out implicit threats to slavery from Congress and its northern majority became less and less necessary, as the growing abolitionist movement made such attacks unmistakable. Edgefield and Barnwell watched the rising tide of abolition with fear and disgust, then vented their wrath at both abolitionists and any among their own who seemed less than willing to defend their most vital interest. An 1836 public meeting in Edgefield lauded the uncompromising stand of Francis W. Pickens "in his prompt and bold resistance upon the floor of Congress to abolition fanaticism, as in every respect according with our own." A decade later, citizens of Barnwell Court House suspected a visiting lecturer on "the philosophy of magnetism" of being an abolitionist emissary. Town residents responded by forming a committee of ten, which then encouraged the itinerant professor to quit the town forthwith.[3]

The districts' defense of their peculiar society only intensified as the antebellum period advanced from nullification toward secession. An unbroken list of northern actions resulted in a deepening siege mentality among South Carolinians: the Wilmot Proviso, the Compromise of 1850, Kansas-Nebraska, and the ominous rise of the Republican Party. By the time James Henry Hammond addressed the assemblage at Barnwell Court House in the fall of 1858, much of his audience could scarcely recall a time when their ideals and institutions had not been under attack by abolitionists, a hostile congressional majority, and northern commercial interests. In the sectional crisis of 1851, co-operationists carried Edgefield and Barnwell by the smallest of majorities (by fifty-nine votes in Barnwell and just one vote in Edgefield, out of approximately 1,800 votes cast in each district). But the voters merely rejected, barely, the timing and tac-

2. *Charleston Mercury,* August 18, 1830.
3. *Edgefield Advertiser,* March 10, 1836; May 10, 1848.

tic of separate state secession, not the right to secede. Within a decade, the calculus would no longer be in doubt and the two districts followed their state out of the Union almost to a man.[4]

Despite the passion of their speech and the desperation of the act, secession struck few in Edgefield or Barnwell as particularly revolutionary. Indeed, they seceded in large part to avoid being caught up in a revolution. They wanted to preserve their society, not change it. They remained rooted in the past, idealizing themselves as kindred spirits to their forefathers, who likewise fought to shake off the yoke of foreign tyranny. The agrarian world of Hammond's Barnwell audience seemed little removed from that which their fathers and grandfathers erected upon cotton profits and African labor. It was a comforting continuity. Their society provided a last bastion, they believed, against the social, economic, and political revolutions that they had watched unfold in the North. Such was a world in which few, if any, in Edgefield or Barnwell wished to partake. Yet, by 1860, it was a world with which they had more in common than most would admit, or even realize.

Edgefield and Barnwell sent twelve men to South Carolina's secession convention in December 1860. Planters, predictably, dominated the ranks of those sent to the Columbia convention. Agrarian scions Andrew J. Hammond, James Smyly, and James Tompkins were among the Edgefield District delegation, while the aristocratic Lewis Malone Ayer Jr. and planter David F. Jamison led the Barnwell District contingent. In fact, Jamison received the high honor of being elected to preside over the convention by his fellow delegates. But while predominant, planters did not constitute the sole occupation of the Edgefield and Barnwell contingents. Town-dwelling professionals, like Aiken lawyers W. Peronneau Finley and Chancellor James P. Carroll as well as Edgefield physician R. G. M. Dunovant, were likewise elected by district voters to represent them at the convention, as was Barnwell merchant Josiah J. Brabham. Judge Francis H. Wardlaw of Edgefield Court House was among the seven delegates selected to draft a summary of the causes that justified the secession of South Carolina from the Union. Rounding out the Edgefield delegation was William Gregg, whom the convention journal identified as the "founder of Graniteville and the leading industrialist of the State." His attendance was

4. Chauncey Samuel Boucher, "The Secession and Co-Operation Movements in South Carolina, 1848 to 1852," *Washington University Studies* 5 (April 1918): 128.

brief. On December 25, five days after he affixed his signature to the Ordinance of Secession, Gregg was granted leave from the convention "for important business."[5]

On the surface, the two district delegations exuded a remarkable show of unity. As Edgefield and Barnwell followed the rest of South Carolina to the political precipice in December 1860, planters, lawyers, merchants, and even industrialists acted as one mind in the defense of slavery. One strand of this common thread was certainly self-interest. Slaveownership was universal among the Barnwell and Edgefield delegations (even William Gregg owned fourteen slaves by 1860). Similarly, even town-dwelling professionals like Carroll and Dunovant or merchants like Brabham operated sizable plantation interests as lucrative adjuncts to their legal and commercial interests. More significantly, there was little reason to expect district merchants and manufacturers to act otherwise. Besides a shared economic stake in slavery's existence—albeit one that varied widely among district slaveowners—men like Gregg and Brabham were likewise products of a political and social upbringing that unquestioningly defended the right of property in slaves, believed in the innate inferiority of the African race, maintained eternal vigilance against government power, and extolled paternalism as the proper relationship between the "better sorts" and the "lower classes." Immersed in such a social order, the acceptance of the political credo of states' rights, disgust over abolitionist fanaticism, and eventual embrace of secession was hardly out of character for a merchant or any other "man of capital" in the agrarian landscape.

But as the events of three decades amply demonstrated, a shared commitment to the preservation of slavery did not preclude conflict in other areas. Despite the common attachment of district agrarians to the past, the Edgefield and Barnwell of the secessionists was not that of their forefathers. While cotton plantations and yeoman farms blanketed the districts by 1860, the landscape also included towns and factories, business corporations and white wage laborers. But such physical changes, significant as they were by themselves, are only part of the story. As in other parts of rural America, the extent of the capitalist transformation in Edgefield and Barnwell was not always obvious, even to those who experienced it. Factories, towns, and railroads may have brought

5. For the secession convention and sketches of its members, see John Amasa May and Joan Reynolds Faunt, eds., *South Carolina Secedes* (Columbia, 1960), quotations 21.

the districts into closer contact with the industrial and the urban, but agriculture retained its preeminent role in the state and region at the end of the era, and for decades beyond. Even in the Northeast, a section of the country highly industrialized by southern standards, agriculture predominated for most of the antebellum era, even in areas that encountered significant industrial development.[6]

Shifts in attitude, however, were just as important (and arguably more so) than shifts in economic practice. The men of capital in Edgefield and Barnwell succeeded not by overthrowing the agrarian landscape, but by altering it to suit their needs. The urban dwellers, merchants, and manufacturers that resided in Edgefield and Barnwell had not been cowed into submission by the overwhelming hegemony of district slaveholders. Indeed, corporations like Graniteville and the South Carolina Railroad, as well as the rambunctious merchant class of the districts' burgeoning towns, had spent the previous thirty years successfully sculpting the agrarian landscape in the interests of capital. Not the agrarian capital of land and slaves, but the commercial and corporate capital of town merchants, railroads, and cotton factories. And while planters and yeomen certainly benefited politically and economically from these intrusions in their agrarian landscape, they paid a price as well. Southern defenders may have dismissed their commercial and industrial development as self-defense—a means to "out-Yankee the Yankees"—but such mimicking required more than a partial redirection of capital and entrepreneurship. It necessitated an aping of values and attitudes toward capital that left Edgefield and Barnwell a far different place in 1860 than it had been at the end of the eighteenth century.

For modern historians who see the Old South as fundamentally capitalist in nature, South Carolina's embrace of railroads and factories may be taken as part of the region's compatibility with other forms of capitalist enterprise. For counterparts who maintain that the Old South was a precapitalist society, some intellectual gymnastics will be necessary to explain away the legislative succor afforded to capitalist behemoths such as the SCRR and Graniteville. But the significance of the transformation of Edgefield and Barnwell districts does not

6. On the rural component of industrialization in the Northeast, see Jonathan Prude, *The Coming of Industrial Order: Town and Factory Life in Rural Massachusetts, 1810–1860* (Cambridge, 1983), esp. xi–xvi; Steven Hahn and Jonathan Prude, eds., *The Countryside in the Age of Capitalist Transformation* (Chapel Hill, 1985); and Christopher Clark, *The Roots of Rural Capitalism: Western Massachusetts, 1780–1860* (Cambridge, 1990), esp. 7–15.

require a sweeping definition of the South as either capitalist or precapitalist. A transition occurred—one in which the local political economy altered to favor men of capital over men of property. Individual enterprise backed by wealth garnered through land and slaves was no longer guaranteed prosperity or privilege. Rather, those benefits increasingly fell to those who pooled capital, incorporated, and curried government favor, even if their ties to slavery were more tangential than personal. And even though none of the participants saw these dramas as either enhancing or threatening the "peculiar institution," the results, nevertheless, held ramifications for the state's slave society. South Carolina's alternate route to modernity included a good many doses of capitalism, and masters did not find them especially bitter pills to swallow. But in their willingness to accept—and even encourage—change in order to protect themselves as a political class, they blurred the difference between themselves and their northern counterparts. The embrace of capital placed the agrarian landscape of South Carolina in transition from being a society with capitalist features toward becoming a capitalist society.[7]

7. Eugene D. Genovese, *The Slaveholders' Dilemma: Freedom and Progress in Southern Conservative Thought, 1820–1860* (Columbia, 1992), 10–46; idem, "Marxian Interpretations of the Slave South," in *Towards a New Past: Dissenting Essays in American History*, ed. Barton J. Bernstein (New York, 1967, 1969), 90–125; Mark M. Smith, *Mastered by the Clock: Time, Slavery, and Freedom in the American South* (Chapel Hill, 1997), esp. 174–76.

Bibliography

PRIMARY SOURCES

Manuscripts

Baker Library, Harvard Business School, Cambridge, Massachusetts.
  R. G. Dun & Company Collection

Gregg-Graniteville Library, University of South Carolina, Aiken.
  Gregg-Graniteville Collection

Library of Congress, Washington, D.C.
  James Henry Hammond Papers

Massachusetts Historical Society, Boston.
  Holmes Family Papers
  Amos A. Lawrence Diaries

New York Historical Society, New York.
  American Institute Collection

South Carolina Department of Archives and History, Columbia.
  Barnwell County Deeds
  Edgefield County Deeds
  General Assembly Papers
  Manuscript Census Returns

South Caroliniana Library, University of South Carolina, Columbia.
  William Aiken Papers
  Horatio Allen Papers

Orsamus D. Allen Letterbook
Lewis Malone Ayer Papers
Beech Island Farmers Club Records
Iveson L. Brookes Papers
James Edward Calhoun Papers
Cambridge Account Books
Felicia Canfield Papers
William Daniel Account Book
Demosthenian Debating Society Minutes
James Gadsden Papers
Graniteville Manufacturing Company Papers
Edward Spann Hammond Collection
James Henry Hammond Papers
David Montague Laffitte Papers
Robert Latta Papers
George McDuffie Papers
Norris and Thompson Family Papers
Francis W. Pickens Papers
Plantation Journal, Barnwell District
Henry Shultz Papers
Stroman Family Papers
John Eldred Swearingen Papers
David Duncan Wallace Papers
Josiah Wedgewood Papers

Southern Historical Collection, University of North Carolina, Chapel Hill.
David Gavin Diary
Springs Family Papers
Benjamin Cudworth Yancey Papers

Government Documents

Compendia to the United States Census, 1800, 1810, 1820, 1830, 1840, 1850, 1860.
U.S. Congress. House. *Memorial of the Inhabitants of Barnwell District, In S.C. Remonstrated Against Any Additional Duties on Imported Woollen Goods.* 20th Cong., 1st sess., H. Doc. No. 20. Washington, D.C., 1827.
———. House. *Memorial of the Citizens of Edgefield, Against the Woollens Bill.* 20th Cong., 1st sess., H. Doc. No. 24. Washington, D.C., 1827.

———. House. City Council of Charleston, S.C. *Memorial of the Canal and Rail Road Company.* 20th Cong., 1st sess., H. Doc. 246. Washington D.C.: Gales & Seaton, 1828.

———. *Register of Debates in Congress.* 21st Cong., 1st sess. Washington, D.C., 1830.

Court Cases

Addison v. Hard, 17 S.C.L. (1 Bailey, 1830)

Cook v. Gourdin, 11 S.C.L. (2 Nott & McCord, 1819)

Danner v. South Carolina Rail Road Company, 38 S.C.L. (4 Richardson, 1850)

Eaves v. Terry, 15 S.C.L. (4 McCord, 1827)

Ex'rs of Cates v. Wadlington, 12 S.C.L. (1 McCord, 1822)

Kennedy et al. v. Bank of the State of Georgia, et al., 12 U.S. Reports (8 Howard, 1850)

L.C.&C.R.R. Company v. J. J. Chappell; The Same v. Dr. Reese and Mrs. Reese, 24 S.C.L. (1 Rice, 1838)

Lindsay et al. v. Commissioners, 2 S.C.L. (2 Bay, 1796)

Murray v. South Carolina Railroad Company, 44 S.C.L. (10 Richardson, 1857)

Stark v. McGowen, 10 S.C.L. (1 Nott & McCord, 1818)

State v. Cullum; Toney v. Cullum, 29 S.C.L. (2 Spears, 1844)

State v. Dawson, 21 S.C.L. (3 Hill, 1836)

State v. Hickson, 39 S.C.L. (5 Richardson, 1852)

State v. Thompson, 33 S.C.L. (2 Strobhart, 1847)

Published Primary Material

Bagget, J. H. *Directory of the City of Charleston, for the Year 1852.* Charleston, 1851.

Bartram, William. *Travels and other Writings.* New York: Library of America, 1996.

Brookes, Iveson L. *A Defence of the South Against the Reproaches and Incroachments of the North, in Which Slavery is Shown to be an Institution of God Intended to Form the Basis of the Best Social State and the Only Safeguard to the Permanence of a Republican Government.* Hamburg, S.C.: Hamburg Republican, 1850.

———. *A Defence of Southern Slavery Against the Attacks of Henry Clay and Alex'r Campbell.* Hamburg, S.C.: Robinson and Carlisle, 1851.

Brown, Tarleton. *Memoirs of Tarleton Brown, A Captain in the Revolutionary Army, Written By Himself.* Barnwell, S.C.: The People Press, 1894.

Bryant, William Cullen. *Letters of a Traveller; or, Notes of Things Seen in Europe and America.* 2nd ed. New York: G. P. Putnam, 1869.

Buckingham, J. S. *The Slave States of America.* 2 vols. London and Paris: Fisher, Son & Co., 1842.

Campbell, John P. *The Southern Business Directory and General Commercial Advertiser.* Charleston: Walker & James, 1854.

Charter of the Town of Aiken, with the By-Laws and Ordinances, passed by the Town Council, June, 1860. Charleston: A. J. Burke, 1860.

Christy, David. *Cotton is King, or the Culture of Cotton and its Relation to Agriculture, Manufactures, and Commerce.* 2nd ed. Cincinnati: Moore, Wilstach, Keys & Co., 1856.

Cooper, Thomas. *Two Tracts: On the Proposed Alteration of the Tariff; and on Weights and Measures. Submitted to the Consideration of the Members from South Carolina, in the Ensuing Congress of 1823–24.* Charleston: A. E. Miller, 1823.

Cooper, Thomas, and David J. McCord. *Statutes at Large of South Carolina.* 10 vols. Columbia: A. S. Johnston, 1836–41.

Drayton, John. *A View of South-Carolina, As Respects Her Natural and Civil Concerns.* Charleston: W. P. Young, 1802.

Fay, T. C. *Charleston Directory, and Strangers' Guide for 1840 and 1841.* Charleston, 1840.

Featherstonhaugh, G. W. *Excursion Through the Slave States, from Washington on the Potomac to the Frontier of Mexico; with Sketches of Popular Manners and Geological Notices.* New York: Harper & Brothers, 1844.

Folsom, Michael Brewster, and Steven D. Lubar, eds. *The Philosophy of Manufactures: Early Debates over Industrialization in the United States.* Cambridge, Mass.: MIT Press, 1982.

Graf, LeRoy P., and Ralph W. Haskins, eds. "The Letters of a Georgia Unionist: John G. Winter and Secession." *Georgia Historical Quarterly* 45 (December 1961): 385–402.

Graniteville Manufacturing Company. *Report of the President and Treasurer of the Graniteville Manufacturing Company, for the Year 1854.* Charleston, 1855.

[Grayson, William J.]. "The Character of the Gentleman." *Southern Quarterly Review.* New Series 7 (January 1853): 53–80.

Gregg, William. *Essays on Domestic Industry; or, An Inquiry into the Expediency of Establishing Cotton Manufactures in South Carolina.* Charleston: Burges & James, 1845.

[————.] *An Enquiry into the Propriety of Granting Charters of Incorporation for Manufacturing and Other Purposes, in South Carolina.* Charleston, 1845.

————. "Manufactures in South Carolina and the South." *DeBow's Review* 11 (August 1851): 123–40.

————. *Speech of William Gregg, Member from Edgefield District, in the Legislature of South Carolina, December, 1857, on the Bank Question.* Columbia: R. W. Gibbes, 1857.

————. *Letter of William Gregg to Thornton Coleman, Esq., June 8th, 1858.* Charleston: Walker, Evans & Co., 1858.

————. "Southern Patronage to Southern Imports and Domestic Industry." *DeBow's Review* 29 (October 1860): 494–500.

Hamer, Philip M., George C. Rogers Jr., et al., eds. *The Papers of Henry Laurens.* 16 vols. Columbia: University of South Carolina Press, 1968–2003.

Hammond, James Henry. *An Address Delivered Before the South-Carolina Institute at its First Annual Fair, on the 20th November, 1849.* Charleston: Walker and James, 1849.

Hawes, Lilla M., ed. "Letters to the Georgia Colonial Agent, July 1762 to January 1771." *Georgia Historical Quarterly* 36 (September 1952): 250–86.

Hemphill, W. Edwin, Clyde N. Wilson, et al., eds. *The Papers of John C. Calhoun.* 28 vols. Columbia: University of South Carolina Press, 1959–2003.

Holcomb, Brent, ed. *Winton (Barnwell) County, South Carolina, Minutes of Country Court and Will Book 1, 1785–1791.* Easley, S.C.: Southern Historical Press, 1978.

Honour, John H., Jr. *A Directory of the City of Charleston and Neck, for 1849.* Charleston, 1849.

Horry, Elias. *An Address Delivered in Charleston, Before the Agricultural Society of South Carolina, at its Anniversary Meeting, on Tuesday, the 19th August, 1828.* Charleston: A. E. Miller, 1828.

————. *An Address Respecting the Charleston & Hamburg Railroad, and on the Railroad System as regards a Large Portion of the Southern and Western States of the North American Union.* Charleston: A. E. Miller, 1833.

Howard, William. *Report of the Charleston and Hamburg Rail-Road.* Charleston: n.p., 1829.

Jackson, Donald, and Dorothy Twohig, eds. *The Diaries of George Washington.* 6 vols. Charlottesville: University Press of Virginia, 1976–79.

Journal of the House of Representatives of the State of South Carolina, Being the Annual Session of 1852. Columbia: R. W. Gibbes, 1852.

Journal of the House of Representatives of the State of South Carolina, Being the Annual Session of 1853. Columbia: R. W. Gibbes & Co., 1853.

Journal of the House of Representatives of the State of South Carolina, Being the Annual Session of 1854. Columbia: R. W. Gibbes & Co., 1854.

Journal of the House of Representatives of the State of South Carolina, Being the Annual Session of 1855. Columbia: E. H. Britton & Co., 1855.

Journal of the Senate of South Carolina, Being the Extra and Annual Sessions of 1852. Columbia: Johnston & Cavis, 1852.

Journal of the Senate of South Carolina, Being the Annual Session of 1853. Columbia: R. W. Gibbes & Co., 1853.

Kirkland, Wilma Copeland, and Dorothy Havens Wheeler, eds. *Winton County Tax List, 1800.* Greenwood, S.C.: Kirkland and Wheeler, 1977.

Martin, Thomas P., ed. "The Advent of William Gregg and the Graniteville Company." *Journal of Southern History* 11 (August 1945): 389–423.

Mathew, William M., ed. *Agriculture, Geology, and Society in Antebellum South Carolina: The Private Diary of Edmund Ruffin, 1843.* Athens: University of Georgia Press, 1992.

May, John Amasa, and Joan Reynolds Faunt, eds. *South Carolina Secedes.* Columbia: University of South Carolina Press, 1960.

Mills, Robert. *Statistics of South Carolina, Including a View of its Natural, Civil, and Military History, General and Particular.* Charleston: Hurlbut and Lloyd, 1826.

Minutes of the Proceedings of a Convention of Merchants and Others, Held in Augusta, Georgia, October 16, 1837; with an Address to the People of the South and South-Western States, relative to the establishment of a Direct Export and Import Trade with Foreign Countries. Augusta: Benj. Brantly, 1838.

Minutes of the Proceedings of the Second Convention of Merchants and Others, Held in Augusta, Georgia, April 2d, 1838. With an Address to the People of the Southern and South-western States, Relative to the Establishment of a Direct Export and Import Trade with Foreign Countries. Augusta: Benj. Brantly, 1838.

Minutes of the Proceedings of the Third Commercial Convention, Held in Augusta, Georgia, in October 1838; with the Report of the Committee on the Object of the Convention. Augusta: Benj. Brantly, 1838.

Olmsted, Frederick Law. *The Cotton Kingdom: A Traveller's Observations of Cot-*

ton and Slavery in the American Slave States. Edited by Arthur Schlesinger Sr. New York: Modern Library, 1984.

Padgett, James A., ed. "Journal of Daniel Walker Lord, Kept While on a Southern Trip." *Georgia Historical Quarterly* 26 (June 1942): 166–95.

Patterson, Angus. *An Address to the Farmers' Society of Barnwell District, Delivered on the Second Day of January, 1826.* Charleston: A. E. Miller, 1826.

Pickens, Francis W. *An Address, Delivered Before the State Agricultural Society of South Carolina, in the Hall of the House of Representatives, November 29, 1849.* Columbia: A. S. Johnston, 1849.

Proceedings of the Fourth Convention of Merchants and Others, Held in Charleston, S.C., April 15, 1839, For the Promotion of The Direct Trade. Charleston: A. E. Miller, 1839.

Ramsay, David. *History of South Carolina, From its First Settlement in 1670 to the Year 1808.* 2 vols. Charleston: David Longworth, 1808.

Report of a Special Committee Appointed by the Chamber of Commerce, to Inquire into the Cost, Revenue and Advantages of a Rail Road Communication Between the City of Charleston and the Towns of Hamburg & Augusta. Charleston: A. E. Miller, 1828.

Robbins, Walter L., trans. and ed. "John Tobler's Description of South Carolina (1753)." *South Carolina Historical Magazine* 71 (July 1970): 141–61.

Scott, Edwin J. *Random Recollections of a Long Life, 1806–1876.* 1884. Reprint, Columbia: R. L. Bryan, 1969.

Seabrook, Whitemarsh. *Memoir of the Origin, Cultivation and Uses of Cotton.* Charleston: Miller & Browne, 1844.

Simkins, Arthur. *An Address by Arthur Simkins, Esp., Before the State Agricultural Society of South Carolina, at its First Anniversary Meeting, Held During the Month of November, 1855 and Columbia S.C.* Edgefield, S.C.: Advertiser Office, 1855.

Simms, William Gilmore. *The Geography of South Carolina.* Charleston: Babcock & Co., 1843.

South Carolina Canal and Railroad Company. *First Semi-Annual Report, to the President and Directors of the South-Carolina Canal and Rail-Road Company, by their Committee of Inquiry.* Charleston: A. E. Miller, 1828.

———. *By-Laws of the South Carolina Canal and Rail Road Company, adopted by the Stockholders, May 13, 1828, together with The Act of Incorporation Granted by the State Legislature.* Charleston: J. S. Burges, 1828.

————. *Semi-Annual Report of the Board of Directors, of the South-Carolina Canal and Rail Road Company.* Charleston: A. E. Miller, 1829.

————. *Annual Report of the South-Carolina Canal and Rail Road Company, By the Direction. Submitted and Adopted May 2, 1831.* Charleston: Irishman and Democrat, 1831.

[————.] *To the Friends of Internal Improvement in the Southern States, July 24, 1833.* [Coker Springs, S.C.: South Carolina Canal and Railroad Company], 1833.

————. *Semi-Annual Report of the Direction of the South-Carolina Canal & Rail-Road Company to the Stockholders, November 4th, 1833.* Charleston: A. E. Miller, 1833.

————. *Report of the Committee on Cars, to the Direction of the South-Carolina Canal & Rail-Road Company, submitted to the Stockholders, on Wednesday, 20th November, 1833.* Charleston: A. E. Miller, 1833.

————. *Annual Report of the Direction of the South Carolina Canal and Rail Road Company. To The Stockholders, May 6th, 1834, with Accompanying Documents.* Charleston: W. S. Blain, 1834.

————. *Semi-Annual Report of the Direction of the South-Carolina Canal and Rail-Road Company, to the Stockholders, October 31, 1834.* Charleston: J. S. Burges, 1834.

————. *Annual Report of the Board of Direction of the So. Carolina Canal & R.R. Company, with the Semi-Annual Statement of Accounts, to the 31st December, 1835.* Charleston: A. E. Miller, 1836.

————. *Semi-Annual Report of the South-Carolina Canal and Rail Road Company* [January–June, 1836]. Charleston: A. E. Miller, 1836.

————. *Semi-Annual Report of the South-Carolina Canal and Rail-Road Company. Accepted Dec. 31st, 1836.* Charleston: A. E. Miller, 1837.

————. *Semi-Annual Report of the Direction of the South-Carolina Canal and Rail Road Company. July 10, 1837.* Charleston: J. S. Burges, 1837.

————. *Semi-Annual Report of the South-Carolina Canal and Rail-Road Company, To December 31, 1837.* Charleston: J. S. Burges, 1837.

————. *Semi-Annual Report of the Direction of the South-Carolina Canal and Rail-Road Company, to July, 1838.* Charleston: Burges & James, 1838.

————. *Semi-Annual Report of the South-Carolina Canal and Rail-Road Company. Accepted Jan. 18th, 1839.* Charleston: A. E. Miller, 1839.

————. *Semi-Annual Report of the South-Carolina Canal and Rail-Road Company, Accepted July 15th, 1839.* Charleston: A. E. Miller, 1839.

————. *Semi-Annual Report of the South-Carolina Canal and Rail Road Company, Accepted Jan. 18th, 1840.* Charleston: A. E. Miller, 1840.

————. *Semi-Annual Report to the Stockholders of the South-Carolina Canal and Rail-Road Company, Made on the Third Monday of July, 20th, 1840, In Conformity with a By-Law of the Company.* Charleston: A. E. Miller, 1840.

————. *Semi-Annual Report to the Stockholders of the South-Carolina Canal and Rail Road Company, Made on the Third Monday of January, 18th, 1841. In Conformity with a By-Law of the Company.* Charleston: A. E. Miller, 1841.

————. *Semi-Annual Report to the Stockholders of the South-Carolina Canal and Rail-Road Company. Made on the Third Monday of July, 19th, 1841, in Conformity with a By-Law of the Company.* Charleston: A. E. Miller, 1841.

————. *Semi-Annual Report to the Stockholders of the South-Carolina Canal and Rail-Road Company. Made on the Third Monday in January (the 17th.) in Conformity with a By-Law of the Company.* Charleston: A. E. Miller, 1842.

————. *Semi-Annual Report of the South-Carolina Canal and Rail-Road Company. Accepted July 20, 1842.* Charleston: A. E. Miller, 1842.

————. *Thirtieth Semi-Annual Report of the South-Carolina Canal and Rail-Road Company, to January 1st, 1843, Accepted at the Adjourned Meeting, 28th February, 1843.* Charleston: Miller & Browne, 1843.

————. *Semi-Annual Report of the South-Carolina Canal and Rail-Road Company, Accepted 20th of July, 1843.* Charleston: Miller & Browne, 1843.

South Carolina Railroad Company. *Proceedings of the Stockholders of the South-Carolina Rail-Road Company and the South-Western Rail-Road Bank, at their Annual Meeting, in the Hall of the Bank, on the 11th, 12th, and 13th February, 1845.* Charleston: Burges & James, 1845.

————. *Proceedings of the Stockholders of the South-Carolina Rail-Road Company, and the South-Western Rail-Road Bank, at their Annual Meeting, in the Hall of the Bank, on the 10th, 11th, and 12th February, 1846.* Charleston: Miller & Browne, 1846.

————. *Proceedings of a Meeting of the Stockholders of the South-Carolina Rail-Road Company, Held in the Hall of the S. W. Rail-Road Bank, Tuesday, November 17, 1846.* Charleston: Walker & Burke, 1846.

————. *Report by the President of So. Ca. Rail Road Company, and of A Committee of Seven Appointed by the Stockholders, on the Change of Location of the Present Depot, and Work Shops on May and Line Streets, with the Advantages, Objections, and Probable Cost of each New Location Suggested. Also, The Engineer's Report upon Inclined Place, &c.* Charleston: Walker & Burke, 1846.

————. *Proceedings of the Stockholders of the South-Carolina Rail-Road Company, and the South-Western Rail-Road Bank, at their Annual Meeting, in the Hall of the Bank, on the 9th, 10th, and 11th February, 1847.* Charleston: Miller & Browne, 1847.

————. *Proceedings of the Stockholders of the South-Carolina Rail-Road Company, and the South-Western Rail-Road Bank, at their Annual Meeting, in the Hall of the Bank, on the 8th and 9th February 1848.* Charleston: Miller & Browne, 1848.

————. *Report of the Committee of Inspection on the Condition of the South-Carolina Rail-Road. Made at An Extra Meeting of the Stockholders, held on the 2d. of May 1848.* Charleston: Miller & Browne, 1848.

————. *Action of the Stockholders of the South-Carolina Railroad Company, On The Reports and Resolutions of the Committee of Inspection, Held At the Hall of the South-Western Railroad Bank, on Tuesday, 30th of May 1848. To Which is Annexed, in an Appendix, The Report of the President to Board of Directors, Referred to in the Proceedings; and the Report of S. M. Fox (Civil Engineer,) on the Inclined Plane.* Charleston: Miller & Browne, 1848.

————. *Proceedings of the Stockholders of the South-Carolina Rail-Road Company, and of the South-Western Rail-Road Bank, At Their Annual Meeting, in the Hall of the Bank, on the 13th and 14th February 1849.* Charleston: Miller & Browne, 1849.

————. *Proceedings of the Stockholders of the South-Carolina Rail-Road Company, and of the South-Western Rail-Road Bank, at their Annual Meeting, in the Hall of the Bank, on the 12th, 13th and 14th February 1850.* Charleston: Miller & Browne, 1850.

————. *Proceedings of the Stockholders of the South-Carolina Rail-Road Company, and of the South-Western Rail-Road Bank, At Their Annual Meeting, in the Hall of the Bank, on the 11th and 12th February 1851.* Charleston: A. E. Miller, 1851.

————. *Proceedings of the Stockholders of the South-Carolina Rail-Road Company, and of the South-Western Rail-Road Bank, At Their Annual Meeting, in the Hall of the Bank, on the 10th, 11th and 12th February 1852.* Charleston: A. E. Miller, 1852.

————. *Proceedings of the Stockholders of the South-Carolina Rail-Road Company, and of the South-Western Rail-Road Bank, At Their Annual Meeting, in the Hall of the Bank, on the 8th and 9th of February 1853.* Charleston: A. E. Miller, 1853.

————. *Proceedings of the Stockholders of the South-Carolina Rail-Road Company, and of the South-Western Rail-Road Bank, At Their Annual Meeting, in the Hall of the Bank, on the 14th and 15th February 1854.* Charleston: A. E. Miller, 1854.

————. *Proceedings of the Stockholders of the South-Carolina Rail-Road Company, February 1855.*

————. *Proceedings of the Stockholders of the South-Carolina Rail Road Company, and of the South-Western Rail Road Bank. At Their Annual Meeting, in the Hall of the Bank, on the 12th and 13th of February 1856.* Charleston: A. E. Miller, 1856.

————. *Annual Reports of the President and Directors and the General Superintendent of the South Carolina Railroad Company, For the Year Ending December 31st, 1857.* Charleston: Walker, Evans, & Co., 1858.

State Agricultural Society. *The Proceedings of the Agricultural Convention and of the State Agricultural Society of South Carolina, From 1839–1845—Inclusive.* Columbia: Summer & Carroll, 1846.

Suggestions for the Improvement of the Commerce of the State of South-Carolina, As Originally Published in the Charleston Courier, the 27th October, 1827. Charleston: J. S. Burges, 1827.

Thompson, Theodora J., and Rosa S. Lumpkin, eds. *Journals of the House of Representatives, 1783–1784.* Columbia: University of South Carolina Press, 1977.

Thomson, William. *A Tradesman's Travels, in the United States and Canada in the Years 1840, 41, & 42.* Edinburgh, 1842.

Vattel, Emer de. *The Law of Nations; or, Principles of the Law of Nature, Applied to the Conduct and Affairs of Nations and Sovereigns.* Philadelphia: Abraham Small, 1817.

Walsh, Richard, ed. *The Writings of Christopher Gadsden, 1746–1805.* Columbia: University of South Carolina Press, 1966.

Wilson, Clyde N., ed. *Selections from the Letters and Speeches of the Hon. James H. Hammond of South Carolina.* Spartanburg, S.C.: The Reprint Company, 1978.

Wiltse, Charles M., et al., eds. *The Papers of Daniel Webster.* 14 vols. Hanover, N.H.: University Press of New England, 1974–89.

"Winton." *Remarks on Barnwell District, South Carolina.* n.p., 1839.

Newspapers and Periodicals

Aiken Telegraph and Commercial Advertiser
Barnwell, *Palmetto Sentinel*

Charleston Courier
Charleston Mercury
Charleston, *South-Carolina Weekly Advertiser*
Columbia, *South Carolina State Gazette and Columbian Advertiser*
Columbia, *Southern Times*
De Bow's Review
Edgefield Advertiser
Edgefield, *Anti-Monarchist and South Carolina Advertiser*
Edgefield, *Carolinian*
Hunt's Merchants' Magazine
Pottersville, *Edgefield Hive*
Pottersville, *South-Carolina Republican*

SECONDARY SOURCES

Books and Articles

Ackerman, Robert K. *South Carolina Colonial Land Policies.* Columbia: University of South Carolina Press, 1977.

Atherton, Lewis E. "Itinerant Merchandising in the Ante-Bellum South." *Bulletin of the Business Historical Society* 19 (April 1945): 35–59.

———. *The Southern Country Store, 1800–1860.* Baton Rouge: Louisiana State University Press, 1949.

Bacot, D. Huger. "The South Carolina Middle Country at the End of the Eighteenth Century." *South Atlantic Quarterly* 23 (1924): 50–60.

Bailey, N. Louise, Mary L. Morgan, and Carolyn R. Taylor, eds. *Biographical Directory of the South Carolina Senate, 1776–1985.* 3 vols. Columbia: University of South Carolina Press, 1985.

Bailey, N. Louise, et al., eds. *Biographical Directory of the South Carolina House of Representatives.* 5 vols. Columbia: University of South Carolina Press, 1974–92.

Baldwin, Cinda K. *Great & Noble Jar: Traditional Stoneware of South Carolina.* Athens and London: University of Georgia Press, 1993.

Banner, James M. "The Problem of South Carolina." In *The Hofstadter Aegis: A Memorial,* edited by Stanley Elkins and Eric McKitrick. New York: Knopf, 1974.

Barber, Edwin Atlee. *The Pottery and Porcelain of the United States.* 3rd ed. New York and London: G. P. Putnam's Sons, 1909.

Barry, John M. *Natural Vegetation of South Carolina*. Columbia: University of South Carolina Press, 1980.

Bateman, Fred, and Thomas Weiss. *A Deplorable Scarcity: The Failure of Industrialization in the Slave Economy*. Chapel Hill: University of North Carolina Press, 1981.

Bogin, Ruth. "Petitioning in the New Moral Economy of Post-Revolutionary America." *William and Mary Quarterly*. 3rd series, 45 (July 1988): 391–425.

Boucher, Chancey Samuel. "The Ante-Bellum Attitude of South Carolina Towards Manufacturing and Agriculture." *Washington University Studies* 3 (April 1916): 243–70.

———. "Sectionalism, Representation, and the Electoral Question in Antebellum South Carolina." *Washington University Studies* 4 (October 1916): 3–62.

———. "The Secession and Co-Operation Movements in South Carolina, 1848–1852." *Washington University Studies* 5 (April 1918): 67–138.

Brabham, M. M. *A Family Sketch, and Else, or Buford's Bridge and its People*. Columbia: The State Company, 1923.

Brown, Richard M. *The South Carolina Regulators*. Cambridge, Mass.: Belknap Press of Harvard University Press, 1963.

Bryant, Jonathan M. *How Curious a Land: Conflict and Change in Greene County, Georgia, 1850–1885*. Chapel Hill: University of North Carolina Press, 1996.

Burton, Orville Vernon. "Anatomy of an Antebellum Rural Free Black Community: Social Structure and Social Interaction in Edgefield District, South Carolina, 1850–1860." *Southern Studies* 21 (fall 1982): 294–325.

———. *In My Father's House are Many Mansions: Family & Community on Edgefield, South Carolina*. Chapel Hill: University of North Carolina Press, 1985.

Carlton, David L. *Mill and Town in South Carolina, 1880–1920*. Baton Rouge: Louisiana State University Press, 1982.

Channing, Steven A. *Crisis of Fear: Secession in South Carolina*. New York: Simon and Schuster, 1970.

Chaplin, Joyce E. *An Anxious Pursuit: Agricultural Innovation & Modernity in the Lower South, 1730–1815*. Chapel Hill: University of North Carolina Press, 1993.

Chapman, John A. *History of Edgefield County: From the Earliest Settlements to 1897*. Newberry, S.C.: E. H. Aull, 1897.

Clark, Christopher. "The Household Economy, Market Exchange, and the Rise of Capitalism in the Connecticut Valley, 1800–1860." *Journal of Social History* 13 (winter 1979): 169–89.

Clowse, Converse D. *Economic Beginnings in Colonial South Carolina, 1670–1730.* Columbia: University of South Carolina Press, 1971.

Coclanis, Peter A. "Retailing in Early South Carolina." In *Retailing: Theory and Practice for the 21st Century*, edited by Robert L. King. Charleston: Academy of Marketing Science, 1986.

———. *The Shadow of a Dream: Economic Life and Death in the South Carolina Low County.* New York: Oxford University Press, 1989.

———. "The Hydra Head of Merchant Capital: Markets and Merchants in Early South Carolina." In *The Meaning of South Carolina History: Essays in the Honor of George C. Rogers, Jr.,* edited by David R. Chesnutt and Clyde N. Wilson. Columbia: University of South Carolina Press, 1991.

Cordle, Charles G. "The Bank of Hamburg, South Carolina." *Georgia Historical Quarterly* 23 (June 1939): 148–53.

———. "Henry Shultz and the Founding of Hamburg, South Carolina." In *Studies in Georgia History and Government,* edited by James C. Bonner and Lucien E. Roberts. Athens: University of Georgia Press, 1940.

Coulter, E. Merton. "The Georgia-Tennessee Boundary Line." *Georgia Historical Quarterly* 35 (December 1951): 269–306.

Davis, Joseph Stancliffe. "Corporations in the American Colonies." In vol. 1 of *Essays in the Earlier History of American Corporations.* 2 vols. Cambridge, Mass.: Harvard University Press, 1917.

Davis, Robert S., Jr. "The Story and Records of the Winter Iron Works." *Alabama Review* 53 (July 2000): 199–205.

Derrick, Samuel M. *Centennial History of South Carolina Railroad.* Columbia: The State Company, 1930.

Downey, Tom. "Riparian Rights and Manufacturing in Antebellum South Carolina: William Gregg and the Origins of the 'Industrial Mind.'" *Journal of Southern History* 65 (February 1999): 77–108.

Dupre, Daniel S. "Ambivalent Capitalists on the Cotton Frontier: Settlement and Development in the Tennessee Valley of Alabama." *Journal of Southern History* 56 (May 1990): 215–40.

———. *Transforming the Cotton Frontier: Madison District, Alabama, 1800–1840.* Baton Rouge: Louisiana State University Press, 1997.

Edmunds, John B. *Francis W. Pickens and the Politics of Destruction.* Chapel Hill: University of North Carolina Press, 1986.

Egerton, Douglas R. "Markets Without a Market Revolution: Southern Planters and Capitalism." *Journal of the Early Republic* 16 (summer 1996): 207–21.

Eisterhold, John A. "Charleston: Lumber and Trade in a Declining Southern Port." *South Carolina Historical Magazine* 74 (April 1973): 61–72.

———. "Savannah: Lumber Center of the South Atlantic." *Georgia Historical Quarterly* 57 (winter 1973): 526–43.

Faust, Drew Gilpin. *James Henry Hammond and the Old South: A Design for Mastery.* Baton Rouge: Louisiana State University Press, 1982.

Feller, Daniel. "The Market Revolution Ate My Homework." *Reviews in American History* 25 (September 1997): 408–15.

Fishlow, Albert. *American Railroads and the Transformation of the Ante-Bellum Economy.* Cambridge, Mass.: Harvard University Press, 1965.

Fogel, Robert, and Stanley Engerman. *Time on the Cross: The Economics of American Negro Slavery.* 2 vols. Boston: Little, Brown, 1974.

Foner, Eric. *Free Soil, Free Labor, Free Men: The Ideology of the Republican Party Before the Civil War.* New York and Oxford: Oxford University Press, 1970, 1995.

Ford, Lacy K., Jr. "Rednecks and Merchants: Economic Development and Social Tensions in the South Carolina Upcountry, 1865–1900." *Journal of American History* 71 (September 1984): 294–318.

———. "Yeoman Farmers in the South Carolina Upcountry: Changing Production Patterns in the Late Antebellum Period." *Agricultural History* 60 (fall 1986): 17–37.

———. *Origins of Southern Radicalism: The South Carolina Upcountry, 1800–1860.* New York and Oxford: Oxford University Press, 1988.

———. "A Tale of Two Entrepreneurs in the Old South: John Springs III and Hiram Hutchison of the South Carolina Upcountry." *South Carolina Historical Magazine* 95 (July 1994): 198–224.

———. "Origins of the Edgefield Tradition: The Late Antebellum Experience and the Roots of Political Insurgency." *South Carolina Historical Magazine* 98 (October 1997): 328–48.

Freehling, William W. *Prelude to Civil War: The Nullification Controversy in South Carolina, 1816–1836.* New York: Harper & Row, 1966.

Friedman, Lawrence M. *A History of American Law.* 2nd ed. New York: Simon and Schuster, 1985.

Genovese, Eugene D. *The Political Economy of Slavery: Studies in the Economy and Society of the Slave South.* 2nd ed. Westport, Conn.: Wesleyan University Press, 1989.

———. "Marxian Interpretations of the Slave South." In *Towards a New Past: Dissenting Essays in American History,* edited by Barton J. Bernstein. New York: Pantheon, 1968.

———. *The World the Slaveholders Made: Two Essays in Interpretation.* New York: Pantheon, 1969.

———. *The Slaveholders' Dilemma: Freedom and Progress in Southern Conservative Thought, 1820–1860.* Columbia: University of South Carolina Press, 1992.

Genovese, Eugene D., and Elizabeth Fox-Genovese. *Fruits of Merchant Capital: Slavery and Bourgeois Property in the Rise and Expansion of Capitalism.* New York: Oxford University Press, 1983.

"Georgia-South Carolina Territorial Disputes." *Georgia Historical Quarterly* 12 (March 1928): 53–61.

Gienapp, William E. "The Crime Against Sumner: The Caning of Charles Sumner and the Rise of the Republican Party." *Civil War History* 25 (September 1979): 218–45.

Gilje, Paul A. "The Rise of Capitalism in the Early Republic." *Journal of the Early Republic* 16 (summer 1996): 159–81.

———, ed. *Wages of Independence: Capitalism in the Early American Republic.* Madison, Wis.: Madison House, 1997.

Gillespie, Michelle. *Free Labor in an Unfree World: White Artisans in Slaveholding Georgia, 1789–1860.* Athens and London: University of Georgia Press, 2000.

Goldfield, David R. *Cotton Fields and Skyscrapers: Southern City and Region, 1607–1980.* Baton Rouge: Louisiana State University Press, 1982.

Gray, Lewis Cecil. *History of Agriculture in the Southern United States to 1860.* 2 vols. Washington, D.C.: Carnegie Institution of Washington, 1933.

Green, Edwin L. *George McDuffie.* Columbia, S.C.: The State Company, 1936.

Grinde, Donald A., Jr. "Building the South Carolina Railroad." *South Carolina Historical Magazine* 77 (April 1976): 84–96.

Gutman, Herbert G. "Work, Culture, and Society in Industrializing America, 1815–1920." *American Historical Review* 78 (June 1973): 531–88.

Hahn, Steven. "Hunting, Fishing, and Foraging: Common Rights and Class

Relations in the Postbellum South." *Radical History Review* 26 (1982): 37–64.

———. *The Roots of Southern Populism: Yeoman Farmers and the Transformation of the Georgia Upcountry, 1850–1890.* New York and Oxford: Oxford University Press, 1983.

Hahn, Steven, and Jonathan Prude, eds. *The Countryside in the Age of Capitalist Transformation.* Chapel Hill: University of North Carolina Press, 1985.

Hammond, Bray. *Banks and Politics in America: From the Revolution to the Civil War.* Princeton, N.J.: Princeton University Press, 1957.

Handlin, Oscar, and Mary F. Handlin. "Origins of the American Business Corporation." *Journal of Economic History* 5 (May 1945): 1–23.

Harris, J. William. *Plain Folk and Gentry in a Slave Society: White Liberty and Black Slavery in Augusta's Hinterlands.* Baton Rouge: Louisiana State University Press, 1985.

Heath, Milton Sydney. *Constructive Liberalism: The Role of the State in Economic Development in Georgia to 1860.* Cambridge, Mass.: Harvard University Press, 1954.

Henretta, James. "Families and Farms: Mentalité in Pre-Industrial American." *William and Mary Quarterly.* 3rd series, 35 (January 1978): 3–32.

Hobsbawm, Eric J. *The Age of Capital, 1848–1875.* London: Weidenfeld and Nicolson, 1975.

Hollis, Daniel W. "Costly Delusion: Inland Navigation in the South Carolina Piedmont." *Proceedings of the South Carolina Historical Association* (1968): 29–43.

Horwitz, Morton J. *The Transformation of American Law, 1780–1860.* Cambridge, Mass.: Harvard University Press, 1977.

Ingle, H. Larry, ed. "Joseph Wharton Goes South, 1853." *South Carolina Historical Magazine* 96 (October 1995): 304–28.

Jaffee, David. "One of the Primitive Sort: Portrait Makers of the Rural North, 1760–1860." In *The Countryside in the Age of Capitalist Transformation,* edited by Steven Hahn and Jonathan Prude. Chapel Hill: University of North Carolina Press, 1985.

———. "Peddlers of Progress and the Transformation of the Rural North, 1760–1860." *Journal of American History* 78 (September 1991): 511–35.

Jaher, Frederic Cople. *The Urban Establishment: Upper Strata in Boston, New York, Charleston, Chicago, and Los Angeles.* Urbana: University of Illinois Press, 1982.

Johnson, Paul E. *A Shopkeeper's Millennium: Society and Revivals in Rochester, New York, 1815–1837.* New York: Hill and Wang, 1978.

———. "The Market Revolution." In *Encyclopedia of American Social History,* edited by Mary K. Cayton, Elliott J. Gorn, and Peter W. Williams. 3 vols. New York: Scribner, 1993.

Jones, Lu Ann. "Gender, Race, and Itinerant Commerce in the Rural New South." *Journal of Southern History* 66 (May 2000): 297–320.

King, Alvy L. *Louis T. Wigfall: Southern Fire-Eater.* Baton Rouge: Louisiana State University Press, 1970.

Klein, Rachel N. *Unification of a Slave State: The Rise of the Planter Class in the South Carolina Backcountry, 1760–1800.* Chapel Hill: University of North Carolina Press, 1990.

Kolchin, Peter. *American Slavery, 1619–1877.* New York: Hill and Wang, 1993.

Kovacik, Charles F., and John J. Winberry. *South Carolina: The Making of a Landscape.* Columbia: University of South Carolina Press, 1989.

Kulikoff, Allan. "The Transition to Capitalism in Rural America." *William and Mary Quarterly.* 3rd series, 46 (January 1989): 120–44.

Lander, Ernest McPherson, Jr. "Paper Manufacturing in South Carolina Before the Civil War." *North Carolina Historical Review* 29 (April 1952): 220–27.

———. *The Textile Industry in Antebellum South Carolina.* Baton Rouge: Louisiana State University Press, 1969.

Larson, John Lauritz. *Internal Improvement: National Public Works and the Promise of Popular Government in the Early United States.* Chapel Hill: University of North Carolina Press, 2001.

Lears, Jackson. *Fables of Abundance: A Cultural History of Advertising in America.* New York: Basic Books, 1994.

Lesesne, J. Mauldin. *The Bank of the State of South Carolina: A General and Political History.* Columbia: University of South Carolina Press, 1970.

Licht, Walter. *Industrializing America: The Nineteenth Century.* Baltimore and London: Johns Hopkins University Press, 1995.

Livingston, John. *Portraits of Eminent Americans Now Living; Including President Pierce and his Cabinet: with Biographical and Historical Memoirs of their Lives and Actions.* New York: n.p., 1853.

Lord, Clyde W. "Young Lewis Wigfall: South Carolina Politician and Duelist." *South Carolina Historical Magazine* 59 (April 1958): 96–112.

Luraghi, Raimondo. *The Rise and Fall of the Plantation South.* New York and London: New Viewpoints, 1978.

McCoy, Drew R. *The Elusive Republic: Political Economy in Jeffersonian America.* Chapel Hill: University of North Carolina Press, 1980.

McCurry, Stephanie. *Masters of Small Worlds: Yeoman Households, Gender Relations, & the Political Culture of the Antebellum South Carolina Low County.* New York and Oxford: Oxford University Press, 1995.

McPherson, James M. *Battle Cry of Freedom: The Civil War Era.* New York: Oxford University Press, 1988.

Maier, Pauline. "The Revolutionary Origins of the American Corporation." *William and Mary Quarterly.* 3rd series, 50 (January 1993): 51–84.

Majewski, John. "A Revolution Too Many?" *Journal of Economic History* 57 (June 1997): 476–80.

Majewski, John, Christopher Baer, and Daniel B. Klein. "Responding to Relative Decline: The Plank Road Boom of Antebellum New York." *Journal of Economic History* 53 (March 1993): 106–22.

Meriwether, Robert L. *The Expansion of South Carolina, 1729–1765.* Kingsport, Tenn.: Southern Publishers Inc., 1940.

Merrill, Michael. "Cash is Good to Eat: Self-Sufficiency and Exchange in the Rural Economy of the United States." *Radical History Review* 3 (1977): 42–71.

———. "The Anticapitalist Origins of the United States." *Review* 13 (fall 1990): 465–97.

———. "Putting 'Capitalism' in its Place: A Review of Recent Literature." *William and Mary Quarterly.* 3rd series, 52 (April 1995): 315–26.

Mitchell, Broadus. *William Gregg: Factory Master of the Old South.* Chapel Hill: University of North Carolina Press, 1928.

Morris, Christopher. *Becoming Southern: The Evolution of a Way of Life, Warren County and Vicksburg, Mississippi, 1770–1860.* New York and Oxford: Oxford University Press, 1995.

Murphy, Carolyn Hanna. *Carolina Rocks! The Geology of South Carolina.* Orangeburg, S.C.: Sandlapper Publishing Co., 1995.

Nelson, William E. *Americanization of the Common Law: The Impact of Legal Change on Massachusetts Society, 1760–1830.* Cambridge, Mass.: Harvard University Press, 1975.

Oakes, James. *The Ruling Race: A History of American Slaveholders.* New York: Knopf, 1982.

———. *Slavery and Freedom: An Interpretation of the Old South.* New York: Knopf, 1990.

O'Neall, John Belton. *Biographical Sketches of the Bench and Bar of South Carolina.* 2 vols. Charleston: S. G. Courtnay & Co., 1859.

Pease, William H., and Jane H. Pease. *The Web of Progress: Private Values and Public Styles in Boston and Charleston, 1828–1843.* New York and Oxford: Oxford University Press, 1985.

Peterson, Merrill D. *The Great Triumvirate: Webster, Clay, and Calhoun.* Oxford and New York: Oxford University Press, 1987.

Petty, Julian J. *The Growth and Distribution of Population in South Carolina.* Columbia: South Carolina State Council for Defense, Industrial Development Committee, 1943.

Phillips, Ulrich Bonnell. *A History of Transportation in the Eastern Cotton Belt to 1860.* New York: Columbia University Press, 1908.

———. *American Negro Slavery.* New York and London: D. Appleton and Company, 1918.

Poston, Jonathan H. *The Buildings of Charleston: A Guide to the City's Architecture.* Columbia: University of South Carolina Press, 1997.

Prince, Eldred E., Jr. *Long Green: The Rise and Fall of Tobacco in South Carolina.* Athens and London: University of Georgia Press, 2000.

Prude, Jonathan. *The Coming of Industrial Order: Town and Factory Life in Rural Massachusetts.* Cambridge: Cambridge University Press, 1983.

Roediger, David. *The Wages of Whiteness: Race and the Making of the American Working Class.* New York: Verso, 1991.

Rogers, George C., Jr. *Evolution of a Federalist: William Loughton Smith of Charleston (1758–1812).* Columbia: University of South Carolina Press, 1962.

Rose, Willie Lee. *Rehearsal for Reconstruction: The Port Royal Experiment.* New York: Vintage, 1964.

Rubin, Cynthia Elyce. "The Edgefield Pottery Tradition." *Early American Life* 18 (1987): 24–29.

Ryan, Mary P. *Cradle of the Middle Class: The Family in Oneida County, New York, 1790–1865.* Cambridge: Cambridge University Press, 1981.

Saville, Julie. *The Work of Reconstruction: From Slave to Wage Laborer in South Carolina, 1860–1870.* Cambridge: Cambridge University Press, 1994.

Scheiber, Harry. "The Road to Munn: Eminent Domain and the Concept of Public Purpose in the State Courts." *Perspectives in American History* 5 (1971): 329–402.

———. "Property Law, Expropriation, and Resource Allocation by Government: The United States, 1789–1910." *Journal of Economic History* 22 (March 1973): 232–51.

Seavoy, Ronald E. "The Public Service Origins of the American Business Corporation." *Business History Review* 52 (spring 1978): 30–60.

———. *The Origins of the American Business Corporation, 1784–1855: Broadening the Concept of Public Service During Industrialization*. Westport, Conn.: Greenwood Press, 1982.

Sellers, Charles. *The Market Revolution: Jacksonian America, 1815–1846*. New York and Oxford: Oxford University Press, 1991.

Sellers, Leila. *Charleston Business on the Eve of the American Revolution*. Chapel Hill: University of North Carolina Press, 1934.

Sheriff, Carol. *The Artificial River: The Erie Canal and the Paradox of Progress, 1817–1862*. New York: Hill and Wang, 1996.

Shore, Laurence. *Southern Capitalists: The Ideological Leadership of an Elite, 1832–1885*. Chapel Hill: University of North Carolina Press, 1986.

Smith, Alfred G., Jr. *Economic Readjustment of an Old Cotton State: South Carolina, 1820–1860*. Columbia: University of South Carolina Press, 1958.

Smith, Mark M. *Mastered by the Clock: Time, Slavery, and Freedom in the American South*. Chapel Hill: University of North Carolina Press, 1997.

———. *Debating Slavery: Economy and Society in the Antebellum American South*. Cambridge: Cambridge University Press, 1998.

Stansell, Christine. *City of Women: Sex and Class in New York, 1780–1860*. Urbana: University of Illinois Press, 1987.

Stauffer, Michael E. *The Formation of Counties in South Carolina*. Columbia: South Carolina Department of Archives and History, 1994.

Steinberg, Theodore. *Nature Incorporated: Industrialization and the Waters of New England*. Cambridge: Cambridge University Press, 1991.

Stokes, Melvyn, and Stephen Conway, eds. *The Market Revolution in America: Social, Political, and Religious Expressions, 1800–1880*. Charlottesville: University Press of Virginia, 1993.

Stradling, J. Garrison. "The Southern Porcelain Company of Kaolin, South Carolina: A Reassessment." *Journal of Early Southern Decorative Arts* 22 (winter 1996): 1–39.

Tadman, Michael. "The Hidden History of Slave Trading in Antebellum South Carolina: John Springs III and other 'Gentlemen Dealing in Slaves.'" *South Carolina Historical Magazine* 97 (January 1996): 6–29.

Taylor, George Rogers. *The Transportation Revolution, 1815–1860.* New York: Rinehart, 1951.

Taylor, Rosser H. "Hamburg: An Experiment in Town Promotion." *North Carolina Historical Review* 11 (January 1934): 20–38.

Terrill, Tom E. "Eager Hands: Labor for Southern Textiles, 1850–1860." *Journal of Economic History* 36 (March 1976): 84–99.

———. "Murder in Graniteville." In *Toward a New South? Studies in Post-Civil War Southern Communities,* edited by Orville Vernon Burton and Robert C. McMath. Westport, Conn.: Greenwood Press, 1982.

Thompkins, Daniel A. *Cotton Mill, Commercial Features.* Charlotte, N.C.: by the author, 1899.

Thornton, J. Mills. *Politics and Power in a Slave Society: Alabama, 1800–1860.* Baton Rouge: Louisiana State University Press, 1978.

Wakelyn, Jon L. *The Politics of a Literary Man: William Gilmore Simms.* Westport, Conn.: Greenwood Press, 1973.

Ward, David C. "Industrial Workers in the Mid-Nineteenth Century South: Family and Labor in the Graniteville (SC) Textile Mill, 1845–1880." *Labor History* 28 (summer 1987): 328–48.

Watson, Harry L. *Jacksonian Politics and Community Conflict: The Emergence of the Second American Party System in Cumberland County, North Carolina.* Baton Rouge: Louisiana State University Press, 1981.

———. *Liberty and Power: The Politics of Jacksonian America.* New York: Hill and Wang, 1990.

———. "'The Common Rights of Mankind': Subsistence, Shad, and Commerce in the Early Republican South." *Journal of American History* 83 (June 1996): 13–43.

Way, Peter. *Common Labour: Workers and the Digging of North American Canals, 1780–1860.* Cambridge: Cambridge University Press, 1993.

Wayne, Michael. *The Reshaping of Plantation Society: The Natchez District, 1860–80.* Baton Rouge: Louisiana State University Press, 1983.

Weiman, David. "Farmers and the Market in Antebellum America: A View from the Georgia Upcountry." *Journal of Economic History* 47 (September 1987): 627–47.

Weir, Robert. "'The Harmony We Were Famous For': An Interpretation of Pre-Revolutionary South Carolina Politics." *William and Mary Quarterly.* 3rd series, 26 (October 1969): 473–501.

Wilentz, Sean. *Chants Democratic: New York City & The Rise of the American Working Class, 1788–1850.* New York: Oxford University Press, 1984.

———. "Society, Politics, and the Market Revolution, 1815–1848." In *The New American History,* edited by Eric Foner. Philadelphia: Temple University Press, 1990.

Williams, Michael. "Products of the Forest: Mapping the Census of 1840." *Journal of Forest History* 24 (January 1980): 4–23.

Wood, Gordon. "Inventing American Capitalism." *New York Review of Books* 41 (June 9, 1994): 44–49.

Woodman, Harold D. "Itinerant Cotton Merchants of the Antebellum South." *Agricultural History* 40 (April 1966): 79–90.

———. *King Cotton and His Retainers: Financing and Marketing the Cotton Crop of the South, 1800–1920.* Lexington: University of Kentucky Press, 1968.

Woodson, Hortense. *Giant in the Land: A Biography of William Bullein Johnson, First President of the Southern Baptist Convention.* Nashville: Broadman Press, 1950.

Wright, Gavin. *The Political Economy of the Cotton South: Households, Markets, and Wealth in the Nineteenth Century.* New York: Norton, 1978.

Wright, Richardson. *Hawkers & Walkers in Early America.* Philadelphia: Lippincott, 1927.

Wyatt-Brown, Bertram. *Honor and Violence in the Old South.* New York and Oxford: Oxford University Press, 1986.

Theses and Dissertations

Benfield, John Steven. "Judge John Belton O'Neall: The Law of Eminent Domain, Railroads, and Internal Improvements." Master's thesis, University of South Carolina, 1982.

Bennett, Robert B., Jr. "The Santee Canal, 1785–1939." Master's thesis, University of South Carolina, 1988.

Eelman, Bruce William. "Progress and Community from Old South to New South: Spartanburg County, South Carolina, 1845–1880." Ph.D. diss., University of Maryland, College Park, 2000.

Greb, Gregory Allen. "Charleston, South Carolina, Merchants, 1815–1860." Ph.D. diss., University of California, San Diego, 1978.

Majewski, John D. "Commerce and Community: Economic Culture and Internal Improvements in Pennsylvania and Virginia, 1790–1860." Ph.D. diss., University of California, Los Angles, 1994.

Mendenhall, Marjorie. "A History of Agriculture in South Carolina, 1790–1860: An Economic Study." Ph.D. diss., University of North Carolina, 1940.

Raiford, Norman Gasque. "South Carolina and the Issue of Internal Improvement, 1775–1860." Ph.D. diss., University of Virginia, 1974.

Stokes, Allen Heath. "Black and White Labor and the Development of the Southern Textile Industry, 1800–1920." Ph.D. diss., University of South Carolina, 1977.

Terry, George D. "'Champaign Country': A Social History of an Eighteenth Century Lowcountry Parish in South Carolina, St. John Berkeley County." Ph.D. diss., University of South Carolina, 1981.

Index

growth of, 66–69, 164; and railroad schemes, 184–85; as railroad terminus, 98–99, 196, 197–99; SCRR seeks to bypass, 181, 194–201; Whig Party in, 145–47

Hamburg and Edgefield Plank Road Company, 187n, 188

Hamilton, Alexander, 58, 147, 169

Hamilton, James, 112

Hammond, Andrew J. (planter), 146, 147, 224

Hammond, Catherine Fitzsimons, 25

Hammond, Charles (merchant), 185

Hammond, Edward Spann, 84–85, 96

Hammond, James Henry, 7, 25, 26, 29, 58, 60–61, 89, 132, 146; on banks; 154; Barnwell C.H. speech, 9–10, 223; on manufacturing, 122, 128, 137, 141, 142–43; on merchants, 83–84, 85; peach orchard of, 205; on slavery, 11, 33–34

Hammond, LeRoy, 27, 146

Hammond, Marcellus, 128

Harris, J. William, 19, 32

Harrison, William Henry, 145, 146

Hartford Insurance Company, 130

Havird, W. (merchant), 86

hawking and peddling, 81, 88, 149, 158–64

Hay, O. G. (merchant/planter), 80

Hay, R. G. (merchant/planter), 80

hay farmers, 193–94

Hayden, Hezekiah Sidney, 130, 218

Hayden, Nathaniel, 130

Hayne, Robert Y., 112–14

Henkell and Robinson (merchants), 81, 201

Hext, Laurence P. (planter), 174

Hickson, Levi (sawmill operator), 211, 212

Higgins, Francis (ferry operator), 51

Hodges, Elihu (merchant), 82

Holman, John (bridge operator), 48, 49

Holmes, Marcella, 85

Holmes and Gray (factors), 78

homespun, 27–28

Horn's Creek, 29n

Horry, Elias, 89, 109, 120–21

Horse Creek, 7, 8, 57, 146; disputes over, 59–60, 62, 206–7, 209, 212–17, 219, 220–21; manufacturing on, 117, 119, 123, 131, 137, 138, 217–18

Horwitz, Morton, 101

Howard and Garmany (cotton traders), 144

Howland and Taft (factors), 137

Hull, Gideon (shoemaker), 85

Hunt, Freeman, 140

Hutchison, Hiram, 135, 136, 137, 139, 185, 186

indigo, 16, 18

iron, 111–12

Jackson, Hays B. (merchant), 80

Jamison, David F. (planter), 224

Jeffers, Henry L. (cotton trader), 81, 145, 201

Jefferson, Thomas, 10, 20, 30, 58, 82, 116

Jesse (slave), 126

Jews, 85

John Sale and Co. (merchants), 77

Johnson, Mrs. S., 39

Johnson, William (merchant), 86

Johnson, William Bullein, 33

Johnston, Job, 41

Jones, James, 128, 131, 132, 137, 212–13, 214, 215

"just compensation," 41, 108

Kalmia, S.C., 204–5, 219

Kansas, 10

Kansas-Nebraska Act, 223

Kellies Cowpen (Winton County), 42

Kelly, George, 57

Keowee River, 70

Kernaghan, Thomas (cotton trader), 81, 145

Klein, Rachel N., 36

Lamar, Thomas, 48, 59

Lamb, James (merchant), 137

Landrum, Abner, 120, 122